NO LIMITS

NO LIMITS

THE INSIDE STORY OF CHINA'S WAR WITH THE WEST

ANDREW SMALL

 MELVILLE HOUSE
BROOKLYN · LONDON

No Limits

First published in the United Kingdom in 2022 by
C. Hurst & Co. (Publishers) Ltd.

Copyright © Andrew Small, 2022

All rights reserved

First Melville House Printing: November 2022

Melville House Publishing
46 John Street
Brooklyn, NY 11201

and

Melville House UK
Suite 2000
16/18 Woodford Road
London E7 0HA

mhpbooks.com
@melvillehouse

ISBN: 978-1-68589-019-3
ISBN: 978-1-68589-015-5 (eBook)

Library of Congress Control Number: 2022943339

Printed in the United States of America

1   3   5   7   9   10   8   6   4   2

A catalog record for this book is available from the Library of Congress

CONTENTS

ACKNOWLEDGEMENTS

This book could not have been written without the help of a great number of colleagues, friends, supporters, and sources. While the primary phase of research, and all of the writing, was conducted from 2019 on, the book draws on meetings and interviews that go back to 2003, as well as my wider experiences in China since 1998. As such, thanks are owed to a particularly expansive array of people. Given the critical nature of much of the text, however, I will refrain from listing the friends and colleagues in (particularly) Beijing, Shanghai and Guangzhou who have been so foundational to my understanding of China, and provided me with opportunities as a teacher, fellow, intellectual partner, and regular visitor to the country. I appreciate your continued ideas and advice, and hope for better times.

The German Marshall Fund of the United States has been my professional home for most of this period. The range of locations covered in the book is indicative of the space and support GMF has afforded me to rove across so many areas of Chinese policy, and the US and European responses to China's rise. This includes the people responsible for bringing me on board in the first place, and setting in motion GMF's efforts on China and the transatlantic relationship—Craig Kennedy, Bob Kagan, and the late Ron Asmus. Dan Twining was my closest and most impor-

ACKNOWLEDGEMENTS

tant collaborator for many years, and translated the whole agenda of transatlantic cooperation on China and in Asia into reality during a period when few others saw its importance.

I am very grateful to Jamie Fly, who did so much to steer that agenda through a particularly challenging period for the transatlantic relationship, and trusted to include me in so many of the most interesting parts of that process. I'm also grateful to Bonnie Glaser, Kristi Govella and my other colleagues on the program for giving me the chance to push this book to completion well after it was ostensibly finished, and setting the Asia program on its successful course. Thomas Kleine-Brockhoff and the Berlin office provided a fantastic welcome as I relocated there over the course of the project. The Stockholm China Forum, supported by the Swedish Ministry for Foreign Affairs, was at the center of GMF's work on China—both the transatlantic exchanges and continued efforts to engage with Chinese counterparts—and the source of so many of the most useful insights from its participants down the years. I'm grateful for the longstanding cooperation with Borje Ljunggren, in particular, over the lifetime of the forum.

I was hosted as a fellow by the European Council on Foreign Relations for a core period of the book research. I'm grateful to Mark Leonard for bringing me on board, and for all the support and collaboration during my time in Beijing back in the days of the Foreign Policy Centre. I would like to thank the teams from ECFR's offices—particularly in Madrid and Rome—who helped put my visits programs together, as well as the support from the Asia program, especially Manisha Reuter and Rosa Melissa Gehrung. I also benefited from both the expertise of other members of the institution, and opportunities to join their activities, especially Jeremy Shapiro and Jonathan Hackenbroich.

The book would not have been possible without the generous support of the Smith Richardson Foundation. Well before the topic achieved such prominence, Allan Song encouraged me to sharpen a wider research proposal to focus on the shifting approach towards China among US allies in Europe, which is at the heart of the book. SRF's flexibility as the project evolved— not least through the complexities of getting the research conducted through the course of the pandemic—was also greatly appreciated. With the subject exploding politically, even in the early months of the research, I published preliminary versions of the analysis in the book in a variety of outlets, and am grateful to the editorial teams at Foreign Affairs, GMF and ECFR for bringing these essays and reports to life.

I would also like to thank my agent, Jonathan Conway, who translated my early drafts into lucid and sparkling proposals, gave extensive notes on the texts, and made sure the book found the right home(s). I am very glad that one of them is Hurst. I'm delighted to work with them again for my second book, and am grateful to Michael Dwyer for his support, Tim Page for his great edits, and everyone else at Hurst. I am also excited to be working with Melville House, and am very grateful to Carl Bromley for his extensive comments, as well as the rest of his team, and George Lucas at InkWell Management.

A long list of officials, ministers, journalists, members of parliament, and businesspeople, talked freely and candidly to me over the years, and provided the most important material for the book. The bulk of them are in the cities where I have lived— Beijing, London, Brussels, Washington, DC and Berlin—but I am also greatly indebted to many of those in Paris, Rome, Madrid, Lisbon, Stockholm, Warsaw, the Hague, Vilnius, Geneva, Tokyo, New Delhi, Taipei, Islamabad, Male, and Kabul, to mention only those that feature directly in the book. I am particularly grateful to those who not only went on the record but took the time to look at sections of the text and correct my mistakes and infelicities, especially Keith Krach and his team, and Martin Selmayr. With a small number of exceptions, I chose not to cite most on this list by name—in part because most of them are still serving in various capacities, but also because the bulk of the interviews were contemporaneous, and the terms under which the conversations were conducted precluded their being directly attributed.

I can however, thank at least some of those in their personal capacity—rather than as the officials that some of them were or are—where I have benefited from interviews, comments, invitations to helpful events, assistance, or just reading their work, including: Matt Turpin, Tom Wright, Ely Ratner, Michael Schiffer, Stephanie Kleine-Ahlbrandt, Dave Shullman, Tanvi Madan, Ryan Hass, Dan Rosen, Evan Medeiros, Jeremie Waterman, Jonathan Hillman, Jeff Smith, Laura Rosenberger, Dhruva Jaishankar, Mira Rapp-Hooper, Evan Feigenbaum, Abe Denmark, Liz Economy, Dan Markey, Jennifer Hillman, Rush Doshi, Andrew Shearer, Barney Rubin, Siddharth Mohandas, Lisa Curtis, Michael Pillsbury, Randy Schriver, Jennifer Staats, Thomas Kellogg, Kaush Arha, James Schwemlein, Gary Schmitt, Dan Blumenthal, Phil Saunders, Garima Mohan, Dario Cristiani, Dhruva Jaishankar, Chris Buckley, David Rennie, Jörg Wuttke, Kerry Brown, Patrick Chovanec, Aaron Friedberg, Nadège Rolland, Raff Pantucci, Minxin Pei, Frédéric Grare, Sarah Raine, Volker Stanzel, Reinhard Bütikofer, Thorsten Benner, Nils Schmid, Metin Hakverdi, Sabine Stricker-Kellerer, Mathieu Duchatel, Abigaël Vasselier, Agatha Kratz, Giulio Pugliese, Giulia Pompili, Giulio Terzi, Mario Esteban, Todd Hall, Jane Perlez, Alexander Gabuev, Jakub Jakubowski, Vijay Gokhale, SL Narasimhan, Indrani Bagchi, Suhasini Haidar, Shivshankar Menon, Pramit Pal Chaudhari, Saeed Shah, Fazal Rehman, Hamayoun Khan, Mosharraf Zaidi, Mirwais Nab, Thoriq Hamid, and Mohammed Nasheed.

The two clusters of research expertise in Europe that deserve extra mention are MERICS and the world of François Godement, in his various different guises. The former I was able to credit in the text, focused on Sebastian Heilmann's tenure as director, though it has also gone from strength to strength under Mikko Huotari. He and other former researchers, including Lucrezia Poggetti, also generously sat for more formal interviews. François Godement has occupied a crucial role in the China debate in Europe for decades now, magnified by the fact that so many people who worked for him are now leading intellectuals and officials in their own right. The emerging policy consensus looks like the one he sketched out many years ago.

Stuart Lau, Finbarr Bermingham, and—first as journalist, now as colleague—Noah Barkin have changed a dry, insider topic into a juicy set of news, policy stories and analysis, and much of the book has benefited from their work.

I am grateful to Paul Roberts for introducing me to the Maldives, well before any China related questions there were in anyone's minds, and everything that we were able to do together there and in the neighborhood since then, from Hambantota to Hulhumale. I also benefited from a fellowship at the Takshashila Institution in Bangalore for a key part of the Maldives developments; I'm grateful to Nitin Pai, and colleagues—especially Pranay Kotasthane, Manoj Kewalramani and Hamsini Hariharan—for the opportunity and the collaborations.

Amy Studdart was a part of so many of these stories and had to put up with me for swathes of the writing and research process. Her input and support has been invaluable in more ways than I can possibly list, in Washington, DC, in Brussels, in China, in the worlds of technology and democracy support, intellectually, and personally. Po made an important contribution too, albeit with less direct ramifications for the text.

I received many kind offers to read the drafts, but among my friends, I am particularly grateful to Peter Sparding for going closely through the full text. Desmond Shum has helped me sharpen my thinking on all the subjects here, since my early days in Beijing, and I was thrilled that his own book allowed so many others to benefit from his insights and way of thinking.

One person couldn't be accorded the credit she deserved in the text itself. Janka Oertel was a protagonist in many of the dramas outlined in the book in recent years, and much of the 5G story, in particular, is really hers (though she would tell it better). There is little in the book that she didn't provide, help, or improve, from the most practical support to the most challenging critiques. She did more to make this book possible than anyone else, and has been an incredible partner.

My family's love and indulgence during all these travels and relocations has helped make this possible too, and this time also featured my mother's help with Italian material...

All the errors, omissions, eccentric selection of material, and failures to grasp key points about the workings of the Radio Access Network and lawful interception, are mine alone.

INTRODUCTION

THE MESSAGE THAT POPPED up on my phone was a little shocking. It was late January 2020, and COVID-19 was hitting China hard. The note from my Chinese friend initially appeared to be analyzing the impact of the worsening crisis on the country's GDP numbers. But there was more. He was trying to understand the rationale behind some of the Chinese government's decisions and was troubled by what he saw. This was a system he knew from the inside out. Serving members of the Politburo Standing Committee, the Chinese Communist Party's top decision-making body, had once been his dining companions. He understood the way they thought. And his conclusion was a dark one. It seemed to him that the Chinese leadership had reached a decision: if China was going to take a hit from the pandemic, the rest of the world should too.

Although I was skeptical, some of the moves Beijing was making were at least consistent with this analysis. Even as it locked down domestically, the government was demanding that countries around the world remain open to Chinese visitors and denouncing anyone that tried to stop them. China's foreign minister turned up at a security conference in Munich to announce that "China has effectively curbed the spread of the outbreak beyond our borders" while hundreds of thousands of Chinese travelers fanned out across the world.[1] Yet as an attribution of malign intent, this seemed a step too far. It felt like conspiracy-theorizing, though I knew my friend wasn't prone to that. I reflected on the note occasionally in the months that followed, as the world was convulsed by the pandemic, wondering whether I had been sober-minded and judicious or simply failed to make the mental leap that understanding Beijing's behavior increasingly required.

Then later that year I opened Bob Woodward's new book and saw that the US deputy national security advisor, Matt Pottinger, the architect of much of the Trump administration's China policy, had taken the warnings more seriously. "Several Chinese elites well connected to the Communist Party" signaled that they thought the government had a "sinister" goal, the opening pages explained. "China's not going to be the only one to suffer from this."[2] I was sure that the same analysis had found its way to Pottinger, one of the few serving US officials to emerge from the Trump years with his reputation enhanced, not least for his critical interrogation of Beijing's COVID-19 concealment efforts. It was among the reasons the United States shut down inbound traffic from China in February, virtually the sole element of Trump's handling of the crisis that he could legitimately tout as a success. I shot my friend a note: "You're in the first chapter of the Woodward book!" He replied with what I took to be the emoji equivalent of wry, dark laughter.

* * *

When we had first met in Beijing in the early 2000s, it was Zhongnanhai, the Party's leadership compound, that brought us together. The Chinese prime minister, Wen Jiabao, was due to visit London, and we had embarked on plans to launch a new program of think-tank activities during his visit. China's relations with Europe were heading into a new era, and we hoped to help sketch out some ideas for their future course. I was in China to negotiate the modalities of the event with my Chinese counterparts, including the sensitive matter of gaining Wen's personal imprimatur. But the man who was handling the most delicate contacts with Wen's staff, who had got the whole initiative started, was not one of the academics who were my ostensible opposite numbers. It was an intriguing figure from the Chinese business community.

Desmond Shum and his wife, Whitney Duan—to take the anglicized names that they frequently used—were a rarity in the Chinese corporate world. Most of their peers were monomaniacally focused on racking up as much money and influence as possible, with philanthropy only another instrument to facilitate these goals. They, by contrast, were seemingly also on a mission to improve the caliber of Chinese policymaking and intellectual life. This certainly did not preclude the money and influence. Most controversially, their proximity to the Wen family would blow up in a *New York Times* story that detailed Duan's role as the white glove handling billions of dollars that flowed from their stake in China's largest insurance firm, Ping An.[3] But they had other priorities too. They were funding chunks of the economic policy work at China's elite universities and think-tanks, such as Tsinghua and the Chinese Academy of Social Sciences. With China's journalism scene flourishing, Desmond explored plans to put together a Chinese equivalent of the *New Yorker*. He was not satisfied with a hands-off benefactor role either. He was personally engaged in circumventing the layers of what he saw as ossified Chinese bureaucracy to channel ideas and advice directly to the leadership. This was where our work on the Sino-European relationship kicked in.

The early 2000s were a period of near-unabashed mutual enthusiasm among Chinese and European policymakers, and the Beijing of that time seemed physically to incarnate the sense of opportunity. Shanghai had already gone through the most dramatic phase of its transformation in the 1990s, driven by the natives of the city that were then running China. Now it was Beijing's turn. In the lead-up to the 2008 Olympics, the skyline of this far lower-slung city was increasingly punctuated by architectural mega-projects, and the old atmosphere of wood-burning stoves and gritty street life was making way for shopping malls, luxury car dealerships and five-star hotels. For visiting European politicians, it was beguiling. The Chinese government had always done a masterful job at making its political visitors feel like they were far-sighted historic figures deliberating on the fate of the world. Now they could do it in high style too.

The sense of reform and opening was tangible. China had recently acceded to the World Trade Organization (WTO), having accepted and seemingly delivered on the most stringent requirements any new member had ever faced, slashing tariff levels and opening up major industries to foreign competition. If European companies could gain even greater access to the Chinese market during the next phase of economic restructuring that everyone expected to follow, the future of entire sectors of the European economy would look different. Visiting CEOs were confident. The Chinese economy was still comparable to the likes of the UK and France in scale, and its companies complemented European industrial and technological strengths. Those malls and dealerships were selling European cars and luxury goods and were built with the invisible support of innumerable specialist engineering firms from across the continent.

Another group of foreigners was excited too. Few of the budding China hands I knew in Beijing at the time had come to the country because they wanted to prepare themselves for a role in a future great power contest. Instead, most were enthusiasts for the literature, the language, the food, the history, a different civilization, a different way of living and thinking and understanding humanity. As China was stepping out onto the global stage, it seemed that the rest of the world would also come to benefit from a richer immersion in all the things that had first entranced them.

The transformations spanned every dimension. Virtually every visitor in the early 2000s with even the slightest artistic curiosity would make a trip to the vast 798 Dashanzi factory complex that had been turned into a set of workshops and exhibition spaces for avant-garde sculpture and painting, while the likes of Ai Weiwei were already becoming familiar international figures. The so-called sixth generation of Chinese film directors, such as Jia Zhangke and Lou Ye, were making biting neo-realist-style masterpieces about contemporary urban existence. From foreign policy to philosophy, the Chinese intellectual scene seemed to have an anticipatory fizz around it, as thinkers who had once toiled in international obscurity started to realize just how much their ideas now mattered to the world. Despite the political system, it was a China where spaces for self-reflection and critique seemed to be growing again. The mix was a heady one. The old China that people like me had first fallen in love with. A sense of burgeoning possibility for the country and for the rest of the world. The economic boom that never seemed to end. And the intellectual challenge of making sense of what it all meant.

* * *

In the background, ubiquitous, was the Chinese Communist Party. When I walked to the Starbucks in Oriental Plaza from the little house in which I lived near the Forbidden City's East Gate, I would often take the long route that allowed me to peer furtively down the entrance of one particular *hutong*—narrow alleys lined with Beijing's traditional courtyard residences—where Chinese security personnel were always discreetly positioned. A little way down the tiny street was Zhao Ziyang's home, where he still lived under house arrest. Zhao had been the CPC general secretary in the lead-up to Tiananmen in 1989, the hope of the students who saw a kinder, more liberal face who might lead the country down a different path. His unwillingness to launch the brutal crackdown demanded by Deng Xiaoping and the Party elders saw him removed from office and consigned to the house in Fuqiang Hutong where he would live until his death in 2005. At Zhao's side, in the famous photo where he stands amid the students with a megaphone trying to persuade them to leave the square ahead of what he knew would be bloodshed, was his aide, China's future prime minister, Wen Jiabao.

Wen too would end up as the more humane face of the Party, the man who would visibly shed tears after mining accidents and natural disasters, "Grandpa Wen," "the People's Premier." Unlike his immediate predecessor, Zhu Rongji, Wen was not going to tear into any economic reforms with free-market zeal. Unlike the men he once worked for, Zhao Ziyang and Hu Yaobang, he was not going to be a standard-bearer for even the limited version of political opening that once had support in the Party. But, for a time, Wen reinforced the sense among many of his political counterparts in the West that there was a version of this China and the party-state that the world could live with. Not a progressive China, not a democratic China, but not an aggressive or totalitarian China either. With his very demeanor, he conveyed the impression that there were some leaders there with decency. That the mission of maintaining the leadership of the Party was not so distinct from the task of working out how to build a prosperous life for the people of a still-developing country that faced unimaginably large problems.

Wen was also the Chinese government's beneficent face to Europe. Where US presidents and other heads of state dealt primarily with the Chinese Communist Party's general secretary and president, the achingly stilted Hu Jintao, the Europe portfolio belonged to the prime minister. This made sense for an agenda that was so heavily economic in nature. But in the shadow of the Iraq war, minds in Europe and China were increasingly trained on political and strategic dynamics too. Optimism about the European project was at its peak. The EU was tentatively starting to assume a foreign policy role of its own.

A European constitution was in the offing. There were mutterings from European political figures about the desirability of "multipolarity" during a period when US "hyper-puissance" under George W. Bush made everyone uncomfortable.[4] When Europe and China looked at each other, they saw emerging poles in that new order. The cluster of advisors around Wen certainly believed that more Europe was a good thing. They all viewed Europe as the more benign edge of Western power. They saw the growing appetite there for a European profile distinct from the continuum with Washington and thought that China should encourage it.

Europe wanted more from China too. It envisaged Beijing gradually assuming greater global responsibilities: supporting a common development agenda in Africa, taking on the burden of peacekeeping in the world's trouble spots, and a host of other tasks to ensure that the system on which China's economic interests depended continued to function smoothly. The push was for China to step up, to assume leadership, to end its free-riding, to stop "hiding its brightness," as Deng Xiaoping's strategy had once urged. US Deputy Secretary of State Robert Zoellick's call for China to become a "responsible stakeholder" mirrored European thinking to a tee. China wasn't one.[5] But perhaps there was a chance that Beijing could come to see its interests that way, and perhaps Europe could help get it there.

Wen was the man fielding these earnest entreaties from political leaders in Brussels, Paris, Berlin and London. And one staff member, the only official then attached to either Hu's or Wen's offices who came from a diplomatic background, converted them into options for China's leaders to consider. This was Desmond's friend, the scrupulously careful Song Zhe, who later ended up as China's ambassador to the EU and its chief representative in Hong Kong. We would feed him "non-papers," with ideas that had also been quietly bounced off British, French and German officials, to sound out the limits of the possible. This didn't go on for long. Desmond was firmly discouraged from this kind of stove-piping after Song received a warning from the Chinese security services. Other parts of the Chinese bureaucracy were less friendly to foreign policy freelancing.

It was illustrative of a system that seemed simultaneously rigid and permeable, at a moment where China's global role was characterized by a vast spectrum of potential. For all that Chinese politics is supposedly a black box, many of us in Beijing at the time at least had glimpses inside. What we saw looked nothing like the world of unimaginably far-sighted Chinese leaders who supposedly thought in centuries, nor a mythologized Confucian meritocracy, nor the inflexible bureaucracy that many other foreigners were stuck dealing with. It looked like raw politics. The horse-trading for positions. The bureaucrats who wanted to do enough to ensure their own promotion while leaving any mess for their successors to clean up. The endless factional games. The shadowy figures behind the scenes who wielded greater influence than their formal positions implied. The ingeniously concealed and choreographed rules of corruption.

But most striking were the stories of the leaders who were figuring out their own relationship to China's newfound power. Chinese mayors shocked by the level of open graft they found when they met counterparts in places like Moscow that "we'd never get away with here." Politburo members receiving visiting Taiwanese dignitaries and being amazed that "Chinese" leaders could carry themselves like real politicians rather than the stiff bureaucrats they still knew themselves to be. Then there were the stories that felt like darker portents of the country's potential future. One that stuck with me was the account of a visit by Vladimir Putin in 2006, during which he and the Chinese leadership had spent most of their meeting time together exchanging advice on how best to refine their domestic repression techniques in the aftermath of the revolutions that were blowing up in Central Asia.

As it turned out, this was precisely the form of raw politics that would ultimately prevail.

* * *

When Desmond sent me the COVID warning message, he was in exile. His wife Whitney had been detained, seemingly indefinitely, held incommunicado for three years in an unknown location, likely never to be tried but simply held as a standing warning to Wen Jiabao not to step out of line against the new leadership. The Party was now decisively under Xi Jinping's grip, and much of the country's commercial life was under the grip of the Party. Once-potent private sector actors were cut down to size, as Xi moved to neutralize any independent sources of power, and economic goals were subordinated to political and military objectives. A million Uyghurs in Xinjiang were in detention camps. Hong Kong was no longer under the "one country, two systems" model that China had committed to in its handover treaty, instead subjected to Beijing's unadulterated authority. And the rest of the world faced a Chinese government that had moved from free-riding to assertiveness to a level of diplomatic, economic and military aggression that seemed to be intensifying by the month.

Like many other Western think-tankers working on China, I had not visited the country since December 2018, when one of our number, International Crisis Group's Michael Kovrig, was also thrown into a Chinese prison. He was grabbed as a de facto hostage after the daughter of Huawei's CEO, the Chinese telecoms company that will occupy a prominent role in this narrative, was arrested in Canada at the US's behest for her role in sanctions-busting with Iran. Michael's work embodied the efforts of those researchers who were trying to understand China better and find ingenious ways in which cooperation might still be possible despite all the obstacles. It made no difference. Journalist contacts from the early 2000s, like the guru-like Chris Buckley of the *New York Times*, with whom I used to trade speculation about inner-Party workings at Sichuanese restaurants, had been forced out of the country after devoting their professional lives to making sense of its complexities for the world at large. Longstanding friends in the Chinese intellectual community, whom I now only met outside China, had either become excruciatingly cautious or complained darkly about the trajectory the country was on.

Their experience has been replicated in myriad other ways for almost everyone working in this environment: the diplomats, businesspeople, journalists and intellectuals who had spent so many years trying to ensure that things would end up in a very different place. When most of us meet now, it has little to do with the optimistic initiatives that we attempted a decade-and-a-half before. It is typically spent trying to figure out how the rest of the world can deal with the sharp edges of Chinese state and Party power that were once only felt within China's own borders. Many of those who were once so excited about China's arrival on the global stage now debate how the other major powers might best work together to stop the most damaging elements of the Party's agenda from prevailing. This book tells the story of how that happened.

Munich, February 2020

The art deco ballroom of Munich's Bayerischer Hof was packed. German military personnel maintained a perimeter around the assembled heads of government, ministers, senators and parliamentarians as the US Speaker of the House began her remarks. It was the last major gathering of political leaders before the COVID-19 pandemic brought the world to a standstill. The Chinese foreign minister, Wang Yi, was snapped meeting the cheerful-looking head of the World Health Organization, Tedros Adhanom Ghebreyesus, where he denounced "misinformation and stigma" about the origins of the virus and claimed that its spread outside China had been curbed.[6] Nonetheless, the Europeans and Americans in attendance were genuinely confident they would be spared. The only casual nod to the outbreak was a proliferation of little sanitizer bottles with "so that things don't get out of hand" emblazoned on their front. Another China-related matter was on everyone's minds.

Nancy Pelosi was on a repair job for an alliance under severe strain. The hope among many of the Europeans there was that this was a foretaste of the end of the Trump presidency, the soothing prospect of a Democratic administration and the restoration of transatlantic amity after a bruising few years. Yet she had another message to deliver too: that some things were not going to change as much as they might have hoped.

Speaking on the same stage twelve months earlier, US Vice-President Mike Pence had delivered a bracing warning on China. This was far from the norm. The Munich Security Conference was usually the place to talk NATO, European security, Russia, nuclear arms or the Middle East. This was where Donald Rumsfeld tangled with the German foreign minister, Joschka Fischer, ahead of the Iraq war; where Vladimir Putin laid out his baleful warning in 2007 that Russia now stood in opposition to the entire post-Cold War security order in Europe. Stern lectures about the Chinese security threat, on the other hand, were for gatherings of Asian defense ministers in Singapore, not old world Atlanticist confabs in Bavaria.

Two years earlier, China hadn't even merited a mention in Pence's speech. Now the vice-president was identifying it as a core risk to the transatlantic alliance. The United States was in the middle of the biggest shift in its own approach to China in decades, and the most comprehensive overhaul of its approach to national security since the 9/11 attacks. Technology competition was at the heart of this revolution, a cluster of issues that would determine the future economic, political and military landscape and the distribution of global power. While these ranged from artificial intelligence to quantum computing, there was an immediate set of decisions that would have a conditioning effect on virtually all of them, the question of whether Chinese equipment would form the spine of the next generation of the world's telecoms networks. "We cannot ensure the defense of the West if our allies grow dependent on the East," Pence declaimed.[7] 5G infrastructure, a seemingly technical matter, had taken on vast geopolitical significance.

There was a problem with Pence's argument though. Few of the assembled European politicians were listening. For many US partners and allies who weren't looking closely enough at how deep and broad the new consensus on China in Washington was, this was just another episode of Trumpian lunacy that they had to find a way of sitting out until sanity was restored. This ignored the fact that de facto US bans on Chinese equipment had been in place since the Obama administration, while the British intelligence services had moved to ban Huawei's state-run counterpart, ZTE, in 2018. Yet the hope was that it would still be possible to placate both the Americans and the Chinese in the short term and that the situation might look very different when the 2020 US presidential election was over. As a result, the two most critical European capitals on the 5G issue, London and Berlin, were still trying to come up with tortured compromises.

This was where Pelosi came in. No messenger could have been more apt. At the very inception of her long career in Congress, the Tiananmen Square massacre had been her breakout political moment, when she became the leading voice fighting to protect Chinese students in the United States whose open sympathy for their compatriots now put them at risk if they returned. She would remain a thorn in the flesh of the Chinese government for the duration of her time in Congress, from her efforts to condition trade relations on human rights to her support for an Olympic boycott. Her critical views on China had once been seen as excessively hawkish for mainstream tastes. More supposedly sophisticated policymakers claimed that economic growth and closer Chinese integration with the liberal international order would be a more effective way of addressing her concerns. Now Pelosi's position was the mainstream. For European audiences though, it was not the China credentials that gave resonance to her remarks. It was Pelosi's position as Donald Trump's arch opponent. Uniquely able to get under his skin, her disdain for his entire agenda was embodied by the images of her tearing up his State of the Union speech at the conclusion of his address, just a couple of weeks before the conference.

Yet the subject animating the woman who was then the most powerful Democrat on her visit to Europe was precisely the same as Trump's faithful VP a year earlier. What was at stake with the 5G decisions, Pelosi told those helping her to prepare for the trip, was no less than the choice of dictatorship or democracy. "I'm going to say something that may not be agreeable to many of you here, because you invited candor, and that is the subject of 5G and cybersecurity," she started, after pleasantries about the transatlantic alliance were out of the way.[8] "China is seeking to export its digital autocracy through its telecommunication giant, Huawei. Nations cannot cede our telecommunication infrastructure to China for financial expediency." Her unambiguous answer to one of the questions from the floor had even greater piquancy: "Does this mean that you agree in substance with the China policy of President Trump?" Without a pause, she jumped in to respond: "We have agreement in that regard ... Yes, yes, I do believe that it's a real danger to put all that power in the Sinification of 5G." Any European leader in attendance who had hoped that the China question might recede again after the upcoming elections could be under no illusions.

In the months that followed, China was ground zero for an even more immediately deadly threat. Whatever uncertainty there was about whether the inner workings of the Chinese system had ramifications for the world at large was blown away by the manner of the cover-up of the COVID outbreak in Wuhan during the crucial early stages of the pandemic. Supply chain panics exposed dangerous levels of dependence on Chinese production facilities, from pharmaceuticals to basic medical goods. And unlike a decade earlier, where Beijing's judicious, pragmatic approach during the financial crisis won plaudits even from critics, its prickly belligerence instead saw China's standing in international public opinion plummet.[9] Whether it was sanctioning Australia for demanding an inquiry into the origins of the pandemic, dismantling the vestiges of Hong Kong's distinct political system or inducing the biggest crisis on its border with India in decades, China's behavior on a bewilderingly expansive number of fronts intensified the sense that there was an urgent problem to address. By the time of President Biden's own speech at Munich in 2021, the language was even sharper. The liberal democracies had to mobilize if they wanted to win the "race for the future," he argued.[10] Open democratic societies were at an inflection point and needed to pull together to defend a global system facing competition from a powerful authoritarian rival.

The 5G drama was the first point where all of these different dimensions converged, and a template for the battles that will comprise this larger contest. It was the moment when China moved in so many countries from being a foreign policy and commercial matter to being an issue of high-stakes internal politics. When the Chinese government started threatening countries not over their meetings with the Dalai Lama or their dealings with Taiwan but whether or not they were willing to embed

Chinese firms in their critical infrastructure. It was the catalyst for an ideologically diffuse group of politicians who decided to take the challenge on themselves when their governments refused to act. It was the moment when the United States woke up to the fact that critical elements of its China policy could no longer be run as a solo act, that it had to start getting allies on board that had never mattered to US strategy in this way before. When policymakers faced up to the question of how entire ideological, technological, economic and political systems interacted with each other, and whether the long intertwining of those systems needed to start being unraveled.

* * *

To get a glimpse of what is at stake, take a stroll around Ericsson's 5G showroom at their headquarters outside Stockholm. The hardware is a set of inconspicuous white boxes. Surrounding them is a vision of the near-future, the "Internet of Things" and "Smart Cities" given tangible form. There are remote ultrasound tests conducted using robo-gloves. Vehicles pictured on LCD screens are controlled by free-floating steering wheels and pedals. Industrial robotic arms undertake precision-engineering tasks. Colored lights pulsate across model football stadiums, apartment blocks and railway stations to illustrate the breadth and depth of the new network's coverage.

Each further generation of mobile technology has seen a dramatic evolution in the way life and commerce is conducted. The shift from 2G to 3G brought emails into the palms of our hands. The jump from 3G to 4G made possible the apps that have turned mobile devices into near-extensions of our brains. 5G promises something else: constant high-speed data of such a quality that industrial systems, medical operations and fleets of driverless cars can be run through it. It is a prospect that has seen 5G telecoms networks compared to the power grid in their centrality to the new economy.

But in this very promise lies the risk. 5G networks will be even more deeply embedded in the hard-wiring of everyday life. The security questions at stake are no longer solely about spying on phone calls, locations and personal data, but the far vaster flows of sensitive information that will course through the mobile telecoms architecture, as well as the potential to disrupt the functions of the cars, hospitals, companies, production facilities and governments that come to rely on it.

The system works differently from its predecessor. Most of the new functions on display at the Ericsson showroom are made possible by 5G's low latency: data-processing is almost immediate, meaning that autonomous vehicles, for instance, are not subject even to the tiny lags that could be the difference between life or death in split-second decisions. This is achieved in part through processing more of that data at the periphery of the network. Unlike 4G, where the distinction between the "core" and the "edge" was sharply drawn between the brains of the network and the signal transmissions, 5G sees more intelligent functions moving out from the center; the decision to stop a driverless truck speeding towards a pedestrian or respond to rapid adjustments in a patient's condition during remote surgery cannot wait to be refracted through a distant control site. There would also be a point in time when user traffic is unencrypted in the base station: a requirement in the standard to allow law enforcement agencies to intercept communications, but one that could be subverted.

In addition, it requires prodigious increases in the lines of source code that run, optimize and secure the system. Experts characterize the distinction as a move from a hardware-centered model in 4G to a software-centered model with 5G. The perennial security issue—the potential for unnoticed backdoors—was difficult enough to manage already. Government Communications Headquarters (GCHQ), the British signals intelligence agency, had noted in one of its reports that even when dealing with the existing 4G set-up, "it is just impossible to go through that much code and be absolutely confident you have found everything." Now the volume was increasing exponentially. The result was that the United States no longer believed that the old risk-mitigation techniques for Huawei worked. The towers and antennae could be checked. At 5G scale, the code couldn't. One White House official giving his briefings in Europe had a tried-and-tested routine with a pen and a phone that he would lay out on the table. He would quickly disassemble and reassemble the pen: "This you can take apart and inspect and it will not change." With the phone, however, "every new update could change it completely."

And while the public debate was focused on "smoking guns" that would reveal Chinese data-siphoning from the existing systems, US warnings concentrated as much on the opportunities for coercion, and even the military risks of allowing a company beholden to the Chinese state to exercise so much control over such a vital set of economic functions. The ultra-secure communications used for intelligence-sharing may not rely on public 5G networks, but NATO's capacity to mobilize effectively in a crisis with Russia certainly would.

Even if countries ran into more prosaic political disputes with China, they could find themselves subjected to the same kind of deniable "technical issues" that Beijing was already so deft at conjuring into existence for trade partners it wanted to punish, from suspending exports of critical raw materials to Japan to barring virtually all trade with Lithuania through its elimination from China's customs declaration system. In an inadvertent tell, telecoms operators in the UK threatened that the country would face network outages during the 5G transition phase if Huawei was excluded, precisely the kind of scenario that the United States had been warning British politicians the country might face if it made the wrong decision. As one European official put it:

We have meetings with the US on "the proof" but the day you have "the proof" it's too late. It's a fallacy. The problem of espionage is not as important for 5G, it's the risk of sabotage.

But 5G was not only important because it was the subject of an intrinsic level of concern. It was just as significant for the symbolism and the imminence of the decisions. As one of the US officials most closely involved in the campaign put it:

> There are a number of critical technology issues and 5G happened to be the first one ... We put AI, quantum, bioengineering, and these other areas together as if they're like for like. But we're talking about a grid being built and contracts being negotiated now. If you get it right, the other things will be easier. If you get it wrong, half the battle is already lost.

* * *

This book tells the story of how the major democracies broke from decades of thinking to identify China as the critical outside challenge to the system they had built. It explains why many of those closest to China became the agents of this shift, pressing their still-reluctant governments towards a revolution in their dealings with Beijing. It looks at the catalytic episodes, from 5G to the pandemic to the burgeoning Sino-Russian partnership, that finally illuminated the nature of the challenge and galvanized action. It also shows why it took so long to get there, despite countless wake-up calls in the preceding years.

This is not a book about a great power competition. If we were only navigating a Washington–Beijing contest for primacy with a few superficial ideological trappings, it would be far easier for policymakers on all sides to manage. But it is an entire system that the Chinese party-state is challenging, a fact that Beijing has always been far clearer about than most of those on the receiving end. Much of the story is about how political elites in key capitals came to realize that seeing the problem through the prism of a rivalry between major powers is inadequate. Instead, not only would the Western democracies have to take on the military and economic challenge posed by China but they would also have to ensure that their own system still offered the best vision for humanity, at a time when that system had rarely looked more troubled. And they would also have to find new ways to pool their efforts, at a time when levels of mutual trust in the West had rarely looked lower.

Yet China faces an equally profound set of struggles, and the book also tells the story of how Beijing's failings in recent years have provided an opportunity to turn the tide. It looks at how a hubristic sense of Western decline led China to escalate its ideological and political challenge before the conditions were ripe. It details Beijing's troubled efforts to build a rival coalition of its own, and how its plans to externalize the "China model" ran into resistance even from its closest partners. It concludes with the shock of the Ukraine war, and the Chinese vulnerabilities it exposed.

Over the last twenty years, I have had a ringside seat to the China drama, the journey from deep and close intertwinement to the profound rupture with the West that we see in motion today. From my perches in Beijing, Washington, DC, Berlin, Brussels and London, and my research on how Chinese power is being exercised from Harare to Havana, Kabul to Okinawa, I have benefited from conversations with many of the protagonists in that drama at the time, as well as going back to ask them to reexamine those experiences from the vantage of hindsight.

Inevitably, it is in part a story of regrets. The very first thinktank pamphlet I wrote, living in Beijing in the mid-2000s, was entitled "Preventing the Next Cold War": both the costs of this outcome and the risks of it occurring have been evident for a long time, yet it was not inevitable that we would end up here. I am not among those who believe that the attempt to secure the best case outcome—a China integrated into the system, seeing the scope to realize the ambitions of its people within parameters that we could all live with—was not worth trying. But those efforts have failed. If there is a silver lining, it is that the existential threat that China now poses to the system is creating the possibility for a different—and better—version as a result. To achieve that, though, we first need to make sense of how we got here.

NO LIMITS

1

WHEN DOVES CRY

HOW THE UNITED STATES AND EUROPE WOKE UP TO CHINA

Washington, DC, September 2015

THERE WAS ONLY A SINGLE OCCASION where I saw Xi Jinping up close. One of then-Vice-President Joe Biden's advisors had added my name to the guest list for the official State Department luncheon during his 2015 state visit. Few at the time realized that it would be the valedictory occasion for a whole era in the US–China relationship. On a warm September morning, I duly joined the queue of luminaries on C street and trooped up to the Benjamin Franklin Dining Room on the eighth floor. Xi's trip had the usual tensions hanging over it. Cyber-enabled economic espionage and the militarization of the South China Sea were the topics that captured the headlines ahead of his arrival. But it also had the usual bonhomie. Biden and the secretary of state, John Kerry, were there to fete Xi and the friendship between China and the United States, not to denounce their guest. Everything about the occasion exuded normality and the sense of continuity embodied by Henry Kissinger's familiar position as the center of attention in the room.

Watching the speeches on the archives now is like stepping into another age, a language and manner that would look jarring only a couple of years later. Kerry praised the two sides' cooperation, buoyed by the recent climate deal ahead of the Paris talks: "When we're pulling in the same direction, we can bend the curve of progress in a way that few other nations on earth can accomplish," Kerry said.[1] Biden laid out what was then seen as a slightly edgy notion of "responsible competition" between the United States and China but also talked in depth about his personal relationship with Xi, saluting his "candor, determination, and capacity."

I was seated close to the speeches, the senator who would have obscured my view, Orrin Hatch, helpfully absent from the lunch. But as Kerry and Biden spoke it was hard to pull my eyes away from Xi Jinping. I was used to seeing the more stilted Chinese leaders who had emerged in recent times, the figures who were boxed in by the system, operating at its apogee but not fully commanding it, wary about missteps that might cost them back home. They were invariably awkward in rooms with Western politicians, rigidly reading their talking points without their eyes deviating from the text in front of them. The robotic demeanor of his predecessor, Hu Jintao, was a standing joke among many foreign officials.

Xi had none of this. He exuded confidence and ease, as well he might. He had consolidated his power through the ruthless deployment of an anti-corruption campaign that purged some of the highest-ranking figures in the Party and state, as well as hundreds of thousands of lower-level officials. He was escalating China's military posture in the South China Sea, and well into the rollout of ambitious plans for a new geo-economic initiative, then known as "One Belt, One Road," that would augment China's capacity to project power across the globe. But as he listened to the encomiums, he could afford to be sanguine. Despite all the US plans for rebalancing to Asia, there was little sense of urgency to it.

The Middle East and Afghanistan still commanded the lion's share of attention in Washington. There was endless White House agonizing about whether to go ahead with even basic freedom of navigation operations in the Western Pacific, and a pervasive impression that the administration's desire for a climate agreement with Beijing had an unstated influence on wider US policy. One of the supposed successes of the visit, Xi's pledge not to militarize islands in the South China Sea, was broken within the year. No element of his domestic repression or external assertiveness seemed to change the course of the bilateral relationship.

Chinese friends attributed this in part to a long arc of fortune. From 9/11 to the Arab Spring via the global financial crisis, each time the United States seemed poised to take a harder look at its approach to China and concentrate its strategic attention on great power competition, circumstances seemed to conspire to suck it away again. But they also saw the luster of the Chinese market working its magic. The entire US economic agenda with China was steeped in the belief that the aim of US policy was to expand access for American firms.

Whatever reforms US policymakers pushed on their Chinese counterparts were still mostly a means to this end. Even the Trans-Pacific Partnership, the Obama administration's ambitious Asian trade pact, was framed less as the basis of a genuinely alternative order that excluded China and more as a form of pressure on Beijing to return to the path of economic restructuring. Indeed, seen through this prism, Xi's deepening authoritarianism was not even such a bad thing. A number of China hands and US corporate leaders with high-level Party connections in Beijing claimed that Xi's ruthless accumulation of power was intended to make it possible to break the institutional gridlock of the Hu–Wen decade and give reform and opening a new lease on life.

Meanwhile, for all the litany of complaints from foreign multinationals about Chinese non-market practices and forced technology transfer, the sense from Chinese officials was that even if they could no longer count on the corporate world to act as unabashed cheerleaders, the commercial interests at stake were now so large that they would ultimately suck it up. Much of the US tech sector was reaping substantial profits in China selling everything from semiconductors to software to iPhones, and using production bases and integrated supply chains there to keep their costs down. The CEO nearest to me in the queue outside the State Department that day, Tim Cook, had seen his company make $58.7 billion in China that year, 25 percent of Apple's global revenues.[2] And some of the largest firms that were excluded had not given up hope of reaping the same benefits themselves. Before coming to DC, Xi had stopped off in Seattle to attend an internet industry forum, with the architect of China's "great firewall," Lu Wei, in train, the minister in charge of cyber-administration who would later find himself purged in Xi's anti-corruption drive. Even Lu's most prominent victims, the US platforms that his filtering made sure Chinese citizens could not access, gamely showed up anyway, personified by Mark Zuckerberg and his near-adulatory pursuit of Xi that saw him offer the leader of the Chinese Communist Party the opportunity to name his child.

The same dynamics were equally apparent across the Western world. When I headed to a reception at the Chinese embassy near the end of Xi's trip, one of the Chinese officials there was less interested in a postmortem than in talking rhapsodically about the British chancellor at the time, George Osborne. Osborne was the mastermind behind the announcement of a "golden era" of UK–China relations, which saw a virtual open door for Chinese investments even in sensitive sectors such as nuclear power. His rush earlier that year to make sure the UK was first to join China's new Asia Infrastructure Investment Bank (AIIB), over US objections, pushed other Europeans to expedite their own decisions lest they be perceived by Beijing as laggards.

In talking to UK Treasury officials close to the process, they made clear that this was seen by Osborne and his advisors as a long-term bet: Britain had to be positioned to benefit from the next global power transition. The Chinese official commended the far-sightedness of the British and hoped that this approach from the very closest of US allies would blaze a trail for the rest of the West.

The Belt and Road Initiative, as the Chinese government subsequently rechristened it in English, was barely on the US radar screen. Having spent much of the year traipsing around the world hearing about little else from China's friends and rivals alike, returning each time to a curious radio silence about the subject in Washington, DC, I wondered whether it might at least feature during Xi's visit. In a series of speeches in Central and Southeast Asia, he had laid out a scheme for a globe-spanning set of Chinese-financed infrastructure connections, which anyone talking to officials in Beijing or potential recipient countries could already see would have at least hundreds of billions—if not trillions—of dollars deployed behind them. I sheepishly raised questions about this vast Chinese investment initiative in the pre-briefings and readout meetings from the White House and drew slightly quizzical looks as the officials batted me away and went back to Taiwan, trade, the South China Sea and the other traditional staple issues in the bilateral relationship. When I asked a contact who had sat in on the meetings with Xi if the issue had featured even in passing, he shrugged and said that they had prepared talking points but it hadn't come up.

This was not the byproduct of a soft-minded view among the individuals centrally responsible for crafting China policy. Most of the officials were clear-eyed and critical in their views of the Chinese Communist Party and the consequences of China's growing power and assertiveness, just as their predecessors had been. Some were minded to harden US policy considerably and would have the chance to do exactly that a few years later. But this was what China policy looked like in 2015, and had for a long time. Except on the margins, everyone stayed in their separate lanes. The trade people did trade, the security people did security. Problems in the bilateral relationship were at least superficially addressed through meetings and summits, embodied by the unwieldy "Strategic and Economic Dialogue," a vast edifice that brought together virtually every US cabinet official with their Chinese counterparts. One of the highlights of the Xi visit was an earnestly negotiated agreement that China would restrain the extent of its commercial spying activities. The belief was that these deals stuck. As one White House official at the time put it:

> The sense was that when Xi gave his word, it was solid. He said he would get the climate deal done. He said he would get visa reciprocity done ... We felt good about the cyber-deal.

If there was already an impression during the trip that something was amiss, it was still nascent. "At their private dinner, Obama beat the shit out of Xi for two hours over the South China Sea" noted one of the US officials in attendance. The next day, Xi made the announcement in which he pledged the non-militarization of the South China Sea: "He said this on his own—we hadn't expected it." Cui Tiankai, the Chinese ambassador, and the other officials with him were fidgeting when Xi spoke. "We tried to follow up immediately to talk about what it meant, what the definition of 'militarization' was. They were very resistant." Chinese officials would initially claim that "he didn't say that, that's not our policy" and stonewalled US officials on the subject during future meetings.

Looking back, one of the officials noted that the experience would affect the mental frame on China for many of those who returned to serve in the Biden administration: "From that point forward it felt like: these fuckers are acting in bad faith." But at the time, there was little sense that decades of the relationship should be turned on its head, let alone that this was imminent.

* * *

The shift in the years that followed seems so abrupt that it is easy to attribute almost everything to the radical discontinuity of the Trump administration. The story tells itself nicely. Trump arrives, ready to take steps that no previous US government would ever have contemplated in pursuit of a trade deal. After an initial phase of factional battles over the direction of US policy, a group of hawkish officials use the political space provided by Trump's trade war to push through measures that send the US–China relationship into a state of open confrontation. China's access to US technologies is squeezed, its investments and acquisitions are restricted, the two intertwined economies start to decouple, ideological hostility intensifies, and then COVID-19 tips things over the edge. More and more facets of US policy are subsumed in the counter-China agenda as the president blames Beijing for the damage the pandemic wreaks and allows the administration's hardest-edged voices to run the China show as they see fit. The rest of the world is reluctantly forced to adjust to the new US–China rivalry, despite their wish not to "choose sides."

The speed and breadth of the changes bely this account. Within barely a year of the new US administration taking office, a new National Security Strategy and National Defense Strategy were codified and agreed, stipulating that "inter-state strategic competition, not terrorism, is now the primary concern in US national security," with China named as the only all-fronts competitor.[3]

For anyone working in Washington, DC at the time, it was clear that the hardening of China policy was the one issue that many career civil servants and serious political appointees were very happy to take on. During what was otherwise an often-demoralizing time to be working in US foreign policy, the mobilization of energy and inventiveness on any China-related matter was apparent across an array of US government departments and agencies. Where on other topics there was often some combination of disbelief and horror among officials about the measures the Trump administration was considering, when

11

it came to China more often than not there was a degree of relief and enthusiasm.

I personally sat through numerous conversations with US officials in which I was regaled with "it's worse than you think" stories about goings on in the administration before they would pivot to some variant of: "But I have to admit that I like the fact that we're not pulling our punches with China anymore." Well before the Pence speech that gave public expression to it, the scale of the shift underway across the US government was palpable. It was equally evident in Congress. While Trump was still holding up the tougher measures that his staff hoped to pursue, bipartisan majorities passed bills on China-focused export controls, China-focused investment screening and support for the financing and instruments to compete with the Belt and Road. For all the stops and starts, and internal battles, the general direction of flow was clear. Whatever changed in the United States, it ran far deeper than the ephemeral administration-initiated moves in other policy areas.

To make sense of this, career officials closest to the changes in US China strategy point their fingers away from the colorful accounts of Trump administration cabinet members screaming at each other in the Oval Office. They return to a set of debates that played out in the Obama administration at precisely the time that Xi was having his celebratory visit. In particular, a set of initiatives and concepts that were couched in the very driest of bureaucratic defense-speak.

* * *

In April 2016, Obama's deputy secretary of defense, Robert Work, arrived in Brussels for a rare visit, his trips away from the Pentagon being so infrequent that he compared his role to the tethered goat in *Jurassic Park*. It was the peak of the counter-ISIS campaign, and much of Bob Work's agenda was nominally focused on Iraq, Syria, terrorism and a list of issues that had been familiar ones over the preceding decade-and-a-half. But the real purpose was to move beyond them. It was time, he contended in his speech, for NATO to revisit the question of deterrence, "a concept that NATO really hasn't thought about since the end of the Cold War."[4] We were in a "new era of great power competition" with a resurgent Russia and a rising China, and we needed to draw lessons from the Cold War on how to prevent war between nuclear-armed powers.

After over a decade of "out of area" operations in Afghanistan, NATO was only just starting to come to terms with Putin's annexation of Crimea and what it implied for the European security order. Any institutional thinking about China was at best embryonic. His argument was that deterrence relied on "increasing our margin of technological superiority" with China and Russia "that unquestionably has been eroding over the last 20 years."

To contextualize it, he went back to two prior US efforts to offset Soviet capabilities during the Cold War. The first was in the 1950s when the United States used its superiority in nuclear weapons to offset the huge Soviet conventional advantage, including the threat of using tactical nuclear attacks against Soviet forces in Europe. The second was in the 1970s and 1980s, when precision-guided strike and stealth technologies achieved the same effect. Scale would be trumped by technological prowess. He proposed a new effort to "overmatch" not only the Russian capabilities that most worried NATO but the Chinese capabilities that were becoming the graver concern to the United States. Hence the infelicitous name for the initiative: the Third Offset Strategy.

Work was on a mission. "The only reason he took the job was the Third Offset, and he drove the shit out of it," noted one former White House official. The technologies he cited were less important than the principles the strategy embodied. The bare fact of putting Russia and China at the center of US national defense strategy was itself by no means a reflection of the prevailing view in the administration at the time. There was also a big difference between the Third Offset Strategy and its predecessors, with implications for the United States and its allies that went well beyond what its architects envisaged. While the technological advances in the 1950s and 1970s were catalyzed by government-led research and development efforts, now "almost all of the technology that is of importance in the future is coming from the commercial sector, and all of the technology base is global."

It was not just about Lockheed Martin and Boeing anymore. When it came to AI, autonomous vehicles, virtual reality, robotics, blockchain technology and an assortment of other areas, the cutting edge of the research was being conducted by companies that had no such hand-in-glove relationship with the US defense sector. China was drawing on precisely the same technology base. And it was indeed global. Making sure that the United States ran faster was all very well, but if China was able to benefit from the fruits of the most advanced research in the United States, Europe, Japan, Korea and elsewhere, there was still the danger that it would catch up regardless. "Any competitor and any adversary is going to have access to these types of technologies, and they can quickly mimic even the most powerful state." At the time, Work claimed to be "okay with that." The United States simply had to deal with a world of "fast followers." But the thinking would soon change.

A few months earlier, the Pentagon had set up a new unit to do the kind of liaison work with Silicon Valley that the strategy envisaged. After a rocky start, which saw Congressional threats to withhold funding until it tightened up its plans, and a quick turnover of leadership, the Defense Innovation Unit Experimental— DIUx—found its feet with a mission to fund fast turnaround contracts that would get advanced commercial technologies quickly into the hands of the US military. Headquartered down the road from Google in Mountain View, it would finance solutions for tightly defined problems such as how to design drones that could do advance work for US special forces teams going into buildings on kill-capture missions, a bargain at $1.5 million.

When the Trump administration took over, DIU—by then it was no longer "experimental"—was given another task: to see what the competition was doing. Michael Brown had been the CEO of another firm headquartered in Mountain View, Symantec, before joining the Obama administration as a White House innovation fellow. He was sent back over to the Bay Area to look into Chinese investment activities.

The results were troubling. Precisely the early-stage technological advances that DIUx was supposed to be focused on were fully accessible to China too and sucking in ever-greater volumes of Chinese venture capital. It wasn't even clear that the United States was better placed to make use of some of them. China's own civil–military fusion program had its deficiencies but was being turbo-charged under Xi Jinping. Some of it mapped onto an ambitious new industrial strategy that had been laid out a year earlier, called Made in China 2025, which named all and more of the areas that the Department of Defense (DOD) had identified as the most critical. Brown's report argued that "the Crown Jewels of US innovation" were available to a "strategic competitor," and that what China was doing was perfectly legal under existing investment screening and export control rules.[5] When combined with cyber-theft, economic espionage, Chinese research centers in the United States, partnerships with US academia and an assortment of other channels, it added up to a technology transfer strategy that would render plans such as the Third Offset strategy virtually useless. "If we allow China access to these same technologies concurrently, then not only may we lose our technological superiority but we may even be facilitating China's technological superiority."

While the Third Offset terminology would soon fade during the Trump administration, the principles underpinning it were on their way into US legislation and strategic planning well before Trump had imposed a single tariff. The US saw itself losing its technological edge.

The implications cut to the core of US deterrence in Asia and Europe. The openness of the US system was becoming a security liability. But changing a few rules about foreign ownership stakes would only chip away at the problem. The US and Chinese economies had been deeply intertwined, with talent, finance, research, production facilities and supply chains distributed from Zhongguancun to Boston. Decoupling them would be a wrench. And the problem didn't end there: if the United States adjusted alone, China could acquire many of the same technologies, techniques and components from other advanced economies. Semiconductor production spanned Taiwanese fabrication plants, Dutch photolithography and specialized German design tools. Chinese academics denied access to Stanford and MIT could still study graphene in Manchester and autonomous technologies in Tel Aviv.

That would mean getting a wide array of US allies in line too, some of whom had major economic interests in the current state of interactions with China continuing. The scale of what this required went well beyond what could be diplomatically cajoled or legislatively coerced. China was not the DPRK, Iran or even Russia. This was a market really worth fighting for, and some of the world's most powerful lobbyists would do exactly that. But those battles were still to come. What the DIUx paper and the debates around it confirmed for many officials and legislators was that the balance of openness and security was landing in the wrong place. It also posed a fresh set of questions: if the US advantage was eroding, what was the broader plan to support the forms of innovation the country required? What happened to the competitiveness of the US tech sector if it lost its access to the huge Chinese market? How far could US national security rely on the current framework of commercial incentives for its firms? Should the United States consider the notion of an industrial strategy, once unthinkable to market purists?

The proposals emanating from the DOD were only a snippet of the wider debates that had been unfolding over the trade-offs involved in the economic relationship with China. But while US firms and US trade strategists landed in an assortment of different places on what they thought the right balance looked like, this put a floor under them. Whatever the mammoth Trump trade talks with Beijing accomplished, there was now a deeper appreciation that economic, technological and military competition were too intertwined for these issues to be determined purely by questions of market access, trade deficits, production costs and bilateral purchasing agreements. Where negotiations on a trade deal oscillated between hope, crisis and face-saving, the national security dimensions of the nascent US–China decoupling followed a logic of their own.

Even more striking, however, were some of the positions that emerged from Western industry itself. The most illuminating were not coming from Silicon Valley or Wall Street. They were coming from the single cluster of firms that could most unambiguously have been said to benefit from the Chinese economy in the preceding decade, on the other side of the Atlantic.

* * *

In January 2019, an unusual paper started gaining traction. The Bundesverband der Deutschen Industrie (BDI), the Federation of German Industries, embodies what had once been the unequivocal success story of Western economic engagement with

China. Its biggest companies, from the car and chemical companies to the myriad smaller engineering and component firms, had seen the Chinese market as a lifeline during a period that was defined by the eurozone crisis and deep stagnation in the principal European markets. Whatever impact China's economic ascent had elsewhere on the continent, Germany had unfailingly remained aloof. When industries in Spain and Italy had been hit by waves of imports after China's accession to the WTO, their experience was seen as yet another indicator that—unlike Germany—they had not reformed their economies to be sufficiently competitive in this next phase of globalization. As Chinese money started to roll in, and Southern European ministers and European commissioners raised the prospect of European investment screening mechanisms, it was BDI members who lined up to dismiss it as base protectionism.

Yet by 2018, the mood had soured. Some claimed that the turning point was the takeover of the Augsburg-based robotics firm KUKA by the Chinese appliance manufacturer Midea in 2016. After years of acquiring dumb infrastructure and fading brands, China was increasingly training its sights on the crown jewels of advanced German industry, much as it was also doing in California. KUKA was not such a jewel itself, as its lackluster performance after the acquisition confirmed. But the incident demonstrated that there were no ready means of recourse if Chinese firms decided to snap up the firms dubbed the country's "hidden champions," the small and medium-sized companies that dominated niche sectors from tunnel-digging equipment to hydraulic presses.

It set off a flurry of activity. The economics minister, Angela Merkel's former top aide, Peter Altmaier, personally wrote a set of contentious proposals for the state to step in to intervene in comparable cases. But for the people involved in coming up with the BDI's paper, KUKA had little to do with it. The new strain of thinking was not the byproduct of a moment of political shock. It was rueful, considered analysis from the very experts, officials and business leaders who were closest to China and had seen what was unfolding over the last few years. For the cluster of paper drafters and outside advisors, it was evident that an entire way of evaluating the political and economic situation in China had come to an end, which others with a more distant vantage point had not fully understood. And that someone would have to state it clearly if anything was going to change.

As one of the paper's authors put it: "We had a clear focus— that we have to rethink everything. We sat discussing the Xi Jinping era and said, do we really continue with the same line in 2018 as 2017, 2016 and before that about cooperation with China or do we do it differently?" A small group from different government ministries, businesses and think-tanks duly gathered at a retreat outside Berlin to think harder. But a little gang of critical voices would have had limited traction if the wider context was not permissive. "The surprise was that there was no real hurdle to get a consensus on the paper, we expected more challenges on the industry side," as one of its drafters admitted. "In fact, the more China knowledge the firms had, the more supportive they were in the process. They all said: "We don't want our name in the paper but it's exactly the right direction." There was one exception, the CEO of one major firm who called the president of the BDI to try to get it stopped at the last minute, claiming it would endanger German business in China. But by then it was too late.

The paper opens starkly with the description of "China as a systemic competitor." "For a long time it looked as if China would gradually move towards the liberal, open market economies of the West by integrating into the world economy and reshaping its economic system. This theory of convergence is no longer tenable." Instead, it argued that China was "in the process of consolidating its own political, economic and social model [and is now] shaping other markets and the international economic order." "Politicians and companies must adapt" to a "conflict" between the Chinese model and the "liberal and social market economy principles of the EU and many other countries." It would have been one thing if it had been an NGO report or a think tank policy paper. Coming as the consolidated product of a year-long process of consultation across German industry, it represented something almost revolutionary in its implications for economic relations between China and the advanced industrial democracies. There was a "division of labor," as one of the experts close to the process noted: "As individual companies, we can't afford to stick our own heads out. But we must support business associations and think-tanks to say the unpleasant things."

One of those think-tanks was MERICS. Founded in 2013 with the intention of being a "bridging institution" between Berlin and Beijing, and "filling the void" in Europe as the demand for high-quality China analysis now vastly outran supply, it was easily the best-resourced and largest cluster of China researchers working on the continent. It would decipher and translate dry Party papers into sharp data visualizations and was informed by a "principled approach of not treating politics and economics separately." As Sebastian Heilmann, its founding director, put it:

> The Party writes a lot of these things down: their goals and instruments have become more transparent than before. We read all these Chinese documents. It's not easy to communicate a text on ideology or "the main contradiction." China experts would say wow, this is a new stage in history, but most people wouldn't understand it.

A few years later, MERICS would be one of the only think-tanks in the world to be placed under Chinese sanctions.

Heilmann had worked for much of his academic career on the distinctly unfashionable topic of Chinese industrial policy. "It was a no-go area. It was always seen as unproductive, a dead end. Industrial policy was not a topic in the US at all, a blind spot. Yet it was a center-piece of China's whole thinking." Some of the policymakers that Heilmann had dealt with during his research were now taking on even more prominent roles under Xi Jinping, from Yang Weimin to Liu He, Xi's top economic advisor:

> They became market-friendly but they started out as planners, and were very influenced by Japan's experience. They always had a long-term view. They see themselves as guardians of economic and social stability, of China's stability. We saw our systems as superior, and believed that they would absorb anything we taught them.

In the aftermath of the financial crisis of 2008, that was no longer true:

> This was a watershed event for them. Before that they said: the West has found the solution for leading society and the economy into the twenty-first century. After that they thought: the West has no idea, no solution for these problems. "This must never happen in China. We have to go it alone."

Relatively soon after launching MERICS, Heilmann wrote an op-ed in the leading center-left German daily *Süddeutsche Zeitung* that identified precisely how this was translating into Chinese strategy under Xi. He argued that China was in the process of closing down, that ideological content was being taken increasingly seriously, that we were seeing the end of the "reform and opening" era. The infamous internal "Document Number Nine" had been leaked a few months earlier.[6] Bearing Xi's imprimatur, it warned of a comprehensive threat from Western democratic and liberal ideals and heralded a devastating rollback of what little political space remained. Yet Heilmann's article attracted considerable criticism in Germany, outrunning the still-sanguine consensus at the time.

But it was MERICS' study on China's turbo-charged industrial policy plans that really broke through. As one German analyst put it:

> The single most decisive thing that led to a shift in thinking on China for the people that matter in Germany was "Made in China 2025." While "Change through trade" had long been discredited, they could live with an authoritarian China as long as they could profit from it.

That view changed once the nature of the ambitions in the coming years was clearer: "they were out to get us." Heilmann adds: "We were the first to make clear that this is a full-scale plan not just to substitute foreign competition but to get rid of foreign technology leaders, and in very aggressive terms." When they talked to German ministries, their line was: "You may not believe in industrial policy. But your most important trading partner is relying on this." The detailed work on each of the individual pieces of the puzzle in China, from Xinjiang to the social credit system, was adding up to a dark picture. "What we had once seen as authoritarianism, even soft authoritarianism, was instead becoming totalitarian control. From then on people said: "We have to fight this, not just analyze it."

As well as its invocation of this darker vision of the China that was now a competitor of a systemic nature, two other things were striking about the BDI's paper. Previous iterations addressed China with their recommendations. This one did not. That seemingly small distinction in fact encapsulated the entire shift in the way thinking in so many major capitals was now moving. There was no point in pretending that China was going to change. There was no point in spending so much time and political capital trying to induce it. Energies should be directed elsewhere. The bilateral relationship was no longer where the action was in China policy. It was a question of what could be done if Beijing continued on precisely its current course.

It was also a question of who should do it. For the German business association, this would usually have meant Germany itself. When it came to dealings with Beijing, Berlin had a special set of channels that were better developed than those of any other European state, from elaborate joint cabinet meetings to Merkel's role as the single leader in Europe whose voice carried weight at the highest levels in China. Yet as the BDI team batted ideas around, it was also evident that most of the essential steps would have to come at the EU level, with the full weight of the economic bloc behind them, rather than from Berlin alone. "The longer we worked, the more deeply convinced we were that we needed to change any language about the 'German government' to 'the EU,' that a stronger EU was essential." A few weeks after the BDI paper came out, the action would switch to Brussels.

* * *

Much like papers from the BDI, documents from the European Commission don't usually make a splash. They are typically lowest-common-denominator products of twenty-eight rounds of consultation. Even when they have bite, it is often hidden behind the deadliest of prose. In March 2019, two months after the red alert from German business, there was a distinct exception. One senior British official described it as the single best paper he had ever seen the European institutions produce on any subject. It would be cited near the top of the Trump administration's own China strategy as the very encapsulation of shifts in thinking by US partners. The document was a punchy ten-point plan that promised to rebalance the EU's strategy in light of the "growing appreciation in Europe that the balance of challenges and opportunities presented by China has shifted."[7]

And it had a kick. It introduced a term, "systemic rival," that has become part of the European lexicon ever since, to China's deep disquiet. The language itself had already appeared in an in-house document prepared by the German Foreign Office's planning staff the previous year, a first effort to rethink the terms of the relationship from the ground up. The diplomats tasked with the exercise introduced what would be dubbed by some the "holy trinity"—that while China was still a partner in some areas, it was a competitor (which even the Chinese accepted), and rival too (which they decidedly did not).

The notion that the rivalry was "systemic" had an entropic quality to it, as the idea that China could also be a real "partner" started to look decreasingly plausible the more one faced up to what the nature of that rivalry really amounted to. The notion of "systemic rivalry" would later become foundational to European thinking about China, so socialized into common use that it was part of the intellectual furniture. But at the time the concept was still at the furthest edges of the debate. As one of the drafters admitted, "when we included the term, I wasn't sure it would survive." The German policy planning document was internal. This would be public.

The paper was put together in barely two weeks, with most of the work being undertaken in a few crucial days, masterminded by Martin Selmayr, the Commission's gray eminence and most senior official. The manner in which he wielded power across the EU bureaucracy had won him a legion of critics, but his deployment of this approach in the cause of reshaping the continent's approach to China was widely credited as essential to the success of the process. He was single-mindedly intent on demonstrating that Europe—and the EU itself—needed to be treated as a player in the emerging geopolitical landscape. As Selmayr put it: "I was always puzzled how weak the EU must have appeared to the Chinese, and how they treated us—as an irrelevant factor. It was a reproach to us. China sees weakness and treats weakness as weakness." He described sitting next to Juncker through meals with Xi Jinping, who would be slurping his food (as is common in China) while explaining how great China was, and at the same time teasing the Europeans, saying that he had heard that Le Pen was now stronger than Macron in France, and making clear that he saw the European Commission and the European Council president as a sideshow. He would say: "We have made a deal with Merkel", which his dining room companions understood to mean, as Selmayr put it: "'So what do you dwarves want here?' And at the same time they were buying the 16+1."

For many officials in Brussels, China's approach to this grouping of sixteen (and, for a time, seventeen) Central and Eastern European states exemplified Beijing's shift from subtle power maneuvers that exploited intra-European differences to openly drawing dividing lines across the EU. For Selmayr, though, it was an earlier moment of European vulnerability that had left its imprint:

> The experience that woke me up was during the financial crisis, when we were trying to keep the eurozone together. I saw the harbor of Piraeus being bought by the Chinese while we were arguing about how to help. I found it a shame, that we were not showing solidarity, that we were not being geostrategic, and I thought it was dangerous. We are still paying for some of those mistakes.

European political leaders had placed China on the agenda for their meeting in March 2019, one month before the EU–China summit. Merkel and other heads of government wanted to allot time to discuss the big issues that had so often been swamped by Europe's internal crises in the preceding years. "We had been shaken up by Brexit, and several leaders said to us—look, we have a summit coming up and this time we have to prepare it. We should not speak with twenty-seven voices." Selmayr and the Commission president, Jean-Claude Juncker, planned on far more than a careful unity text though. As Selmayr described their goal: "China is very assertive. Let's be as assertive as we, as the EU, can manage to be. Let's have a document that China will read, and that they will not immediately throw into the bin. That will wake them up. That will not be talk. That will have teeth."

This was not about China alone. It was the culmination of a year of intense efforts to demonstrate the EU's capacity to be a geopolitical protagonist, from its ambitious new trade and data deal with Japan to a painfully agreed tariff truce with the United States: "We saw the Chinese as the biggest challenge to the international rules-based system, but there was also Trump." The G7 summit in Canada in June 2018 had been a bruising experience, immortalized in the German official photographer's image of the US president sitting alone with his arms folded, glaring up defiantly at an exasperated-looking cluster of European leaders. Juncker himself was dubbed a "brutal killer" by Trump in the course of the meeting. "In our hearts we are always more transatlantic, even then we knew what side we were on. We share the values of the West," noted Selmayr: "But this [China paper] was a message in all directions: we don't shy away from calling a spade a spade."

It was written by a small, closed group, with only six people formally permitted to see the full text before it was sent into the formal adoption procedure among the twenty-seven members of the European Commission—who liked the document so much for its clarity and concreteness that they adopted it without changing a comma. Selmayr killed an earlier version of the paper, "very nice diplomatically, very thin operationally," and sent the drafters back to deliver something with more communicative and operational heft. It arrived whole and intact, the outcome of a tight political-level process rather than consultations across the full bureaucracy, and without any opportunity for EU member states to soften the edges. One of the paper drafters noted gleefully that while a document like this would usually have been picked to pieces by various EU senior officials from across the bureaucracy, "Selmayr terrified them all. It was fantastic."

Even more importantly, Beijing had no opportunity to lobby any of them to water it down, and no warning of the paper before its publication. It came as a shock. The EU is not generally set up to keep secrets. When documents kick around twenty-seven member states, they leak. As a result, China was used to inserting itself and acting as a shadow party to exercises of this nature. And while strategy documents come and go, it was clear that this represented something more. As well as using language about China that would have been unthinkable only a short while ago, the approach it outlined was no longer constructed entirely around the classic areas of trade and foreign policy. It promised to deploy the entire spectrum of European economic, political and security instruments behind it and looked like the first inklings of how China might recondition European grand strategy rather than being a China policy paper alone.

As one French official put it:

> When we got the EU document, we were taken aback by its sharpness. It was so to the point. No paraphrasing. Tough but not unfair. But the surprise for us, even more than the paper itself, was the European Council. We thought it would trigger never-ending discussions. That it would be torn apart. What surprised us was that the Council accepted. That was even more striking. The fact that the overall assumption now was that everyone agreed.

The "systemic rival" terminology was expected to be one of the biggest points of contention and was the subject of fierce debate in the final stages of the paper's preparation. While it was European diplomats who inserted the language in the first place, their higher-ups were skittish. "The diplomats in the negotiations were all against it," Selmayr stated, "But Richard Szostak and I insisted that it was inserted. And Juncker insisted on it. We had a mandate from the president to put it in there." When EU member states met in the aftermath, they were still too cautious to endorse the text wholesale; that would only come the following year. Even then, some European leaders could never bring themselves to echo the language themselves. But none of them, from Merkel to Viktor Orbán, objected to it. There was a slight headiness to being able to describe reality as it was with China without this bringing about the end of the world. "No-one challenged it," Selmayr noted, "in fact, the member states lauded it. They said 'can you really say that?' We had never dared to say it." This included the German chancellor:

> I'd heard people say that Merkel didn't like it. It wasn't true. She was the first to take to the floor to say that she liked the style. She has never used the term "rival" but she liked that it was in that document, she knew that the Chinese would take it seriously.

The French president, Emmanuel Macron, would claim that it signaled that the era of European "naïveté" on China was over. With Xi Jinping due to visit Paris shortly afterwards, Macron made a point of bouncing the Chinese leader into accepting that his supposedly bilateral trip would feature Merkel and Juncker too. As one official involved in the trip preparations put it to me at the time: "For us, it was a twofold narrative to China—united we stand and: go fuck yourselves." But they also sought to make a point to other Europeans: "Europe could stand up to China, and it still wouldn't stop them buying our products."

Beijing's unhappiness with the new European strategy was evident. As one of the participants in the meeting noted: "In the EU–China summit they were very irritated. For an hour they spoke about nothing else." Chinese diplomats would embark on a witch-hunt for which EU officials were behind it. If the Commission's bureaucratic ambush had been a success in putting Europe's approach on a different footing, it was only the starting point. As Selmayr reflected later:

> It was surprising that we needed to surprise our systems, to get them out of their comfort zone. It showed that people were very naive if

it was already seen as surprising and courageous to go that far. If you've ever sat on the other side of the table with Xi, it's absolutely common sense. It's the minimum. This change should have happened much earlier.

* * *

To make sense of why it was not just the language that represented a break, some disentangling is required. For outsiders, the Brussels institutions are an opaque blob. A jumble of acronyms and a mostly unlovely set of buildings clustered around a roundabout at the end of a multi-lane highway. China policy had largely been the purview of two of these institutions, which wielded far from equal clout. The European External Action Service ostensibly acts as the EU's diplomatic service, with its chief often dubbed the European foreign minister. But the unwieldy name—pointedly not the EU foreign ministry—reflects the discomfort that European states had for handing over their foreign policymaking powers. It is also hobbled by the requirement for unanimity, which means that not even a joint statement can be issued in the EU's name if, say, Hungary or Greece decide to block it. Much of the new agenda, however, would fall to the more powerful beasts in town.

The Directorate-General for Trade was near the top of the food chain. With the capacity to marshal the full economic force of the world's largest trading bloc, no inhibiting veto for individual member states affecting its decisions, and the unalloyed status that trade is a full EU competence, it was already deeply embroiled in the China game. The new proposals envisaged giving DG-Trade even more capacity to block Chinese investments, enforce reciprocity in the EU's enormous government procurement market, level tariffs on Chinese imports with additional robustness, and tighten restrictions on high-tech exports. But it would also unleash other Brussels powerhouses on the China account. The

Directorate-General for International Partnerships, which controls the world's largest aid budget, was supposed to reconfigure its approach to deal with China in a more competitive manner, though it would prove exceptionally painful to persuade them to do so. The digital wing of the EU, DG-Connect, was tasked with rethinking technology rules and regulations to deal with the growing presence of Chinese firms in the European market. But one of the most interesting cases was the heaviest of the heavyweights, the Directorate-General for Competition, "DG-Comp."

* * *

DG-Trade is part of the newly empowered Europe that emerged with the establishment of the European Single Market in the 1980s, turning diffuse national economies into the world's largest trading bloc. DG-Comp's roots run even deeper, back to the founding mythology of the entire European integration process. Decartelization had been a critical part of the Schuman plan, with the language originally drafted by a US official and Harvard professor, Robert Bowie, the leading expert on US antitrust legislation, "which the Americans applied as rigorously as morality itself" as Europe's founding father, Jean Monnet, put it in his memoirs.[8]

Breaking down concentrations in the coal and steel industry had been central to US policy in the post-war settlement, part of the plan to limit the re-emergence of the forms of German industrial power that had existed under Nazism. As such, the competition provisions in the Schuman plan were highly contentious, resisted by the West German government at the time. But they stuck. Monnet later noted that "the extensive antitrust legislation now applied by the European Community essentially derives from those few lines in the Schuman treaty." And they had in their DNA a US spirit and philosophy of highly competitive markets, which would now become hard-wired into the way the new European institutions worked.[9]

In more recent years, DG-Comp had emerged as the bane of Silicon Valley, trying to regulate and take on concentrations of market power where US antitrust authorities, fixated since the 1970s almost exclusively on keeping consumer prices down, were no longer willing to go. US companies and officials complained that they were too often the targets, Trump himself calling the responsible commissioner, Margrethe Vestager, a US-hating "tax lady."[10] European officials, by contrast, lamented the fact that the United States no longer seemed meaningfully committed to the very competitive values it had helped to inculcate in Europe in the post-war settlement. But now a new problem was on the table: the China question.

The trigger was what would typically have been an open-and-shut case, the proposed merger of Alstom and Siemens in 2017, the French and German companies that were Europe's largest suppliers in the rail market. In normal circumstances, this would barely have merited a debate. Yet the companies involved had a different argument to make than in years past. The Chinese high-speed rail sector had consolidated rapidly and was now posing a threat in every international market. European champions were required to take it on. EU competition authorities should therefore no longer restrict themselves to looking at the position of these firms in the European market alone but take a global view. DG-Comp officials were bitterly resistant to this line of argument, seeing it as a new form of anticompetitive special pleading. Even when Vestager was hauled in front of European leaders to explain the decisions, the merger was blocked in early 2019.

When I dropped by to talk to the China hands in the DG soon after the decision, it was striking how few of the EU's powerful competition tools the institution believed could actually be deployed to take the China problem on. Blocking Chinese mega-mergers was too much of a reach, and "European champions" were antithetical to their mandate to ensure competitive markets. Everything that might have looked like a job for DG-Comp actually belonged in the trade realm, they contended. "Competition law is not the answer to all evils." Taking on large, well-connected European and US multinationals was challenging enough already for the embattled officials. China risked becoming their get-out-of-jail-free card.

By 2020, everything had changed. "There is a reflection in the house on how to approach the overall state of affairs and the detonator for this is China," as one official put it. The first public sign of what was going on was a series of proposals that year laying out an ambitious set of plans for how the EU could go after Chinese subsidies. Beijing's untrammeled capacity to back its firms with cheap land, electricity and other inputs, as well as outright finance, had been a headache for Western firms in China but was now becoming one in third markets and even in their home markets. It was one of the single biggest advantages that Huawei had over European telecoms firms. How to level the effect of this was a problem that virtually every competitor was wrestling with.

It was the European Commission that would lay out the single most comprehensive approach to address it, even if they rarely mentioned China by name in the process. For the various foreign officials who contacted me enthusiastically the week the EU's proposals were released, the most exciting part of it was that DG-Comp was now in on the game. "This is lightyears ahead of us," one US official commented. "Once it was us with Brandeis," she noted, referencing the anti-monopolist Supreme Court justice who had dubbed economic concentration the "Curse of Bigness": "We trained you on antitrust, and now you're going to train us."

In private, there was a changed spirit. When I went back to the European officials who covered the account, they were fizzing with ideas for how to overcome China's non-transparent practices, how to target cartel-like practices among Chinese firms, metrics that could indicate anti-competitive behavior, methods for blocking subsidized takeovers, models for thinking about China's use of data, and a long list of other proposals. Bolder arguments suggested treating all Chinese firms as a single "China Inc.," given the role of the state and the Party across the totality of the Chinese economy, a decision they had already hinted at when they decided that Chinese firms in the energy sector should be seen as a single entity for the purpose of merger assessments. "We went through a long reflection process on what's legally possible. We had to come up with a solution," they noted in priestly fashion. When it really mattered, Commission lawyers could suddenly become very creative. Now, even core EU doctrine needed reinterpreting with China in the picture.

* * *

Dwelling on the arcana of European competition law may seem like a sideshow in the context of militarized islands in the South China Sea, vast infrastructure investments and mass detentions of Uyghurs. But China has long understood the base of its power to come from its access to the Western-created system and its ability to game it at the same time, whether that be technology acquisition by fair means or foul, or the freedom to access international markets while ensuring only the most selective access to its own.

The reluctant revisiting of fundamental orthodoxy about anti-trust practices was more emblematic of the newfound impetus to think differently about how to deal with these basic asymmetries than any statement of European criticism about Hong Kong. China didn't represent a narrow challenge. It posed questions about whether the foundational principles of the existing system could still function in the same way. As one French Treasury official commented· "We haven't changed our understanding of economics. We still don't think that the Chinese model will succeed in the long run. But how many decades are we supposed to wait for it to fail? And what will happen to our industry in the meantime?"

Talking to European officials at the time, there was the sense of a dawning recognition that an era was coming to an end, if not full acceptance of the revolution it implied. But the first step was simply to face up to the problem. As one of the officials reflected:

> There was Trump, we have to recognize that he had a role in getting us to rethink our position. There was the promise fatigue—China would keep making announcements and nothing happened. There was the evidence accumulation, the long track record, the depth of understanding of how the Chinese economy was really working.

There was also a coming to terms with past mistakes. "We gave a lot of access to China, believing that we had to be the first movers and then we'd be rewarded. We were fools." But just as the United States had started to wake up to what the changing nature of China's economic and technological ambitions would mean for their military rivalry, so too was there a growing awareness in Europe. "We also saw more clearly what was happening systemically—it was Made in China 2025 meets the Belt and Road. We didn't take some of these things as seriously in the first place." It was not just about seeing China more clearly though; it was also about training the mirror on themselves. As one French official put it:

> "We saw our own weakness: the openness paradigm. That no matter what people do outside the EU, we were convinced of the virtues of being open. This way of thinking can work when you don't have the likes of China playing on these rules to their advantage."

* * *

It was no longer tenable. "We needed to have a way to ensure that this openness and freedom were sustainable. The sheer magnitude of the China problem puts it at risk."

Tokyo, July 2018

It was my last meeting in Tokyo. I was in town to give a talk at the National Institute for Defense Studies and had my usual round of meetings at the foreign ministry and the prime minister's office. But the appointment I was keenest to get to was at the Ministry of Economy, Trade and Industry. METI's forerunner had been responsible for Japanese industrial policy and was alternately vilified and admired by US policymakers back in the 1980s when Japan was the locus of American anxieties. Chinese planners had used elements of Tokyo's approach as a model, even as they took it to a whole new level.

Times had long changed. METI was now at the cutting edge not only of the drive for ambitious new trade agreements but all forms of economic and technology cooperation among the world's free-market democracies. The tradition of strategic economic thinking in which they were steeped often gave METI officials an edge when they saw industrial strategy being pursued on an even grander scale by their overbearing neighbor. The Japanese government had been quick on the draw in providing countries with alternative financing to China's Belt and Road Initiative while the Americans and Europeans lagged well behind with their own efforts. It had reached an ambitious trade and data agreement with the EU. It had held together and revived the pan-regional Trans-Pacific Partnership trade pact despite Trump withdrawing the United States from the unratified deal. I was told I would be meeting an interesting China hand in the department and that I "wouldn't be disappointed."

Even by my standards of being outflanked in a meeting, this was a singular record, as I arrived to find nearly a dozen officials sitting round the table. At the center of the conclave was the head of the ministry's economic intelligence division, which analyzed competitive threats to the Japanese economy. The issue he wanted to expound on was artificial intelligence.

The Japanese officials were concerned that China was poised to take advantage of its closed data market to gain considerable edge over its international competitors. The phenomenon was a familiar one: China's market in many sectors was of such vast size that if its own companies were able to benefit from the scale advantage while foreign firms were effectively excluded, it gave them an enormous leg up. Some economic analysis assessed it as an even more critical factor in tilting the playing field in favor of China Inc. than the Chinese state's vast subsidies.

But this was even more worrisome. Data was the lifeblood of AI. If Chinese companies were able to tap into far larger datasets, while Japanese companies were confined to their own national market, the benefits would extend not just to the Chinese AI firms themselves but all the industrial sectors that would benefit from its application, whether that was advanced manufacturing, healthcare or transportation. This was not a flimsy, speculative assessment, a wide-eyed "data is the new oil" analysis, or a claim that only data mattered among the many different dimensions of competition in the AI space. It was run with numbers as best they could approximate and stitched together into one of the typically meticulous collections of slides that the Japanese government departments produce with such facility. In this instance, I was asked not to remove the documents from the room.

Taking the challenge on required a number of different measures, but one of the most important was pooling data on a scale that could plausibly allow the advanced industrial democracies to compete. Therein lay the problem. Data flows were a matter of high contention. The agreements that had permitted data to move freely from Europe to the United States had been struck down twice by the European Court of Justice as the result of the insufficient privacy protections for European citizens from US law enforcement. Japan and the EU themselves had just established the biggest area of free data flows in the world, based on an EU determination that Japan's entire privacy regime, by contrast, was "adequate." Japan would spend much of its presidency of the G20 promoting its "data free flow with trust" concept. But METI's message was that the advanced industrial democracies would collectively lose out to China if transatlantic privacy standards could not be sufficiently aligned.

For European and American officials and legislators, this was still a leap beyond current thinking. The data agreements they had reached, Safe Harbor and Privacy Shield, were workarounds rather than a comprehensive solution. There was no attempt to bring the underlying approach on the US side in line with European privacy concerns, and certainly not yet any sense that doing so might represent part of the collective process of systemic competition and rivalry with China. This was a highly charged battle over the preservation of distinct European and American models, with China a factor that had not even been seriously considered during the early rounds. But the need for a truce, and preferably a settlement of various long-running transatlantic disputes in order to focus on a common threat, was becoming increasingly clear, even if METI was ahead in identifying its salience to perhaps the single most important general-purpose technology. As one European official working on digital issues put it: "On the one hand, you have questions about whether the protections under Privacy Shield are adequate. But you contrast that with a Chinese system that is veering off into totalitarianism and it puts it in a different perspective."

* * *

From privacy to competition, industrial policy to investment screening, a range of areas that had never been touched by the China question were now being transformed. But most of the decisions in these areas would play out over many years. In one area, it had become very urgent indeed. As Heilmann put it:

"Made in China 2025 was closely connected to the Huawei debate. Many people would treat that as the attack they had seen coming. It was a debate that then sunk down even to many smartphone users, a unifying and focusing event." 5G, he argued, "was the manifestation of bigger things; the bifurcation of the technological ecosystems for the next generation; the new means that China has to reshape societies; and how their ideas of social order and surveillance are translating to us." The question was whether policymakers in London and Berlin could be persuaded of this in time.

2

NOBODY DOES IT BETTER

BRITISH SPIES AND THE 5G QUESTION

Washington, DC, March 2019

THE QUESTION TO ME WAS FRAMED by a pair of raised eyebrows and a vexed look: "Have the Brits gone wobbly?"

I was sitting with my colleague, Jamie Fly, in one of the grander suites of meeting rooms at the Pentagon with a couple of concerned Trump administration officials who oversaw much of the US intelligence apparatus. The allusion to Margaret Thatcher's fortifying injunction to George H. W. Bush on the eve of the first Iraq war—"Remember George, this is no time to go wobbly"—was knowing and pointed. A disturbingly long list of European allies was ready to buck Washington's warnings and allow Huawei to take a sizable role in their 5G networks. But none of them prompted as much incredulity and exasperation as the country that had long framed its relationship with Washington as uniquely "special." I would hear much blunter language in the year that followed, especially in January 2020 when Boris Johnson's Conservative government announced that Huawei would not be excluded from swathes of the UK's 5G infrastructure.

By then, however, the Trump administration had a better handle on how to fix the problem and was approaching the home stretch of what would prove to be a successful political offensive to turn the tide. That previous spring, as I bounced between meetings to see an array of similarly disturbed US Defense, State and White House officials, it was floundering. The 5G issue lay somewhere between China policy, Europe policy and cyber policy, with a host of questions around telecoms regulation, export controls, industrial policy, intelligence-sharing, military mobilization and much else thrown in besides. The result, as one of the other officials in our Pentagon meeting lamented, was that "it's not just that there is no strategy. No-one is even in charge of this."

* * *

The issue was ostensibly simple. Huawei had already made vast inroads into the world's 4G architecture, but its presence there was seen by US officials as something they could just about live with in other countries, even if it was not a risk they accepted themselves. Any use of the Chinese company's kit in 5G networks, however, posed security risks of a different magnitude. Washington just had to convince its allies of this before the new grid was built. Two cases loomed over all the others.

The first was Germany. As the largest European telecoms market, the lynchpin of the European economy and the most politically influential actor in the European Union, decisions in Berlin were expected to set the tone for much of the rest of the continent. The second was the UK. London's verdict would be closely watched by every country that was still deliberating over its 5G equipment suppliers.

The UK had been the first major Western state to become deeply enmeshed with Huawei. It had the most advanced risk mitigation processes to deal with what were euphemistically called "high-risk vendors," with British spies crawling all over the company's equipment and code. But it was the hand-in-glove relationship between the US National Security Agency (NSA) and the UK's GCHQ, the Western world's two most capable signals intelligence agencies, that gave the decision so much symbolic resonance.

Many countries had followed the UK's path of integrating the Chinese company into their telecoms networks and were reluctant to exclude it altogether. Now they were trying to figure out what the Trump administration could live with. It was hard for Washington to argue that any country should be applying more stringent standards than those of its very closest defense and intelligence partner. As one US official put it: "The way we saw it, if London goes, we can roll everybody else. It had to do with the position of GCHQ, the perception of their technical powers. It was the crutch that others used to justify their inaction."

For US officials who were used to thinking about China through the prism of strategic competition in the Indo-Pacific, it became clear in the early months of 2019 that Europe had become the most critical battleground. As one of the US officials leading the diplomatic efforts on 5G remarked in a meeting at the time: "If we can't even get our NATO allies on board, we're not going to make much progress anywhere else. We have to prioritize, and Europe is the priority."

For Huawei, the stakes were high. Its very nature as a company hung in the balance. The Chinese firm was already largely excluded from the United States and, more recently, Japan. The verdicts in Europe would decide whether it was going to be confined to China and the developing world or if it still had the chance to consolidate its position at the heart of the industrialized democracies. But the issue went well beyond one Chinese firm. It was clear to both Beijing and Washington that this was a test case in China's wider push for global technology leadership. The scope for Beijing to set standards, access data and acquire specialized components would be far more limited if its leading companies were restricted by virtually every advanced economy.

As a result, the Chinese government decided to swing in firmly—if often ham-handedly—behind the company's fierce lobbying efforts to persuade European governments to find in its favor. And to prevent that from happening, the United States was preparing to run a campaign of unprecedented scope, the most significant mobilization of political resources on a China-related issue in Europe that it had ever undertaken.

* * *

Washington's realization did not come quickly. It had concluded during the Obama administration that the use of Huawei equipment was not an acceptable risk for its own national networks. Aside from a few rural operators, the major US telecoms operators understood to steer well clear of Chinese suppliers. Even this was starting to come under creeping pressure. Privately, as the planning for the 5G transition got underway, US telecoms firms started raising questions about whether the "gentlemen's agreements," whereby Huawei had been excluded without the need for a full panoply of legislation, needed to be firmed up. As one US official put it:

> They were starting to say to us "Okay, we haven't been using their equipment, you've sent your teams in to show us the intelligence and persuaded us not to do this. But it's becoming harder for us to justify to our boards and our shareholders to keep doing it with a wink and a nod when Huawei is 30 percent cheaper."

As they started to move towards tightening the legislation in 2018, it started to become clear that the allies were going to be a far bigger problem.

Canberra raised the warning flag first. In August 2018, the head of the Australian Signals Directorate, Mike Burgess, announced that, despite its best efforts at trying to figure out a British-style risk-management approach, "At the end of this process, my advice was to exclude high-risk vendors from the entirety of evolving 5G networks."[1] Australian officials had war-gamed scenarios that replicated Huawei's presence in the existing networks for the new ones and determined that they could no longer credibly secure them from Chinese intrusion. Their US counterparts began waking up to the consequences if its other partners did not reach the same conclusions.

At first, the Trump administration hoped the whole thing could be dealt with quickly and discreetly. That had been their experience handling the first country at which they directed their energies in late 2018: Japan. It was a remarkably uncomplicated case. Shinzo Abe's government needed little persuasion from Washington that Chinese technology firms might represent a threat, nor the importance of aligning Japan's security position with that of its military guarantor.

Only one Japanese company, SoftBank, had any Huawei equipment in its 4G networks anyway, and Japanese officials were already looking to deal with the problem even before the US weighed in. Corporate Japan was not as hawkish on China as Abe and his cabinet advisors, and indeed SoftBank's prodigious success owed much to its early investments in Alibaba, the Chinese commercial giant. Without any need to name Huawei in Japanese government guidelines, it was made clear to SoftBank's billionaire CEO, Masayoshi Son, that making the move away from Chinese suppliers was a precondition for any allocation of 5G frequency. There was no public agonizing about the lack of alternative suppliers and no blood-curdling threats from Beijing over the firm's decisions. Huawei was out. Nokia, Ericsson and the more experimental cluster of 5G efforts from Fujitsu, NEC, Rakuten and Samsung were in. When Washington trained its sights on Europe, it expected a repeat.

Instead it would face an almighty political battle. European and Japanese security anxieties about China were not of a remotely similar scale. European governments did not have to spend their time planning to face Beijing in an outright war or deal with an ongoing barrage of air and naval intrusions by China's People's Liberation Army (PLA). Their view of the relationship with China was nonetheless growing increasingly jaundiced. The cyber-domain was the one security arena where Europe was in the same boat as other Chinese targets, not least when it came to the forms of economic espionage at which Beijing was so skilled. This was estimated to cost the US economy alone $320 billion each year, but also encompassed over 80 percent of the theft of trade secrets, market data, software, source code and manufacturing techniques in Europe too.[2]

There was a major problem, however, even for governments on the continent that might have been minded to follow Tokyo's example. European telecoms operators were simply far more beholden to Huawei and ZTE, Huawei's Chinese state-owned sibling, than their Japanese, American or Australian counterparts.

One of the main reasons that European mobile operators had ended up in this invidious position was the cumulative effect of a seemingly innocuous public policy choice: the model used by European governments to issue rights to telecoms frequencies. Japan assigns them for free and then imposes various obligations on the firms that are the beneficiaries. Most of the European markets use spectrum auctions, an ingenious process that helped win the economists who designed it, Paul Milgrom and Robert Wilson, the 2020 Nobel Prize for economics. Spectrum auctions have been a lucrative cash cow for governments who require the telecoms operators to make a large up-front payment for the privilege of operating within the frequency they are allocated. The scale of that payment depends on what the operators expect to recoup, but it can run stratospherically high, the German government alone recouping over €50 billion from a single 3G license auction at the turn of the millennium.[3] And while there are many uncertainties about how lucrative these contracts will prove to be, it is absolutely clear that driving down operating costs will make them more so. Chinese firms offered a way to do this at the cheapest imaginable rate.

Huawei's rise was fueled by a mix of theft, genuine technical ability, vast research and development spending, and prodigious subsidies. The company was founded in 1987 by Ren Zhengfei, a former member of the PLA engineering corps, and spent its early years selling telecom switches to connect phone calls in rural China before it reverse-engineered them and produced the switches itself. One of its breakthrough deals was a contract to build the first national telecom network for the PLA, but it was when Huawei was accorded "national champion" status in the 1990s, with all the government backing this afforded, that its take-off really began. The volume of special lending arrangements, tax breaks, deals on cheap land and outright grants was estimated in one study at $75 billion.[4] Its international competitors complained particularly forcefully about the vast credit lines offered to Huawei's customers, the major telecoms operators, by China Development Bank and the Export–Import (EXIM) Bank of China. Not only were Western firms' equipment prices often undercut by 30 percent or more, the generous financing terms that Huawei offered made it almost impossible for the likes of BT and Deutsche Telekom to resist.

As one expert on the European telecoms industry put it, though:

> The story about Huawei wasn't a story just about the price, it also integrated well with how Europeans did business. They were extraordinarily forthcoming, diligent, and professional in their service. It was a good story of how a Chinese company became an exceptional business partner for European companies in a crucial industry. They trusted them.

The consequence was that many of the other telecoms equipment suppliers were driven into the ground. Back in the 2000s, the telecoms market was a competitive space in which an assortment of mostly European and North American firms vied for the market. The arrival of Chinese competitors on the scene was one of the main factors behind a brutal consolidation that is still underway. Lucent, Alcatel, and Siemens' communications arm were swallowed up by Nokia. A struggling Marconi was bought by Ericsson, which also took over most of Nortel's assets after it filed for protection from creditors, the former Canadian giant's situation hit not only by cost issues but Huawei's large-scale industrial espionage, which saw Chinese hackers stealing hundreds of Nortel's sensitive internal documents over the course of a decade.[5] For the leading US firms, such as Cisco, it was ever-more evident that equipment provision was turning into a low-value business that they wanted to transcend. They got out of the market altogether to focus on higher-margin products—the routers and the software—rather than the heavy-lifting of radio infrastructure building.

By the time it came to the 5G bids then, in 2018, there were only two major competitors left standing who could match Huawei toe-to-toe, both beaten and bruised by the whole experience: Finland's Nokia and Sweden's Ericsson. In 2019, there was even the risk that they would be driven out of the business too, as they struggled to compete on pricing with the state-backed behemoth from Shenzhen. As one US official put it:

> What dawned on us, when we talked to the telcos, was that 360 million people in the US and Australia is not enough to support the companies who are providing an alternative. It used to be that we could agree—okay, you made a different decision. Increasingly it was becoming: your decision to "mitigate risk" with Huawei is undermining our ability and your ability to maintain an alternative.

The European Commission had attempted to step in to deal with the damage years earlier, but the case brought against Huawei by the European Commission in 2013 was knee-capped by member states whose telecoms operators were already hooked on the very Chinese subsidies that it sought to address. Not only was the course adopted by European governments over the preceding decade leading to a deepening dependence on Chinese suppliers but it had also brought about the near-destruction of one of the largest-scale advanced technology sectors where Europe retained a genuine global edge: constructing the spine of the world's telecommunications networks. When governments defended their Huawei decisions on the grounds of a "lack of alternatives," they rarely acknowledged that it was their own choices that had led them there.

* * *

The country that made the biggest early Huawei gamble was the UK. In 2005, the Chinese firm was at best a regional actor, its only serious international contract being with Hutchison Whampoa, a short hop over the border in Hong Kong from its South China headquarters. Huawei's international reputation was transformed by a breakout deal pioneered by BT, the UK's former state provider and the largest telecoms firm in the country, which handed it a £10 billion contract to supply routers, transmission and access equipment for an upgrade of the UK's networks. BT did so with remarkably little scrutiny. Ministers were not even informed until a year after the contract was signed, foreshadowing the curious process that would keep the most important decisions away from politicians until they could be presented with faits accomplis.

From that point on, the UK would act as Huawei's most important reputation-launderer. Prior to the BT contract, the firm had been dogged by concerns not just over its technical competence but its proximity to the Chinese state, not to mention Ren Zhengfei's military background. Most governments steered well clear. The cost proposition, the firm's improving technology and the stamp of validity from a charter member of the Five Eyes, the Anglosphere intelligence club that comprised the United States' closest allies, opened many more doors. In the decade that followed, Huawei would become the world's largest telecoms equipment supplier, winning a string of contracts across advanced economies as well as the developing world.

This didn't mean that Huawei had carte blanche in the UK. An arrangement had to be found to address the unique lack of trust in the firm. Several years after its groundbreaking deal was completed, BT had detected suspicious behavior in Huawei's core switches, necessitating a bending-over-backwards level of reassurance from the Chinese firm about the security of its equipment and its code. This took the form of a two-story building on the outskirts of Banbury, about an hour's drive across the Cotswolds from GCHQ in Cheltenham. The Huawei Cyber Security Evaluation Centre, more commonly known simply as "the Cell," was described by the *Economist* with uncharacteristic hyperbole as the "fulcrum for the balance of power in the world of telecoms."[6]

The Cell was supposed to be the place where Huawei's hardware and software was scrutinized and tested. Instigated by the British government, but paid for by the Chinese company itself, it was initially staffed by Huawei employees until a 2013 report by the UK parliament's Intelligence Committee baldly noted that whatever advantages GCHQ believed this provided "do not, in our opinion, outweigh the risks of Huawei effectively policing themselves."

This was less outrageous than it looked. The staff were security cleared, and the hiring decisions lay with the former deputy-director of GCHQ who was running the operation. But it was one of a growing number of blurred lines between Huawei, the British civil service and the telecoms operators. Government officials took up roles with the company, personnel rotated out of operational and oversight roles in the telecoms firms into slots at Huawei, while the firm's money was liberally dispensed among leading specialist researchers in the field. The visible apogee of this process was a 5G hearing held by the House of Commons' Science and Technology Committee in 2019.[7] The principal technical expert, Rahim Tafazolli, was the recipient of £5 million in financing from Huawei for his research center at the University of Surrey,[8] while the Chinese company itself was represented by the reassuring face of the man who had for several years been the British government's chief information officer, John Suffolk, now employed as Huawei's head of cyber-security.

Although the Cell was deemed a success by the British intelligence services, it was yet another iteration of the UK providing a stamp of credibility—in this case the AAA "GCHQ-approved" rating—and it formed part of the steady entrenchment of Huawei as a foundational and respectable part of the country's telecoms establishment. This was part of a fundamental difference in mindset between the British signals intelligence world and that of its most important Five Eyes partners, which would blow up when the 5G clash reached its final stages. For the US government, Huawei's journey down the path to respectability was part of the problem. For GCHQ, which saw improving engineering standards at the firm as an essential objective if the UK's networks were going to be secure, it was precisely the point.

The United States was not just asking countries to make their firms pick up a higher tab for the construction of their networks, it was asking them to wrench themselves away from an entire model for the relationship between the telecoms operators, the equipment suppliers and the governments that had been built up over more than a decade. The immediate challenge was that 5G would build on the foundations of the existing 4G equipment. Sticking with Huawei would be cheaper and make the 5G rollout faster. The more that the telecoms firms were dependent on its subsidized products, the bigger the bill for switching. Exactly how long the delay and how much the cost difference was something that only the telecoms operators themselves knew, and—along with Huawei—they would use this information advantage to commission and steer "expert" reports and feed out numbers that grew ever-more astronomical the more panicked they became.

These accounts dominated the early stages of the European debate. The United States, slow to realize this, would repeat some of the very talking points that had been crafted by Huawei and the European telecoms firms in their information campaigns with its underlying message: "Switching from Huawei is certainly expensive but how can you place a price on security?" If you were a member of parliament who was minded to believe your own country's intelligence services, technical experts and telecoms firms, all of whom made reassuring noises about the navigability of those security risks, this was not terribly persuasive.

* * *

In the early stages, the issue was treated as a narrow technical one: could networks with Huawei equipment in them be "secure"? This was a matter for the cyber-agencies to decide. Indeed, the pretense throughout much of the process was that their verdict on this was the only question that needed to be resolved. If they gave Huawei a sufficiently clean bill of health, there were no grounds for any other factors to be taken into consideration. This narrow issue was interpreted even more narrowly. It was generally taken to mean: can Huawei, at the behest of the Chinese government, use its vantage point in the 5G networks for surveillance purposes? The initial conclusions reached reflected the different standing, capacity and political cultures of the different agencies across Europe.

Virtually every cyber-institution on the continent is either party to NATO intelligence-sharing arrangements or, like Sweden, has a comparably close and longstanding partnership with the United States on these issues outside alliance structures. Yet the status of bilateral intelligence ties, the capacity of the agencies and their outlook on the China question all varied considerably.

In some cases, such as the Czech Republic, the country's cyber-agency took on the role of lead Huawei skeptic, to the extent of boxing in their more Beijing-friendly political leadership. As early as December 2018, the agency's director, Dušan Navrátil, issued a public warning to network operators that Chinese equipment suppliers posed a security risk: "China's laws ... require private companies residing in China to cooperate with intelligence services, therefore introducing them into the key state systems might present a threat."[9] It was no surprise that Prague was the venue for a US-initiated gathering of thirty-two countries in May 2019 to thrash out some common security principles around 5G networks.

The situation was harder when it came to two of the higher-powered cyber-actors in Europe. The real juggernaut was GCHQ. If the UK had lost its superpower status in most areas, its signals intelligence capabilities were undoubtedly one of the exceptions. It was never able to keep pace with NSA spending in areas such as satellite surveillance, and most of the imperial territories that once housed its global network of listening stations were long gone. But the British government kept it sufficiently resourced to justify the maintenance of the genuinely special arrangements between the HQs in Cheltenham and Maryland that meant that it was the only foreign intelligence service to have regular access to the highest tier of US intelligence. But GCHQ did not carry itself as a modest junior counterpart to its dominant US sibling. If ever there was an embodiment of former British Prime Minister Harold Macmillan's fanciful notion of the UK playing Greece to America's Rome, GCHQ was it.

This is partly borne out by outside assessments of the capabilities of various governments. In the cyber-domain, separate rankings by the Economist Intelligence Unit and the International Telecommunication Union put the UK ahead of the United States and China in the number one spot as the top cyber-power.[10] And its continued utility for the NSA was evident. The Snowden documents revealed that in the vast intercepts of internet traffic, GCHQ was actually producing more metadata than the NSA itself, while the hacking of major US internet firms that was among the most explosive Snowden scandals was a British operation. The idea that cleverness could compensate for the lack of raw financial and technical firepower was deeply ingrained in the history of the institution. One US official who had close dealings with the UK through the 5G affair dubbed it "Bletchley syndrome."

Bletchley Park, the celebrated home of the World War Two codebreakers, was GCHQ's predecessor organization. For many years a state secret, its role in the Allied victory has increasingly been the subject of Hollywood-ized acclaim that turned Alan Turing into an unlikely counterpoint to James Bond. The powerful notion that a cluster of brilliant Cambridge mathematicians could, as Churchill put it, be the "deciding factor" in the defeat of fascism, "effectively winning the war," has been a central part of GCHQ's founding mythology.[11]

In the case of Huawei, Bletchley syndrome had some clear implications. The UK would reach its own assessment, and if it disagreed with the United States it would be unabashed about saying so. GCHQ also treated threats of intelligence-sharing cut-offs with a pinch of salt. While the UK stood to lose more, there was little belief that the NSA would damage ties with its most capable partner over a legitimate difference of opinion about the UK's own national security, which would have no impact on the most secure intelligence-sharing channels. Underlying this was a whiff of arrogance. While recognizing its capability, other Five Eyes agencies thought that the UK had an inflated sense of its ability to mitigate the threat.

When Australian officials went to brief their British counterparts in detail on their wargaming exercise on 5G, they were sniffily told that UK cyber-experts had conducted a similar exercise themselves but that, unlike the Australian Security Intelligence Organisation, they had been entirely successful in securing British networks. Many UK officials saw themselves as a *sui generis* case, uniquely able to ride the Huawei tiger. As one of them put it to me after the contentious, later-reversed call was made in 2019 not to exclude the Chinese company's equipment from the country's 5G networks: "Just because we decide on this course of action, doesn't mean it's one we'd recommend to anyone else." Yet from a US perspective, what was even worse was that GCHQ was, as one official put it, "running around the world undermining us. They told anyone who would listen that the Americans and the Australians have gone off the deep end. That this is not that big of a deal. It was particularly unhelpful."

The elaborate edifice with the Cell and the very notion of "high-risk vendors" recognized that there was a China problem. Indeed, GCHQ had all sorts of China-related worries on the domestic front alone, from the vast scale of cyber-intrusions that even disrupted UK social care services during the early months of the pandemic to illicit Chinese efforts to acquire cutting-edge technologies from British universities. It was also one of the few agencies with a long history of handling China material at the highest levels, in close cooperation with the United States. Until its edifice on Victoria Peak became a victim of the 1997 handover, the GCHQ listening station in Hong Kong was, for the United States, its single most important, providing crucial information to US policymakers about Beijing's decision-making over Tiananmen Square in 1989.

No-one thought GCHQ was ignorant or naive about China. But like most other cyber-professionals, they simply saw the Huawei equipment question as a lower-tier matter. As one industry expert put it: "A lot of people in IT security are convinced that no IT infrastructure is safe. There are backdoors in everything. And if no infrastructure is safe then the step in letting Huawei in is not so high. They think we're talking about a chimera." GCHQ officials would quietly brief the press that their NSA counterparts—the serious people, not the Trump administration political hacks—thought likewise. One British intelligence official told me that "not a single US official disagreed with our assessment. This was just about 'with us or against us.'"

One US official involved in the accounts disputed this in an interview:

> They continually treated this as if people were challenging their technical chops. Our view was, we're not there to question you on that. We know you've been given an instruction from above to "mitigate." But it's not true that we agreed on the technical side. Why are you running a center that sees no improvements? Those reports alone should have led to a rethinking. They ignored their own conclusions.

Indeed, from the US perspective, it was the UK's consistent effort to treat the question as a matter exclusively for its spooks that was part of the problem:

> Professionally it was a challenge to them—how could they say that what they had said was a method that worked now didn't? That those pesky Australians who are not as technically qualified as us are right and that we're wrong? That's what it became. But our view was that we shouldn't just be having technical exchanges. There was an absolute unwillingness to enter into the policy discussions on the UK side—they only fielded technical people.

There was an additional element to their case, which they did not make public. The arrangements with Huawei gave GCHQ a high level of insight into both the firm's physical equipment and its coding. Placing GCHQ staff as Huawei "employees" offered certain advantages too. British intelligence was engaged in a dual effort—helping Huawei reduce the sloppy practices that would make UK networks accessible to any attacker, Chinese or otherwise, while also identifying vulnerabilities that British—and for that matter American—cyber-agencies could exploit. Huawei provided the telecoms architecture for some of the most important Western intelligence targets. As NSA documents leaked by Snowden revealed, through the Shotgiant program they were looking to penetrate the networks of major Huawei clients, including Iran, Afghanistan, Pakistan, Kenya and Cuba. The Cell gave GCHQ an inside track. "GCHQ believed it could best gain an intelligence advantage at the expense of weakening the systems that the whole of society is increasingly dependent on," as one historian of the agency put it in his book; "Bletchley Park is deeply buried in its DNA, and so when GCHQ looks at a mobile phone or a laptop, it thinks it sees an Enigma machine—and wants to crack it."[12]

By 2019, it was no longer the US government's view that these trade-offs made sense. Of course they would continue penetrating Huawei-built networks, and there was a legitimate debate to be had about the relative weight of concerns from a pure cyber-security perspective. But in private, they were scathing:

> It was continually trotted out by GCHQ. We found it to be a completely bullshit argument. They knew in the back of their minds that it was weak-assed. "It enables us to look inside the equipment and find vulnerabilities." Do you think we're not looking at their equipment? "We get to have interactions with Huawei." Give me a break.

This was not a narrow debate anymore. Indeed, the idea that the decision was solely a matter of assessing the cyber-risks had always been a convenient fiction. If that was the only matter at stake, Huawei would never have featured in the UK's networks in the first place. A series of other considerations—economic and political—meant that GCHQ was encouraged not to reach the blindingly obvious conclusion that the UK would be more secure if Huawei had been kept well away from the country's telecoms infrastructure. The instruction from the top of the British political system was rather: make it work. And so, over the course of a single year, the National Cyber Security Centre (NCSC) ended up producing three separate, lengthily laid-out assessments: Huawei in the radio access network is okay; Huawei in the radio access network is okay if its level of participation is restricted; and finally, Huawei is not okay, even in the radio access network. US sanctions would ultimately help bring about that end result by threatening to prevent the Chinese company from having access to essential equipment for its 5G rollout. But what really changed was the politics.

For most of 2019, the British government had virtually become a brick wall for the United States. Officials were getting no traction at any level. A decision by the cabinet in April 2019 kept Huawei out of the core "brains" of the UK's 5G networks, as expected, but otherwise left their presence in the radio access network unrestricted, a distinction that the US government no longer believed was meaningful. The administration bided its time. The British cabinet had been split cleanly down the middle, with every minister responsible for security or intelligence matters supporting tighter limitations. The prime minister, Theresa May, instead gave the casting vote in favor of the Treasury-led position. But it was a government that was almost a lame duck, and no-one was giving any serious thought to China, Huawei, the United States or any matter other than the single issue that had dominated British politics for the preceding three years, Brexit. Boris Johnson was on track to take over from May in a couple of months, and everyone on the US side was well aware that the decision could be revisited. Trump-world was far closer to Johnson and hoped to have greater pull with him. Once the all-consuming Brexit battles were out of the way, they knew they had another shot at getting the Brits in line. As one US official put it:

We were frozen in the amber of Brexit. All of this discussion was going on during the messiest bits of it. And there was fear—the risk of retaliation from the Chinese government to other parts of the UK economy as they were trying to emerge from Brexit. That was the dirty secret. It was clear to GCHQ that there was zero interest in ministers reopening the settlement on Huawei. Then all of a sudden we were in a very different position.

The political picture for 5G in the UK would go through a convulsive set of shifts. And the same would prove true for the biggest holdout of all: Germany.

3

TAINTED LOVE

TRUMP, MERKEL AND GERMANY'S CHINA PROBLEM

IN MARCH 2017, ANGELA MERKEL returned to Berlin from her first meeting with Donald Trump and went immediately from the airport to join a leaving party for Joachim Gauck, the German head of state. The trip had not gone well.

She laid out the story in clinical, unemotional detail to a small huddle among the assembled guests, stripped clean of value judgments. The public narrative had been dominated by Trump's seeming unwillingness to shake her hand and by his demands for money from Germany for NATO, which he at least pretended to believe was a debt rather than a commitment to raise national defense spending levels to 2 percent. But Merkel's agenda was focused on Russia. One of her main goals had been to convey the scope of Putin's ambitions to the new US president, which she saw best reflected in his statement that the collapse of the Soviet Union had been the greatest geopolitical catastrophe of the twentieth century.

Having been told he needed visuals, she brought a map of the Soviet empire, which she laid out in the meeting, pointing to how Russian interventions mapped on to its former territories. Beyond a momentary flicker of interest in the fact that the color coding included Slovenia, his wife's birthplace, in the Soviet sphere of influence, it elicited no reaction or comment from Trump. It was all irrelevant to him. In fact, as the meeting went on, she found that he operated with no historical references at all. The Cold War didn't register, let alone any talking points from his staff about the longstanding US–German alliance. For Trump, there is no history, everything starts now, she observed to the little gathering of politicians and officials.

Germany, and Merkel personally, would be the subject of considerable animus from Trump and his associates throughout his presidency. The phone calls from the White House were so unhinged that they were put on a specially restricted distribution list in the German government. Trump sent a political agitator, Richard Grenell, to act as his ambassador in Berlin, who described his agenda, weeks after arriving, as "[empowering] other conservatives throughout Europe"[1]—which decidedly did not mean Merkel's center-right Christian Democratic Union (CDU)—and would routinely denounce a government that believed itself to be a close US ally.

Meanwhile, Trump held the German car industry hostage to the threat of being slapped with substantial tariffs, which was given credibility by his already-demonstrated willingness to hit allies with steel and aluminum duties. The president's attacks on the European Union cut at a project so close to the heart of German national strategy that Wolfgang Ischinger, the former ambassador to Washington and chairman of the Munich Security Conference, warned that if Trump pushed for other countries to follow the UK's Brexit example, it "would amount to a kind of non-military declaration of war."[2]

But it wasn't just the political attacks on Germany and the economic threats to its industry that were the problem, nor the fact that the populism that Trump and his friends in Europe represented harked back to darker times on the continent. Merkel was also trying to hold together a certain version of world order. Trump's tabula rasa approach threatened to unravel the fabric of the entire global framework that Germany relied on; the economic globalization that had generated remarkable prosperity for the country even in the midst of the last decade of crises; the multilateral institutions that had navigated differences without resort to the destructive power politics that had bedeviled European history for centuries; the relative peace that ensured the German government could be spared the costs of serious military expenditures.

China itself was not perceived as a security threat, but it was not really viewed as an economic one either. Despite growing concerns from sections of German industry, explained in the previous chapter, China remained at the core of that globalization story. Germany was almost unique among major economies in continuing to run a trade surplus with China. Whether this was a product of superior German production quality, prescient labor-market reforms or the advantages of forgoing the Deutsche Mark for the euro was beside the point. If the Trump administration's China policy was going to threaten this framework, Merkel believed she needed to figure out how best to keep at least some version of it alive. Germany had simply not experienced the "China shock" that upended lower-wage employment across the Western world and helped create the political conditions for the resurgent populism in the United States, the UK, Italy and elsewhere that Merkel feared being replicated at home. The rise of the far-right Alternative für Deutschland in the shadow of the refugee crisis was a baleful specter that had the potential to influence figures in her own party, who mulled joining them in coalition governments at the state level.

It was also extremely difficult to determine whether to take the US position seriously. If Germany and Europe were being asked to join forces with the United States in a long-term rebalancing of their approach towards China, there was a conversation to be had. Indeed, it had already started. After Russia's annexation of Crimea in 2014 saw it kicked out of the G8, the remaining seven heads of government, and the EU leadership, had a discreet space at which to discuss their mutual concerns about China once the formal summit agenda was over. The only voice of dissent among the G7 leaders to the notion that they had a worsening China problem that they needed to figure out was not

Merkel but the British prime minister, David Cameron, who was then in the grips of the "golden era" China mania. But any hope of these exchanges continuing and turning into common action after Barack Obama left office was quickly curtailed. When the French president, Emmanuel Macron, raised the prospect of joining forces to take on China's problematic economic practices, the response from Trump was stark: "The EU is worse."[3]

The capricious nature of the Trump administration's decision-making also made it hard to determine what was going to stick and what was just a means of building leverage for the trade deal with China that Trump craved. The particular scenario Berlin feared was a repeat of what they had watched playing out with ZTE, Huawei's state-owned counterpart, which was subjected to punishment from the US government not only for its initial sanctions violations but then for breaking a subsequent agreement with the Justice Department and shipping US goods to Iran and North Korea.

While US officials had insisted that the crippling restrictions on ZTE's access to essential components that they enacted in 2018 stemmed purely from the wheels of the justice system grinding into gear, Trump soon revoked them after reaching an agreement with Xi Jinping to keep the company alive for the sake of the two sides' trade talks. A set of documents that US authorities found on a laptop belonging to ZTE's chief financial officer, after he was detained in Boston's Logan Airport in 2016, had not only exposed ZTE's sanctions-busting with Iran but fingered Huawei for its involvement in the same practices. Indeed, it highlighted them precisely as justification for why ZTE had to follow suit or lose out to its Chinese competitor. Meng Wanzhou's arrest in Canada, just as Xi and Trump were meeting in Buenos Aires, was one of the dramatic results of the investigation that followed. But the fear was that there was nothing to stop Trump and Xi reaching a similar agreement over Meng, and

Huawei too. And many in the German government trusted Trump even less than they did Xi.

Politicians and important sections of German business worried less about the actual security risks that might result from Huawei's presence in 5G networks and more about the risk that German industry would be caught in a pincer. The United States was never going to use Huawei equipment for its own 5G networks, but it feared that the administration could ease up the pressure on the company elsewhere as part of a similar ZTE-style quid-pro-quo with Beijing. Then, if the United States concluded a bilateral trade deal with China, every indication was that Trump would train his tariff-slapping energies on the EU, with German cars at the top of the list. For its part, Beijing had been none-too-shy about signaling what the consequences would be if Germany reached the "wrong" verdict over Huawei. "If Germany were to make a decision that led to Huawei's exclusion from the German market, there will be consequences," Wu Ken, China's ambassador to Germany, warned.[4] "The Chinese government will not stand idly by." "See, last year, 28 million cars were sold in China, 7 million of those were German."

While the German economy as a whole is not excessively dependent on China, a couple of sectors—chemicals and cars—remain highly exposed. Turning the taps off for chemical companies like BASF, on which China's own industrial base relies, would be difficult. A decision by the Chinese government to "encourage" businesses and consumers to turn away from VW and Daimler would be easier to enact, though the preponderance of those cars were now made by Chinese workers in Chinese factories, which gave the threat a slightly mythical air. It induced deep German nervousness nonetheless. Like Brexit-troubled London, there was a sense that they couldn't afford to treat it dismissively. The result, if paired with US actions, would have been the economic equivalent of a two-front war, as some of

Germany's largest employers faced escalating tariffs in one of their two largest markets and the use of deniable but devastating state-directed measures in the other.

It was not only a portion of the 600,000 existing car jobs, and those tied to the wider array of associated suppliers across Europe, that were potentially at stake. 5G was supposed to provide the underpinnings of Germany's broader industrial future. The telecoms firms played on these anxieties about falling behind. The likes of Deutsche Telekom issued dark claims that Germany would be vastly outpaced by its international competitors unless it stuck with Huawei. As a result, for all the German economics ministry's talk of building "European champions," there was not the level of love for Scandinavian equipment suppliers that the government's language might have implied. In much of Europe, this was already understood as code for "Franco-German champions," and few cases illustrated this better than the disregard given to any notion that support to the Finnish and Swedish champions should feature in German decision-making over 5G. As one industry expert noted: "If Nokia or Ericsson had been a German firm, we wouldn't even be having the Huawei debate."

Those who talked to Merkel did not find her naive about what China was becoming under Xi Jinping. Indeed, some German companies were unhappy about her private warnings that they needed a plan for the fact that their days making hay in the Chinese market were drawing to a close. Her hopes and illusions of the past were the illusions shared with most other Western leaders. But one of the issues she came back to, that framed her dealings with Beijing in the final years, was the United States. If Europe was facing an era in which it could find itself subjected to a Donald Trump, relations with China couldn't be allowed to slide too far. There was little confidence that the EU could act with sufficient weight alone to address crises with Washington and Beijing at the same time, not least given the threats from Putin she had been at such pains to point out to Trump. As one German expert put it:

> Ultimately her thing was that there are large world historical forces at work. China is getting back to its rightful place as the dominant power, and she has very little faith in US staying power or in German society doing what it needs to do to become an independent power that stands up for its own interests.

It was a resignation to fate. Better to "cut deals now and enjoy the party while it lasts."

Whether it was Huawei or a new investment agreement with China, the substance was less important than keeping a floor under the relationship. She would seek to do so to the very end of her tenure as chancellor. But the scale of the foot-dragging on the most basic readjustments of the European position was bemusing even to many of those working most closely on it. Rarely have I encountered so many officials in a democratic government as exasperated as those dealing with the black hole of the chancellery on China policy in the last couple of years of Merkel's term.

* * *

In Germany too, the 5G question was kicked to a technical agency, though this one was a very different beast. The Bundesamt für Sicherheit in der Informationstechnik (BSI) has a less storied history than GCHQ. The Federal Office for Information Security was the former cryptographic department of the foreign intelligence service, the Bundesnachrichtendienst (BND), which still houses the country's external signals intelligence activities. The BSI was spun off in 1991 from the BND headquarters in Pullach, near Munich, to the country's soon-to-be vacated seat of government in Bonn. While the BND has since moved most of its operations into a vast new building near the site of the Berlin Wall, the BSI stayed put in the former capital alongside a small number of other federal ministries. Bonn is not only the home of the old West German government, however. It is also the headquarters of Europe's largest telecoms provider, Deutsche Telekom. The proximity between the two has been contentious. If the question of regulatory capture was an acute one in the UK, it was at least clear that GCHQ and its relatively recently created cyber-security center had a complex agenda with respect to Huawei. Less so the BSI, an entity without NCSC's clout but that would play an outsized role in the decision-making process relative to its capabilities and bureaucratic weight. Other German industries had to make a beeline for the chancellery on the really important decisions, which Deutsche Telekom made sure to do too. But they also had a friendly agency in closer proximity, run by a former lobbyist with close industry links rather than a dyed-in-the-wool spook. One executive on the wrong end of this coziness complained in a more exasperated moment that in the telecoms sphere they felt like Germany was a "banana republic."

The United States also faced a deeper problem in Germany than in the UK, one that pre-dated Trump: the long shadow of the Snowden revelations. For parts of the German security establishment, these were no big deal. Indeed, one of the reasons the leaks blew up in Germany was precisely because they laid out for the public so comprehensively the close collaboration between the NSA and the BND. German intelligence was perfectly well aware that, despite the close linkages between their services, they did not occupy the same rarefied sphere as the British or other Five Eyes nations, who were exempt from US targeting. The supposed shock of US spying on Germany, including the aggressive targeting of Merkel's personal phone, was not really a surprise at all to those in the know—allies spied on allies. But the dismissive "get real," "don't be naive," "grow up," "everyone does it" attitude from various US policymakers and some of the harder-bitten German officials and experts did not land well politically. A wider public steeped in the dual legacies of totalitarianism, which polled at the very highest levels in Europe for concerns over data privacy, did not believe that their allies should be their biggest surveillance problem. It also resulted in a very jaded environment for any American officials coming to Berlin to tell Germans that they should be worried about Chinese spying.

In the second half of 2019, the situation in Germany did not look promising. In mid-October, the German government released its security catalogue, a set of draft security requirements for the 5G network, in a form that was so outrageous that one White House official I met at the time openly wondered whether the real intention behind it was to provoke a political backlash. Beyond a couple of certification requirements, there were no criteria with teeth for dealing with sensitive vendors. The US delegations to Berlin in recent months had clearly not made much headway. Numerous German officials wanted Huawei excluded, but not officials in the places that counted most.

The barrage of US messages and visits was becoming a little relentless, especially given how poisonous the wider political atmosphere had become. German participants in the meetings with US officials described some of them as "actively counterproductive." In their darker moments, even arch Huawei-skeptics muttered that they were minded to say "no" to the Trump administration just to spite them. There were similarly unhelpful musings in the Trump administration, which was weighing up whether to unleash retaliation on Germany after the news broke about the security catalogue. German officials would also repeat the messages they heard from their British counterparts—"that's not what GCHQ says" was perpetually used as cover. But much as the United States ultimately ended up relying on the changing politics in London to get the outcome it wanted, behind the scenes in Germany the situation was set to take a tumultuous turn. It would affect not just the 5G decision but the wider politics of German China policy. A revolt was brewing—and from an unlikely source.

* * *

Norbert Röttgen was once a rising star on the German political scene. A brilliant career politician from a powerful North-Rhine Westphalia CDU party background, he was among the progressive, green-minded faction close to Merkel during her first term in office, with a George Clooney-esque look to boot. As her environment minister, he appeared poised for greater things and was even spoken of as a potential successor. Then he crashed to earth. A failed run to be prime minister of his home state, Germany's most populous, saw the CDU plummet to its lowest voting numbers in decades. He was personally blamed by Merkel for the party's performance, told he had to take responsibility and summarily removed as minister.

He would have to reinvent himself. His vantage point was the chairmanship of the Committee on Foreign Affairs in the Bundestag, which he took over from its longstanding chair Ruprecht Polenz, who described it to him as "the nicest job you will ever have." Polenz had shaped the role into the parliamentary face of German foreign policy, both in the domestic media and to the rest of the world, a mantle that Röttgen eagerly took on. The position suited him, and even if he was not able to rebuild his base in the party, the vantage point it afforded— internationally connected, somewhat non-partisan, sharper and more outspoken on foreign policy than any government minister could afford to be—was well-suited for picking up issues and running with them in ways that shape the public debate. And Röttgen had not lost his political instincts. When the 5G question started bubbling up, he grabbed the opportunity.

China had not featured so prominently on the German foreign policy agenda in his early years in the role. 5G was not just a "China" issue, however, nor even a foreign policy one. Its position at the intersection of so many fields may have created bureaucratic headaches, but it was ideally suited for politicians who could stitch them all together. In Germany, it was Röttgen who first took this task on. As the international debate took off, he started to brief up on it.

He was an Atlanticist, so already minded not to do anything that would blow up relations with a Washington that was exhibiting a striking bipartisan consensus on the issue. He was also closely connected to the British Conservative parliamentarians that would go on to fight their own government on the issue. Digging into the subject further, it became clearer that 5G was even more a question of the fundamental values that would be compromised if a deeper dependency on Beijing resulted from a Chinese company controlling the enabling infrastructure of the German economy. He looked harder at the China that had been emerging under Xi Jinping and did not like what this would entail.

There was an additional dimension—it was an issue where he could take a stand against Merkel's own position, where he would be firmly in the right and where, indeed, much of the party would end up supporting him, not to mention the German public and what looked increasingly like a cross-party majority of parliamentarians in the German Bundestag. Indeed, he was not alone in seeing both the vital nature of the issue and the political value of taking a stand. After Pence's 2019 speech at Munich, a small huddle of senior Bundestag members with a foreign affairs brief were called in for a closed-door meeting by the BND, who laid out the case for why Huawei's presence in critical infrastructure had to be understood as a national security issue, not just an economic or technical one. From then on, it would be the foreign policy voices in the major parties, which also included Nils Schmid among the Social Democrats (SPD), who would persuade and mobilize their colleagues to push the issue forward. Huawei's lobbying meetings, which participants described as being conducted over breakfast at the Adlon Hotel, were no longer having the same effect.

After the security catalogue issue blew up that October, Röttgen wrote an op-ed in the German business daily *Handelsblatt*.[5] He argued that there were limitations to what can be achieved by technical checks. That the issue at stake was therefore the trustworthiness of the Chinese Communist Party, with which Huawei is obliged to cooperate. That handing over such large swathes of critical infrastructure to Chinese companies posed an existential threat to Europe's technological sovereignty. And that for an issue of such far-reaching consequence, the Bundestag, not an obscure technical agency, needed to make the decision. It was co-signed by a cluster of CDU parliamentarians. They were not the party heavyweights but a carefully assembled group that represented many of the topics at stake: the rapporteurs for IT and cyber-security, industry, trade policy and 5G, and the coordinator for transatlantic relations.

The United States was not even mentioned in the opinion piece. The debate had moved into a different place. The Washington versus Beijing frame had been a sticky one and suited Huawei quite well—if you didn't trust either side on espionage matters, as Altmaier suggested, what difference did it really make whose technology you used? But as politicians got their heads around the issue, this "plague on both your houses" mindset started to fade.

One by one, each of the justifications for Huawei's inclusion started to look shaky as it was subjected to closer scrutiny by independent experts. The rollout would not be extraordinarily delayed. The cost was not prohibitive. The alternative equipment operators were all European and they did not lag behind technologically. Ericsson alone held more essential 5G patents than Huawei, and as one US telecoms executive explained, "We've tested the Huawei equipment and gone to the European firms to make sure they can replicate its capabilities—there's nothing Huawei can do that they can't."

As Röttgen staked out a public position on the issue, sections of the German press that had not normally gone near these topics started to pick them up. It was no longer solely a matter for the most serious newspapers, the *Frankfurter Allgemeine Zeitung* and *Süddeutsche Zeitung*, but the mass-market *Bild*, which attacked Merkel's position that same October. It was a shift of major political resonance. With 5G, China was no longer solely a broadsheet matter, it was finally becoming a tabloid issue too and a matter of domestic politics. German politicians could see very well what this meant, and the way the debate was likely to flow. For all Merkel's popularity and her dominance of the CDU, she was heading into her final year and the China question was going to outlast her. It was unclear whether, if the vote did indeed go to the Bundestag, Merkel would be able to carry her own party on the Huawei issue.

Her coalition partners, the SPD, who controlled ministries that were essential to the decision-making process on any 5G legislation, went further. The SPD had once been firmly at the softer edge of the spectrum on China policy. As one of their parliamentarians put it:

> The SPD is usually linked with the idea of dialogue and convergence with a Communist Party that might reform itself and become a social democratic party. We have a privileged relationship with the CPC, an annual political dialogue that goes back decades—the idea was to have real exchange on programmatic ideas around left ideology.

It was clear to them that those days were over: "Our ideas and the CDU's ideas of business leading to convergence were falsified by reality. We now have system competition. Merkel's view on China is out of date." A group of leading SPD figures, led by Schmid, Metin Hakverdi and Christoph Matschie, issued a striking position paper on China. "Our main point," one of the authors noted,

> was that, yes we should regard it as a partner, competitor, and systemic rival. But not as a partner on Monday, competitor on Tuesday, rival on Wednesday. Systemic rivalry conditions and limits the scope for partnership and competition. It puts breaks and restrictions on how we deal with China in the future. We have to understand the overarching effects of systemic rivalry.

With the Greens and the Free Democratic Party in the same place, the prospect of passing any Huawei-supportive legislation dwindled to near-zero. By the end of 2019, the situation was essentially deadlocked. The German government could not command a parliamentary majority for its position. So it chose to bring no legislation at all. The situation was in limbo. For the likes of Deutsche Telekom, this still gave it the space to create facts on the ground, as it already started to roll out base stations that featured Huawei components. But the ground was shifting. At the beginning of the year, Germany had been the decisive actor for the European debate that would set the pace for the rest of the continent. Now it was starting to look like a laggard.

Washington, DC, June 2019

When Keith Krach arrived at the US State Department, he had the same question as our frustrated interlocutors at the Pentagon. "Who owns this thing?" Krach was taking on the role of under secretary of state for economic growth, energy, and the environment, or simply "E." His agenda as the country's lead economic diplomat, however, was best summarized by another "E." "Economic warcraft is not taught in the US government," as Krach put it in an interview. While a few of his colleagues at the Treasury may have disagreed with the sweep of the statement, they were generally used to taking on opponents with little economic firepower of their own. Krach wanted a strategy for outcompeting China, not financially pulverizing a rogue state. He was a Silicon Valley veteran, new to government but armed with a set of experiences, a rolodex of contacts in government and industry, a strategic clarity and a communicative brio that was particularly suited to the mission at hand. "We wanted to deliver a proven, executable and repeatable model for competing with China," he told me: "To build a coalition of countries and companies to stand against authoritarianism. And to use 5G as the beachhead to build that alliance for all areas of economic competition—cable, cloud, carrier, drones, currency, infrastructure." As one White House official put it: "Once Keith Krach was brought on, he picked [5G] up as a topic and was laser-beam focused."

When Krach was running DocuSign, he had visited China to explore whether the company should enter the market, spending two weeks there on a "listening trip." He had been going to China on occasion for business since 1981 and professed deep admiration for China's culture, its history and its people. But it became apparent to him that this time was different. The aggression of the propaganda was not the same, it left the foreboding sense that a new set of rules were at play. It was the first time he saw their drone swarm technology and heard about the Belt and Road. "It looked like a military supply chain to me," he noted. He found it odd that every thirty minutes at the conference he was being asked to download Chinese applications on his phone.

He came back to the States wondering how this was seen in Washington and who was leading the US government's technology strategy. Shortly after his return to Silicon Valley, he flew to DC to find out. He would be asked by the secretary of state,

Mike Pompeo, to take the task on himself. In Krach's Senate confirmation testimony, he outlined his strategy to address the China challenge: "My focus will be on harnessing three powerful areas of competitive advantage: strengthening our partnerships with friends and allies, leveraging the innovation and resources of the private sector, and amplifying the moral high ground of our democratic values."

He had started with a more self-contained initiative: the Blue Dot Network—named for the view of earth from space as a mere blue dot—which was part of the pushback against the Belt and Road but embodied many of the trust principles that would then be deployed in the 5G battles. It sought to define a set of standards for infrastructure that could then be assessed and certified: high-quality, transparent projects whose stamp of approval could act as a market signal for private sector capital. Launched with Japan and Australia, it would go on to form part of the counter-Belt and Road architecture.

But the 5G efforts went beyond this in both the urgency of the task and the sense that it needed to form a template for future US efforts. "It was a political hot potato in the interagency. And officials were just banging on the table saying 'Don't buy Huawei.'" It wasn't working. A few days after Pelosi's remarks at the Munich Security Conference in 2020, Huawei announced a blistering ninety-one commercial 5G contracts globally, including forty-seven in Europe, outpacing Ericsson and Nokia by some margin.[6] "It looked like they were going to run the table," Krach noted: "Huawei had all the momentum and seemed unstoppable."

He was given the authority to recruit a dozen executives from the private sector to pair with foreign service officers: "You needed to bring in people from the business world, not just lawyers or investment bankers but the value creation guys, hi-tech, manufacturing, and combine them with the skills of the people in government ... It was the integration of Silicon Valley strategies with foreign policy tools." Rather than dealing solely with counterparts in government, they would go directly to the companies themselves. This included the CEOs of the telecoms operators who so often acted as Huawei's biggest cheerleaders but were privately anxious about where their dealings with the company were headed. The Chinese government "seduces with money and then reinforces with intimidation and retaliation," Krach noted, but "there's strength in numbers; it created a security blanket. I can't tell you how many CEOs and PMs told us: this is what we've been waiting for."

The framework they developed, the Clean Network, was based on the principle of states committing to use only "trusted" equipment in their 5G infrastructure. "In my first sixty bilaterals, I asked 'how's your relationship with China?' They'd say: 'it's important,' and then they looked around the room as if someone was there, 'but we don't trust them.' Nobody trusted China. And 5G is the ultimate trust exercise." "We would say, who do you trust with your citizens' data? Who do you trust with your company's proprietary technology? Who do you trust with your government's most precious information? Is it the Chinese Communist Party? The answer is invariably no," he told me. The US government's past approach to addressing Huawei's 5G network with other countries had been more sticks than carrots. Krach said:

> It involved a lot of banging on the table and saying, "Don't buy Huawei." That's the dumbest thing I've ever heard. If someone told me that when I was CEO, I'd tell my chief of staff "Check it out, it must be some pretty good stuff." Where I come from, you never mention your competitor's name.

Krach told his team, "Why don't we treat these countries and telcos like customers? Nobody likes to be told what to do. We need to offer them a value proposition if we expect them to partner with us."

The approach was unusually well-aligned with the approach the European institutions were developing, and indeed Brussels was one of Krach's earliest destinations after taking on the job. The EU's approach to China-related problems was invariably to establish a tool that did not reference China by name, that was "actor-agnostic" about states, let alone companies. This was partly out of legal propriety, partly for the sake of having instruments that could be used to deal with a wider array of threats, and partly out of fear of Chinese retaliation. In the case of 5G, it was harder to conceal the China-ness of what was being proposed than with most other new EU tools, given that this was virtually a straight up battle between Chinese and European companies. But the principles were generic, much as with Krach's Clean Network scheme—"it put China in a Catch 22: they either have to live by and practice the trust principles or they're excluded." The aim of the Clean Network was to give China Inc. the hard choice of either sacrificing the largest market or altering its behavior.

The EU was in the process of establishing its own 5G security toolbox, and US officials consistently found their counterparts in the European institutions to be more like-minded than some ostensibly closer allies. Another US official closely involved in the 5G process noted that the EU's approach was so well-crafted that the US government would draw on aspects of the model itself. "A really big juncture for the campaign was our announcement with the EU and with NATO," Krach stated: "It was the first place we went in Europe. We did them together, combined the Clean Network with the 5G toolbox. That meant it was not America alone." Rather than Huawei being excluded by fiat, it would find itself facing a set of hurdles that its very nature as a company beholden to the Chinese system would make it impossible to clear. As one EU official put it at the time, referring to evidence of Huawei representing a security threat:

Some say, "Where is the evidence?" Well, the 2017 National Intelligence Law is there. It's difficult to understand what more you would need. The law is so blunt. And we think economic partners should generally follow laws. We don't find it reassuring from the perspective of our own legal system when they say they won't.

Huawei's tactics had including paying for legal opinions from prominent Western law firms like Clifford Chance that suggested that the National Intelligence Law's demands—that Chinese companies were obliged to cooperate with the Chinese government's intelligence work—did not apply outside China or had "safeguards" that meant firms didn't have to act against their "legitimate interests."[7] Since this elicited incredulity from virtually any informed observer, Huawei founder Ren Zhengfei was ultimately moved to state that they would "firmly reject" any demands from the Chinese government to abide by the law.[8]

The EU's "toolkit" would not-so-subtly ask national governments to consider questions such as what surveillance rules the firm is subject to, and whether it can challenge governments' requests through "democratic checks and balances." Thierry Breton, the European commissioner Krach knew from their time in the corporate world—Breton as CEO of France Telecom—encapsulated the approach as he launched the toolkit: "There is zero discrimination. I'm very honest when I'm saying this." But added, "I'm not naive. I know that for some it will be easier to comply than for others."[9] Krach and Breton issued a joint statement highlighting their "commitment to shared principles on 5G security and the synergies between the EU 5G cybersecurity Toolbox and the Clean Network."

If the UK and Germany were moving slowly and reluctantly towards the inevitable outcome, the dynamics elsewhere had shifted. "In a rapidly changing technology market, everybody wants to go with the leader, and leadership is not determined by size, but by momentum. Huawei had it. In the short term, our goal was to take away that momentum and replace it with our own momentum ... a rolling thunder of wins and announcements," Krach said in his reflection on the campaign.

The US effected a near clean-sweep in Central and Eastern Europe, where relations with the US had even more of a life-or-death dimension. Privately, the NATO secretary general had told US officials: "We need a clean NATO network because we need these 5G systems in peacetime or wartime. We can't have some countries with trusted ones, some with untrusted ones, because you're only as strong as your weakest link." Nowhere did that weigh more heavily than for the states that wanted not only US security guarantees but active US military presence in their countries as a deterrent to Russia. The remaining pieces of Northern Europe were clicking into place too. And in the south, the few holdouts were starting to look anxiously over their shoulder. China also proved adept at making the situation worse for itself. As Krach put it:

> The more they tried to defend against it the more they proved they couldn't be trusted. We used the fact that China's foreign service officers were working for Huawei to our advantage: Huawei is part of the government, the government is the Chinese Communist Party, it has created a surveillance state.

The Chinese ambassadors in Berlin and London were doing the US government's work for them: "We kept saying: 'they're going to bully you, they're going to bully you' and then boom, they'd make the threat."

By the time the interim German decision was finally reached in April 2021, nearly one year later, attention had moved on. Huawei's ninety-one 5G deals went down to barely two dozen, a collapse that the shifting tides of opinion in Europe and a relentlessly effective US campaign had helped to bring about. There was no longer any question of Chinese retaliation or Germany deciding the fate of the continent. But by then, the entire politics of China policy in Europe had changed, in exactly the way that Röttgen and others had anticipated, and Germany was nearing a political tipping point of its own. The COVID-19 pandemic, the arrival of the Biden administration, and Chinese behavior in the intervening period had accelerated every trend that was now underway. The time when China was perennially "important but not urgent" was over. Krach and his colleagues were justifiably able to take a victory lap. According to former US National Security Advisor H. R. McMaster: "The Clean Network's defeat of the Chinese Communist Party's masterplan to control 5G communications was the first time a US government-led initiative proved that China's economic warfare is beatable because it exposed their biggest weakness: nobody trusts them."

Yet it was a victory barely snatched from the jaws of defeat. The fact that the major European liberal market democracies had been so close to simply accepting the inevitability of China controlling the enabling infrastructure of their economies was long in the making. It reflected a decades-long process of refusing to take the problem seriously until it was almost too late.

4

BURNING DOWN THE HOUSE

CHINA'S SHOCK TO THE SYSTEM AND THE CRISES THAT MATTERED MORE

Beijing, 2010

TWO YEARS AFTER THE GLOBAL financial crisis had blown up, I had a meeting in Beijing with one of China's most eminent foreign policy intellectuals. A colleague, Dan Twining, and I were sitting in his office engaging in the usual to-and-fro about the latest twists in the US–China relationship. At a certain point in the conversation, he stopped speaking. Indicating obliquely that listening devices in the room were getting in the way of what he needed to say, he suggested that it would be better if we moved somewhere livelier. We resumed with the clatter of crockery and the chatter of a loud restaurant around us. His message was stark, and one that was doubtless being delivered to many other Americans passing through town. The real debate about Chinese assertiveness in Beijing was over, he said. The advocates of broad-based cooperation with the United States, even those as prominent as him, were not meaningfully in the policy conversation anymore. The question for Chinese foreign policy now was only about timing—should it be assertive now or assertive later? Was China positioned to make a more full-throated push for its interests or would it be advisable to bide its time a little longer? Whatever the tactical calculations, the strategic course was set, he said, and US policymakers should be under no illusions about what to expect.

In the years following the Lehman Brothers meltdown, there was a jarring shift. Even if it did not reach the later excesses that would see China's diplomats dubbed Wolf Warriors, after a popular 2015 Chinese patriotic war movie, a growing sense of assertiveness was already changing China's approach. The events around the turn of that decade were an embryonic form of everything that followed. The bald statement of Yang Jiechi, the Chinese foreign minister, at the ASEAN Regional Forum that "China is a big country and other countries are small countries and that is just a fact" was in 2010, not an aggrieved reaction to Trumpian excesses.[1] China's decision to cut off rare earth supplies to Japan came that same year, amid tensions with Tokyo over a detained Chinese fishing trawler, well before any pandemic-induced debates about supply chains or restrictions on semiconductor sales. Beijing's freezing of economic and diplomatic ties with Norway over the award of the Nobel Peace Prize to the writer and activist Liu Xiaobo was later that year. The man who would later transform Xinjiang first into an open-air prison and then into an actual network of concentration camps, Chen Quanguo, started developing started developing his techniques in Tibet in 2011.

For a while, it was only a question of which of the many triggers would elicit a reaction. For some European leaders, it was China's behavior at the Copenhagen climate talks in December 2009 that gave them pause. As one participant in the meetings characterized it: "China's strategy was simple: block the open negotiations for two weeks, and then ensure that the closed-door deal made it look as if the West had failed the world's poor once again." But while much of this was orchestrated through proxies, it included shocking moments such as the chief Chinese negotiator, Xie Zhenhua, wagging his finger at President Obama and declaiming "Get out!" when he tried to enter a room where the BRICS leaders were meeting.[2] The role Beijing played in derailing the final efforts to reach an agreement saw heads of government coming home burned by the experience: "We got our assumptions about China wrong," one of the prime ministers in the talks at the time noted to his staff, "we need a complete rethink." When I conveyed his remarks to a French official, he smiled—"we already had our rethink. When all your meetings are canceled, it gives you plenty of time to write strategic plans."

Paris had only recently been in the doghouse after Nicolas Sarkozy met with the Dalai Lama in late 2008, barely a few months after the chaotic Olympic torch relay in France, disrupted by protests over Beijing's crackdown in Tibet, led to "boycott Carrefour" protests in China. Indeed, the punishments for meeting him had become so routinized that one European academic had sufficiently ample data to quantify a specific "Dalai Lama effect" on countries' economies.[3] Despite the modest nature of that economic impact, the tradition of Western leaders sitting down with the Tibetan people's spiritual leader quietly came to an end, while Hollywood's enthusiasm for the matter waned in proportion to the growth of the Chinese film market. It was not commercial ties alone that even mattered—Norwegian officials acknowledged that the economic consequences of the Chinese "freeze" after Liu Xiaobo's Nobel Peace Prize were trivial, they just did not want to be cut off from normal political exchanges with such an important global power.

Privately, many Western politicians as early as the late 2000s acknowledged that a revisiting of their China strategy needed to take place. It would be another decade before it happened. Even at the moments where they saw what was unfolding, their capacity to focus on it was painfully limited. As crisis after crisis roiled the system, policymakers who would ordinarily have been thinking about how to address the looming long-term challenge were instead embroiled in a fight for survival. And at each critical juncture until the COVID-19 pandemic—the financial crisis, the eurozone crisis, the refugee crisis, Crimea—China was seen as a stabilizer rather than a vital threat, playing its hand with notable deftness. It was an approach that went back even before the Hu–Wen era, to a strategic juncture that some Chinese foreign policy strategists who are critical of Xi's approach cite as a model to this day.

* * *

When the 9/11 attacks took place, China's president, Jiang Zemin, was watching a Hong Kong cable news network. Since China's own state broadcasters were not running the story, he called Li Zhaoxing, the Chinese foreign minister, to tell him to turn on Phoenix TV. Barely two hours later, Jiang put a call in to George W. Bush to convey his condolences and assure Bush of China's willingness to fight terrorism together. It was one of the first messages of sympathy that he received. Beijing followed up with practical assistance. It offered minesweepers and intelligence support ahead of the invasion of Afghanistan, including an offer to put at the Pentagon's disposal the man who had run Chinese intelligence operations in Afghanistan in the 1980s, Chen Xiaogong, who was serving as military attaché in Washington, DC. While the United States took up the offers of cooperation in sharing intelligence on terrorist financing and the establishment of an FBI office in Beijing, they did not call on a disappointed Chen, nor use any of the Chinese minesweepers.

Donald Rumsfeld's lack of interest in Chinese assistance for the war in Afghanistan was of no real concern to Beijing. The political intervention had its effect: "They were immediately on board with the war on terror, and that just shredded the agenda of anybody who wanted to get going with the new Cold War," as the State Department's Asia head at the time, James Kelly, later noted.[4] Jiang did so despite a certain glee from sections of the Chinese population who thought that the United States had it coming. "As the news spread, people came out to dance and cheer," as one Beijing hotel manager recalled: "They were screaming and lighting firecrackers—it was like a big party."[5]

Bin Laden himself had positioned himself with scrupulous care on China, seeing Beijing's potential support or neutrality as part of a potential bloc to push back against Western power. One drunk Chinese friend close to the PLA told me a story of Beijing sending agents to meet with the Al Qaeda leader, a claim he then retracted when he was sober again. But Jiang would not play to this strand of public opinion nor seek to use the moment to dabble with anti-American coalitions. This was a juncture to keep China's head down. 9/11 alone would have eclipsed the nascent plans for the Bush administration to refocus US energies on great power competition, but Jiang's clear and immediate positioning of China as a partner to the United States on its most urgent security interests guaranteed it.

The final year of the Bush administration followed a similar pattern. As Hank Paulson, the US Treasury secretary, recalls in his memoirs:

> China bashing grew louder through the presidential primaries. In May the Democratic rivals, Senators Hillary Clinton and Barack Obama, endorsed legislation that would have allowed punitive duties on Chinese goods in response to currency manipulation. I spent hours on Capitol Hill ... trying to deflect such knee-jerk protectionism.[6]

For Paulson, the close and trusting relationships with the likes of Wang Qishan, who was the Chinese vice-premier in charge of finance, and Hu Xiaolin, who oversaw China's foreign reserves, were essential to manage the crisis that was roiling the US financial system. Over a trillion dollars of those reserves were invested in US Treasury bills and agency paper. The alternative prospect was on vivid display when Paulson visited Beijing for the 2008 Olympics. He received news on the trip that Russian officials had approached the Chinese to propose that they take the coordinated step of selling their stakes in the federally backed home mortgage companies Fannie Mae and Freddie Mac, a means of heaping pressure on the US government at a moment of real systemic fragility. The Chinese declined.

They would hold on to their US securities throughout the crisis. Indeed, when reports emerged of Chinese banks withdrawing funds from the money market and pulling back on overnight lending, Paulson called the governor of the Chinese central bank, Zhou Xiaochuan, who reassured him that the sales were not coordinated and that "we're going to give some guidance."[7] The Chinese institutions reversed course. Beijing would consolidate its reputation as the power whose interests were bound up in keeping the global system functioning, its interests closer to those of the West in some crucial areas than Moscow's anarchic desire to see it come crashing down. Any role that the Chinese contribution to global imbalances might have played in contributing to an unsustainable level of liquidity in the US economy was set to one side. Indeed, Wang Qishan made sure that there were no references to global imbalances at all at the critical G20 meeting: that might "look like you're pointing the finger at China" for the crisis.[8]

Across the Atlantic, it was the same story. Talk to policymakers who were in the throes of the eurozone crisis and there is still a residue of credit for Beijing even today. A couple of weeks before the fateful Copenhagen climate summit, the new Greek government revealed that its budget deficit would be double the original estimates, exceeding 12 percent of GDP. The years that followed would see the continent enveloped in cycles of market and political panic that pushed dangerously close to the unraveling of one of the EU's signature achievements and frayed the trust between parts of Europe almost to breaking point.

It was an existential crisis for the European project rather than just an economic one. It was also a very immediate political crisis for the heads of government in the states that were closest to the edge. As the likes of Spain, Greece and Portugal came under sustained attack in the bond markets, as Germany was called on to play an enlarged role in bankrolling the survival of the euro-zone itself, and as decision-makers at the European Central Bank and the new eurozone financing entities struggled to come up with solutions that would staunch the bleeding, almost every political question ended up being refracted through the week-to-week decisions that could have after-effects lasting decades.

With China holding $3 trillion in foreign exchange reserves, the war-chest that was once understood as a byproduct of the economic imbalance that helped bring the crisis about in the first place was now seen as a potential means of market reassurance. The head of the EU's bailout fund trooped off to Beijing in 2011 to look for Chinese buy-in to the European Financial Stability Facility. Politicians from Madrid to Athens were keen simply to have statements of support for their treasuries, a few commitments to bond purchases and some friendly words during a visit by the Chinese prime minister. As countries were pushed to sell off assets, from the Portuguese energy grid to Piraeus port, China was there as the willing buyer. As one confidant of the Spanish prime minister at the time put it:

> In Portugal and Greece, the catalytic effect was pro-Chinese. When the northern Europeans kicked our asses, the Chinese bailed us out. People really worried that Spain would default. Our so-called friends like Germany were helping to put us in this position, while the Chinese helped. The signals from them were crucial ... The figures were not big but the timing was important.

Meanwhile, the vast Chinese stimulus acted as a lifeline for the eurozone's most important economy, which could more than compensate for recessions in the nearest markets with buoyant growth in Asia. After the crash of 2009, Germany would not see negative growth again until the COVID-19 pandemic. Other major economies had not been as fortunate.

* * *

China had joined the WTO three months after the 9/11 attacks. The terms of its membership were exceptionally onerous, necessitating a far more comprehensive set of economic reforms than any other new member had faced. But the hope on the part of the Western negotiators was that this was part of a thoroughgoing commitment to dismantling market access barriers and paring back the role of the state, one that would continue and deepen with membership. The prevailing view in Beijing however was that, if anything, it had already conceded too much.

The immediate impact of China's accession was profound. Well after the fact, it would be described by economists as the "China shock."[9] The original version of the theory by a trio of academics, David Dorn, David Autor and Gordon Hanson, laid out the case that, while the impact of technologically driven changes on income inequality and unemployment were largely dispersed across the economy, exposure to trade competition was geographically concentrated. In other words, China's membership of the WTO hit particular income groups and local areas in the West exceptionally hard, and with political consequences that would be clear only many years after the peak of the economic effect in the 2000s. In a series of papers, the economists who developed the theory, and others who used their methodology, were able to trace the causal impact of the China shock on a series of real-world events and trends: the 2016 US elections, the UK Brexit vote and the longer-term ideological polarization reflected in both.

The effects ran well beyond the developed world and well beyond the raw numbers. It was soon straining the global trading system to its limits. My most vivid experience of it was in the run-up to the conclusion of the WTO's Doha round talks back in 2007. My colleagues at the German Marshall Fund were organizing a vast shadow simulation of the process in Salzburg, against the backdrop of the setting to the *Sound of Music*, Schloss

Leopoldskron. The WTO director general, Pascal Lamy and the chairs of the various WTO working groups opened up the deliberations to a range of outsiders to roleplay the complex array of trade-offs over agricultural subsidies and market access commitments. I was there to follow the China dimension of the process.

Lamy gave the remarks at the opening dinner to set the scene. China, he said, was the "specter at the table." Whatever was happening on the surface, in the background more and more countries were privately saying that they did not want to make any moves that would open their economies up to a further wave of Chinese imports. Beijing would need to accept a new bargain if it wanted to keep the whole WTO process alive, and it had no intention of doing so. A negotiating round that was supposed to have liberating effects for the developing world was instead defined by deep skepticism among states across the Global South about what they might be asked to sign up to if it involved even greater exposure to the Chinese juggernaut.

The talks collapsed in mutual acrimony within the next year. India accrued blame for walking out of the final negotiating session. The United States accrued blame for being seemingly unwilling to make concessions for the protection of poor farmers. The EU emerged unusually unscathed but was assumed by campaigners to be somehow responsible too. Unlike at Copenhagen a couple of years later, when insiders to the process quickly went public, it was left to the very wonkiest of journalists and officials to try to make sense of the events and little filtered out beyond the trade cognoscenti. But as I talked through the final stages with WTO staff and outside negotiators at the time, the story kept coming back to China.

It was not acting as the outright spoiler. There was no finger jabbing or political drama, and its negotiators hid masterfully behind others throughout the process. Its spectral presence, however, meant that if Beijing refused to budge beyond its accession commitments, the world faced a stalemate. Developing states publicly criticized the failure of the talks but privately signaled that they had not been so unhappy with the outcome. Although a very thin agreement was reached in Bali in 2013, the moment for a big compromise had passed that year. It never returned. The WTO became a framework for litigation, not a vehicle for liberating trade. In the aftermath of the Doha debacle, the very notion of a global framework was abandoned in favor of regional and bilateral arrangements. The most important of them were characterized by the need to construct new deals that specifically excluded China.

The sense of something amiss was only expressed *sotto voce*. Developing countries did not wish to alienate the country that was starting to have an ever-greater influence over their political and economic fate. But the effect of surging Chinese imports and heightened competition was acute. African and Latin American states that had been looking to diversify their economies were now having to revert to natural resource exports that would feed Chinese industry instead, a benefit to some, but not the economic path they had wanted. If weaker developing countries believed that they simply had to learn to live with it, among the advanced economies the unwillingness to act while they were in a position of such relative strength was more striking.

China's membership of the WTO armed Western policymakers with an array of legal instruments they could use if they thought that China was not playing by the rules. Yet attempts by the few officials and politicians who tried to do so were actively undermined. Perhaps the best example of this was the abortive effort in 2012 by the European commissioner for trade, Karel de Gucht, to bring WTO cases in two exemplary sectors. The aim was to issue China with an across-the-board warning about Europe's willingness to defend the very industries on which its long-term economic future depended. One of the officials at the time tells the story:

In DG-Trade [the directorate in charge of the EU's trade] by then we thought they were not a friendly partner. We believed our companies were under attack. The people who were really working on China saw these things—the overcapacity, the dumping on our markets, the massive subsidies. De Gucht was a grumpy old man, but he always saw where things were going. He read up a lot on it, drew in a lot of outside advice, and acted on his conviction.

They drew up a couple of symbolically important cases that would act as a warning to China that Europe was ready to stand up for its interests, at least in industries that were critical to the fate of the continent. "We tried to act in two strategic sectors, solar and telecoms, where we were very strong and where the Chinese were eating our markets. These were core European industries of the future, not just typical trade defense cases." The first problem that Commission officials faced was that they would have to do all the heavy lifting themselves, in the absence of industry's active support. But given the political value of the effort, they believed they had the wider politics squared:

> The companies themselves were scared to come forward, we had to do it without them, on our own initiative. If we'd been able to move ahead with the full case, we thought we were in a position to reach a strong settlement with China or hit them with duties immediately if not. We talked to member states, we thought we were there with a majority, but then at last minute it all changed.

In May 2013, the Chinese premier, Li Keqiang, headed to Berlin to ensure that the unfriendly behavior from Brussels was squashed. It was a remarkable success. He appeared beamingly at a press conference with Angela Merkel. "Germany will do what it can so that there are no permanent import duties and we'll try to clear things up as quickly as possible," Merkel told reporters: "We don't believe that this will help us so we want to use the next six months intensively."[10] DG-Trade was in shock:

> It was horrible. It was a very high-level decision in Germany; when we met people at the working level, they were very embarrassed about it. Ultimately the member states were not there. It took them ten years to get to where we were then. The position was always—you are exaggerating, China is a partner. Certain people, especially in that member state, considered China a friend.

The same problem held for European firms too. As another European official puts it: "European industry was often paralyzed when it came to their interest in the Chinese market. The problem wasn't just Germany, it was the hesitation from the companies themselves, who feared retaliation." The difficulties getting European solar and telecoms firms on board were indicative of a wider pattern:

> It illustrates the difficulties we have as investigators working on a very important European economic interest—we could often show a prima facie case, an evidentiary picture with market reports, how dumped imports are causing injury, but it was always harder absent real commitment from European industry. And they would often bring the complaints themselves only at the last minute, at the point where the sector was almost eradicated.

Beyond occasional forays from the likes of De Gucht, there was little political capacity to think about China except in instrumental terms. For many politicians in Europe from 2010 to 2018, it was largely there to be pulled in to reinforce their position in other more important games. As long as Beijing handled the most vital system crises in a manner that suggested that it didn't want everything to fall apart, it could buy itself ample room for maneuver, as Li's visit to Berlin demonstrated.

The contrast between China and the more problematic neighbor next door was also seemingly clear. The eurozone crisis resulted in an upsurge of populist parties from right and left, who were gleefully supported by Moscow. This would worsen considerably in the subsequent years. The refugee crisis saw millions fleeing Syria and Afghanistan and arriving at Europe's shores and borders. Populism in Southern, Central and Eastern Europe was turbocharged, as Western European states asked for a fair sharing of the distribution of refugees, which some states such as Hungary refused point-blank. Moscow would inflame these tensions through every propaganda outlet and influence operation going. If the authoritarian threat from Russia was seen to be fusing with fault lines in Europe, China's role at the time appeared far more restrained. Chinese cyber-capabilities were not deployed to subvert Western elections or undermine confidence in democratic political systems. China did not finance, host, support or direct its propaganda outlets to back extremist parties across the continent. It did not look to promote "civilizational conflict" or try to destroy the European project itself. Even Xi Jinping, in his earlier days, seemed to see the virtues of being perceived in Europe as a source of stability rather than Russian-style anarchy. China was always happy to be the beneficiary of any chaos but not yet ready to be a catalyst for it.

* * *

While China was not treated as an issue of the highest salience, it was certainly used for intra-European positioning and signaling relating to the issues that did. The 16+1 was the most mythologized of these efforts. The grouping was launched in 2012. It drew together both EU and non-EU European states, already raising eyebrows about Chinese interest in undercutting the unity of the bloc. But the enthusiasm for the initiative came from states that felt like they had been playing second fiddle to the major Western European powers in their interactions with China. Germany and France had their major bilateral summits, regular government-to-government consultations and trade and investment relationships totaling in the tens of billions. The 16+1 gave regular face-time for Central and Eastern European heads of government with the Chinese top leadership and a chance to demand economic commitments from Beijing that could potentially close the gap. Economic ties with China in the region were barely a dribble by contrast. And as the EU and Western European states threatened to withhold EU money given the increasingly authoritarian proclivities on the part of Budapest, there was a neat positional game in suggesting to Brussels that other outside resources were available if they chose to go down that route.

The same also held true for a cluster of states across Southern Europe that had once been dismissively grouped together as the PIGS. Portugal, Italy, Greece and Spain had all been subject to some of the most intense pressure from bond markets through-out the sovereign debt crisis. Where Spain emerged strongly from the crisis, Portugal had sold critical parts of its industry, including a major stake in its power grid, to the Chinese, while Greece demonstrated its affinities by joining the 16+1 grouping itself. But perhaps no country illustrated the combination of all these trends, from the China shock to the political gamesman-ship that Beijing played into and sought to exploit, than Italy.

After China's WTO accession, Southern European economies were the hardest hit. Artisanal industries from shoemaking to textiles that had been in family hands for generations were deci-mated. Italy's small and midsize family-owned companies had accounted for 85 percent of the country's GDP.[11] A book by the businessman-turned-author Edoardo Nesi, which would win the most prestigious Italian literary award, told the tale of how he was forced to sell the weaving mill that had been in operation in Prato since the 1920s, and the decline of the Tuscan city from its role at the center of the "Made in Italy" garment industry to a hub for Chinese sweatshops. Industry groups in Italy were per-fectly well aware that some of these were less competitive sectors, ripe for displacement by lower-priced firms in Asia. But they had been through waves of this competition before and survived. And their assessment was that while elements of the cost advantage were genuine, the Chinese state also tilted the playing field in an assortment of ways that would later become familiar to more advanced economic sectors too. With a mix of anger and pathos, Nesi's book describes Italian industrialists "being torn limb from limb by the Chinese, in the certainty that no-one would raise a finger to defend them."

"Right before China became a member nation of the WTO and its products were allowed to flood the markets of the West like a raging river," he goes on,

> our politicians traveled the world with smiles on their faces signing agreements that would ultimately undermine Italy's prosperity, with the enthusiastic support of our economists ... they said that the opening of the Chinese market would be doubly advantageous to us Italians because as soon as they emerged from poverty ... what's the first thing the Chinese would rush to buy? But of course, Italian style. When a few observers timidly began to point out the sharp rise in bankruptcies and layoffs, the economists furrowed their brows and said that maybe there were a few Luddites in circulation who hadn't read the memo about how we all now live in a single global market.[12]

Talk now to the major Italian business groups about the awakening of German industry to the challenge China poses and the reaction is one of weary exasperation:

> For us, China was a systemic rival since forever. We said this from the very beginning. We've been brushing things under the carpet since they joined the WTO. But the attitude from Germany was: don't touch them, sure they're bad guys but we're doing a lot of business ... We've been waiting for them for years to get to where they are now.

Italian and Spanish complaints attracted little attention. Officials and politicians from Rome were among those proposing toughened trade measures and mechanisms for investing screening. Yet they were seen in almost Canute-like terms—globalization was a force of nature, China was its embodiment, and the tide would inevitably displace whatever was in its path. It was the same story in Madrid. As one Spanish official put it:

> Fifteen years ago, China was identified by the Spanish public as an economic threat. Companies here saw it as a systemic threat, they were complaining for a long time. Our industries weren't generally the technology companies. Twenty years ago, it was toys, furniture. There were even assaults against Chinese businesses—people burned the storage areas for Chinese goods. They were hit with social dumping, environmental dumping. The message from Northern Europe was—you're not competitive enough, suck it up. Now it's their problem too.

By 2019, the Italian government was virtually the embodiment of all the trends in European politics from the preceding decade. A right–left populist coalition led by inexperienced figures from outside the usual political class had swept to power on a mandate of disaffection that fused the two most potent areas of contention, austerity and immigration. The leadership in Rome was engaged in pitched battles with Brussels over its budget deficit, which left it highly constrained when it came to any of the large spending pledges that helped bring the parties to power in the first place.

If other capitals in Europe insisted on tying the Italian government's hands with eurozone fiscal pacts, Beijing could play a helpful theatrical role in demonstrating what the consequences would be, whether or not it ever delivered on any of its investment commitments. Xi Jinping was the lead actor in a drama that was entirely constructed around local and European politics. For most politicians in Rome, China as such was an afterthought. But Xi's visit there that year would give it an unusually prominent role.

On the outside, Xi's trip looked like a repeat of all the political games-playing of the last decade. Xi was due to arrive with pledges of investment in a series of Italian ports, from Vado Ligure to Trieste. He would be received in high style with a full honor guard at the Quirinale, the presidential palace. His schedule included an unusual visit to Sicily, with its potent symbolism as a channel for US power in the country, with some of the most significant military infrastructure in the Mediterranean. The setpiece would be the signature of the Belt and Road memorandum of understanding, a vivid demonstration that a G7 state and founding member of the EU was also willing to pay homage to Xi Jinping's pet initiative.

The whole occasion was the product of the kind of policy entrepreneurship that would only be possible for a government so lacking in executive experience. The man behind it was not some powerful behind-the-scenes industrialist or political dealmaker but a relatively obscure Sicilian banker-turned-academic. Michele Geraci occupied the role of under secretary of state at the Ministry of Economic Development, a vantage point from which he had been running a virtually autonomous China policy. Geraci until a few years earlier had been at a university in Beijing, a position he had acquired during an era when foreigners with a business background had a much higher cache than they do today. His Mandarin was, by all accounts, exemplary. Geraci had decided to trade in Chinese academic life for Italian politics, and the two populist parties offered a different set of political opportunities for outsiders. He was happy to deal with either or both.

The pitch was all about how China would solve every problem Italy faced, which he was happy to sell—and himself as part of the solution too—to whoever would take it up. A version was ultimately laid out in an article he wrote in June 2018 for Grillo Blog, the comedian and Five Star Movement founder Beppe Grillo's widely read online magazine.[13] Who can solve Italy's weak export situation? China. Debt problems? China. Need for investment? China. Infrastructure deficiencies? China. Migration challenges? China. Public security issues? China. Had this come from one of the dubious array of China-friendly academics, it might have been seen as crank work. It elicited an open letter from many Italian Sinologists, summed up by one of them as "what the hell are you saying?" But that same month, Geraci joined the new government.

The coalition was a strange one. The League, once a Northern secessionist party, had extended its writ to the rest of Italy under the leadership of Matteo Salvini. Its hard-right anti-immigration and euroskeptic platform brought it into affinity with the likes of Marine Le Pen. The Five Star movement had a cyber-utopian/direct-democracy/green/anti-establishment flavor, topped off with its own strand of euroskepticism, and pulled in voters from the left and the south. That China had accelerated many of the conditions that led to this form of politics was long forgotten. Precisely the regions of Italy that had once been reliable voters for the center-left and the Communists in the past, and the heart of its artisanal trades, had now swung to the far right, catapulting once-fringe figures to power. The inability of establishment politicians to protect them from the sharpest edges of globalization had led to their replacement by voices who channeled the antipathy towards other targets, and immigrants above all.

Figures who were capable of spanning both parties were few and far between, but Geraci with his China shtick was one. Indeed, his good relations with the two sides even saw his name implausibly floated on a list of potential prime ministers during a febrile phase of the coalition negotiations. Technically he was connected with the League, but his ministry was run by the Five Star movement, and it wasn't clear that either party leader fully understood the implications of what he was up to. As one Italian minister put it: "Di Maio thought that Salvini had an eye on him, and vice versa. So he slipped through the middle to do something that neither of them wanted, and was too late to walk back." The positional game was ostensibly straightforward, a byproduct of the antagonistic relationship between the new government and the major European powers-that-be. As one Italian analyst explained: "We had a euroskeptic government, and wanted to signal to France, Germany and the EU that we had friends abroad: Putin, Xi and Trump. But it coincided with the worst US–China relations since 1972. It was a car crash."

In many ways, the Xi visit would act as the tail-end of the long era of European distraction. By 2019, none of this was playing out below the radar anymore. In transatlantic and European politics, China had started to move far higher up the agenda, and while the Italian government's antics with Beijing in the preceding months had already attracted a certain level of attention among the China experts, a state visit and the seeming embrace of the Belt and Road was inevitably going to bring it to the attention of the White House.

Even a couple of years earlier, a Belt and Road MOU would have attracted no more than raised eyebrows in Washington. The same, standard document had been kicked around a number of European ministries, officials across the continent had compared notes on it, and it was clear that no serious government was going to sign up. But only because it seemed like a worthless political concession to China for little plausible benefit, not because anyone was in the least bit concerned about the US reaction. Those issues had not gone away—in private, one Italian industry group dismissed the agreement:

> If you know the Italian political system, you know that it's nothing. But we paid a lot for that "nothing." It's all white noise. We will see no results from the MOU, it's a desperate MOU ... We stick to the principles of reality. Not the political surface of the MOU about selling wine and cheese in China—it's bullshit. Anyone who thinks it will bring economic benefits doesn't know what they're talking about.

In 2018, however, there had been a marked change in the international context surrounding the Belt and Road. That summer had seen the United States launch its Indo-Pacific Economic Vision. The substance was still underdeveloped, but it was clear to anyone attending briefings at the White House ahead of its rollout that the Belt and Road was now wholly in the US cross-hairs. American efforts to persuade governments to steer clear, and the surrounding public diplomacy drive to point out the risks involved, were soon in full flow. No-one had really noticed yet that a major US ally was just about to lend it an important symbolic boost. The Italian government had in fact been keen to get the thing signed during Foreign Minister Luigi Di Maio's trip to China the preceding year. But the Chinese side suggested that Xi's state visit would be a far better occasion. Then the US embassy in Rome clocked what was going on.

The final period before the visit was a pitched battle, as the US embassy and the White House intensified their pressure on the politicians and officials over whom they had leverage. The two political parties dealing with the issue were in distinct positions. The Five Star movement was liaising closely with the Chinese embassy, with Huawei and other entities in the Chinese system. But the League was still trying to play itself into a position of legitimacy with the US government, shoring up its dominance of swathes of the political spectrum that extended beyond its original far-right base. The China issue was now unexpectedly getting in the way. One of Salvini's advisors lamented to me over coffee near the Italian Chamber of Deputies: "It was probably impossible to avoid joining BRI [i.e. the Belt and Road] despite powerful politicians from the League opposing it very strongly. We didn't stop it. Geraci was put there by the League. Salvini could have stopped the signature at the last minute. He didn't. We worked hard to persuade him. We failed."

Giancarlo Giorgetti was the powerful politician in question, the number two in the party, close to the US government, the institutional man to Salvini's rougher edge. Attempts to tell the

Chinese that the MOU couldn't be signed, however, received the unequivocal response: "Then the state visit is cancelled." With a cluster of other deals lined up and threats of retaliation mounting, it was too late. Some of those closest to the affair muttered darkly about the Vatican weighing in on Beijing's behalf. A 2018 agreement between the Holy See and the People's Republic of China on the appointment of bishops was expected to pave the way for a normalization of ties, which would now hang in the balance. Salvini himself decided to skip participating in the entire visit, as a pointed act of political distancing. Italian officials worked on rewriting the text to ensure that it was no longer the Chinese boilerplate language but instead fully consistent with EU principles, after other European powers weighed in too. But the Chinese got their MOU. One official joked that it was the first BRI agreement that fixed the Chinese spelling mistake that always appeared on page five.

It was a Pyrrhic victory. The episode roundly demonstrated that the kind of political maneuvering that had gone on in recent years was not going to fly anymore. China policy was now a primetime matter, as other European states started to get their act together at an EU-wide level, and even more so in Washington. It was well understood that it would affect the quality of countries' most important security relationship if they decided to play fast and loose with Chinese investment, technology transfer, telecoms networks or even the symbolism of handing Beijing political victories. And countries were coming under growing pressure to be "good Europeans" too, which no longer meant carte blanche for dubious side-deals or quiet blocking of common European positions.

For years, China had benefited from the fact that it operated below the urgency threshold of other matters. It wasn't that the importance was unclear, especially in countries such as Italy that had already borne the brunt of the China shock. But when the likes of Greece and Portugal were in a state of economic desperation, they could not afford to be choosy about the country that threw them a lifeline. When intra-European feuds over the refugee crisis were at their peak, China simply appeared to be another clever bargaining chip with Brussels. By 2019 though, the crises had passed. When the next one hit, Beijing would shred much of the trust that remained.

5

FEVER

THE POLITICS OF THE PANDEMIC

AS EUROPEAN POLICYMAKERS DECIDED how to handle the darkest days of the coronavirus outbreak in China, there was no suggestion they would gloat over, or politicize, the situation. Instead, Europe rushed to help. As the virus ravaged Wuhan, the EU provided nearly 60 tonnes of medical material to China, often from national strategic stockpiles, and did so discreetly—at Beijing's request.[1]

Given the explosion of criticism inside the country over the cover-up of the crucial early stages of the virus's transmission, the quasi-martyrdom of whistleblower doctor Li Wenliang, and Xi's temporary disappearing act, European leaders were well aware that this was a moment of extreme domestic sensitivity for the Chinese Communist Party. European leaders decided they would save recriminations about the party-state's culpability for a later date. This would be an example of the quiet cooperation-when-it-mattered that was supposed to characterize the Sino-European relationship. "They will remember it when the time comes," French President Emmanuel Macron reportedly told his aides.[2]

But, just weeks later, Europe was subjected to a Chinese propaganda and disinformation barrage that would never let up. The performative nature of China's provision of medical supplies alone would have grated on European leaders, as would its crude linkages to points of controversy—from Huawei's role as one of the public vehicles for the supply of face masks to the videos of medical deliveries traveling along Belt and Road railway routes accompanied by soaring music. Where Europe had provided China with critical supplies for free, with no fanfare, from among its highest-quality stocks, Beijing would sell its supplies to Europe, many of which were faulty, and demand to be publicly thanked for it. This did not go down well among European leaders. Yet Europe could have, in the most generous of interpretations, attributed all this to inept and desperate propagandizing on Beijing's part rather than malign intent.

It quickly became clear, however, that Chinese officials and propaganda outlets were going beyond clumsy and graceless efforts to showcase their "assistance."[3] It formed part of an active campaign that involved playing along with European populist leaders, who used the crisis as an opportunity to attack the EU and other European governments, and coordinated anti-EU messages from Chinese bots on social media.[4] Chinese state-controlled outlets promoted conspiracy theories that the virus originated in the United States or Italy.[5] The Chinese embassy in France published an article by one of its diplomats claiming that care workers in French nursing homes had left residents to die, and that Westerners were "beginning to lose confidence in liberal democracy." A PLA colonel published an article, the unintentionally ironic "Why the US and Europe Need to Draw Closer to China and Drop the Hubris," claiming that European solidarity was gone, the EU would not last the next twenty years and that a "divided Europe's" turn towards China was, therefore, inevitable. "The West is not in decay," Zhou Bo wrote, "It is falling apart. The novel coronavirus is a further blow to a West already at the nadir of its self-confidence since the eighteenth century."[6]

China's attacks on the United States were somewhat to be expected, given the geopolitical tension between the countries. But Beijing also appeared to have decided to instrumentalize Europe, at a moment of deep internal strain, in a broad information battle over the supposed inadequacies of Western democracy. It was no longer enough to argue that the Chinese Communist Party had succeeded; it seemed that others had to be seen to fail.

Far from giving European governments or the EU breathing room during the crisis, Beijing would instead make a concerted effort to take advantage of their situation. The Hungarian government rushed through a highly contentious railway deal that the EU had been trying to block.[7] Financed by the EXIM Bank, all of the details around the deal were classified for a decade under emergency legislation that the Hungarians had enacted in response to the pandemic. A Chinese state-owned venture fund sought to seize control of the United Kingdom's major graphics-chip maker, Imagination Technologies, necessitating an emergency intervention by the British government.[8] Huawei and its advocates among European telecoms operators publicly argued that the crisis created an even greater need to accelerate the deployment of 5G.[9] Beijing's use of the crisis as a cover became a familiar story elsewhere too, from the brutal crackdown in Hong Kong to the escalation of military incidents in the South China Sea and a border crisis with India, which attracted little attention from much of the understandably distracted world.[10]

Beijing also explicitly linked its political interests to countries' economic and health needs. In March, a Chinese state media outlet suggested that the US government's treatment of Huawei could affect its access to face masks.[11] After the Netherlands changed the name of the Dutch representational office in Taiwan—a modest upgrade from the "Netherlands Trade and Investment Office, Taipei" to "Netherlands Office Taipei"—Chinese state media outlets contended that Beijing might react by suspending essential medical supplies, supposedly demanded by angry Chinese netizens.[12] The most egregious case was Australia, however, where the country's demands for an inquiry into the origins of the virus resulted in sweeping economic sanctions on its exports of barley, wine, timber and coal.[13]

In the very short term, European officials scrambled to respond. The EU's top diplomat, Josep Borrell, denounced China's "aggressive" tactics and abuse of the "politics of generosity."[14] France summoned the Chinese ambassador amid outrage among French lawmakers about the articles published by his embassy.[15] There was a newfound willingness in Europe to call out Chinese information operations. A contentious EU report that did exactly that was subjected to intense diplomatic pressure from Beijing in advance of publication. While much of the press reporting was absorbed with claims it had been watered down, the report nonetheless starkly laid out China's "conspiracy narratives and disinformation," "covert Chinese operations on social media" and "the coordinated push by Chinese sources to deflect any blame for the outbreak of the pandemic."[16]

European policymakers also moved to address China's attempts to snap up assets on the cheap. Within days of each other, the EU trade commissioner and the NATO secretary general warned governments to exercise extra vigilance in dealing with efforts to acquire infrastructure and sensitive technologies, while the EU's competition chief suggested that European governments should consider taking stakes in strategically important companies.[17] Germany, France, Italy and Spain all announced new protective measures. Sweden, which did not have an investment review process in place, moved ahead with plans for an emergency stopgap.

* * *

If China's handling of the pandemic tipped the Trump presidency into an outright political and economic confrontation with Beijing that has not abated since, the effect in Europe was no less profound. As with so much about the European outlook on China, it happened despite the fervent hope and wish that things could be otherwise. If there was an article of faith through the previous couple of decades, it was that although China may erode the liberal, democratic and market-based elements of the international order in ordinary times, it seemed driven by self-interest to hold things together when the system itself—which included the EU—came under threat.

The behavior of the Chinese party-state during the crucial early weeks of the outbreak in Wuhan, and the exposure of Europe's dependency on China for critical supplies, would have been grounds enough for a reassessment of their relationship. The way Beijing handled one of the most acute tests faced in recent times by European governments—and by the European project itself—guaranteed there would be a political reckoning. Deliberations in Europe about long-term issues ranging from supply chain diversification to telecoms security would afterwards take place in an atmosphere of intensified distrust of the Chinese government, as well as greater clarity about the nature of the actor China had become under Xi Jinping's leadership.

This perception of China as a revisionist power, but not an actively destructive one, had long conditioned European policy. European policymakers were taking steps to end their long period of asymmetric openness to China. A suite of new defensive economic instruments had already been created or set in motion. Yet, for all that, there had been a high degree of restraint on the part of European political leaders—and not only because of the need to maintain the smooth functioning of one of their countries' largest economic relationships. Many of them expected competition, and even rivalry, with China to proceed under a cloak of civility. Neither side would stick the knife in at politically inopportune moments. Cooperation would continue wherever possible. And, if the sides faced a mutually threatening crisis, channels for close coordination between them would operate smoothly. This had been the lesson from 9/11, the financial crisis, the eurozone crisis and even Crimea.

When the pandemic hit, European policymakers had hoped to address the urgent health and economic challenges they faced with geopolitical competition largely suspended. Pragmatic cooperation with Beijing to secure essential medical supplies and reviving shell-shocked economies would have been reason enough to set concerns aside for a time. But this crisis was different. Beijing's willingness to exploit the pandemic, threaten countries, use the situation as cover for further repression and turn its propaganda outlets towards a full-blast denunciation of liberal democracy soon brought about a backlash from the governments and institutions on the receiving end of its political maneuvers. It would also tilt the balance for some of the most important remaining 5G holdouts.

London, 2020

In January of that year, the UK appeared to be partially emerging from the psychodrama that had overwhelmed its political system for the better part of four years. Between June 2016 and December 2019, the country had seen one convulsive referendum, two general elections and three different prime ministers. Brexit was all-consuming. While British officials continued to beaver away on their usual issues, at the political level—and in parliament—foreign policy matters were refracted almost entirely through Brexit politics. China itself occupied an ambiguous role here. On the one hand, ambitious new free-trade deals with China were part of the Brexiteer promise that might beguile people who didn't look into the matter too closely. Analysis by economists who specialized in the "China shock" showed that the existing trade impact of China's WTO accession had been one of the swing factors affecting some of the critical Brexit-voting constituencies.

Most officials and politicians knew very well that an actual free-trade agreement with China was a non-starter, unless the intention was to wreak further economic damage on them. The more plausible-looking option was the United States. Anyone who looked into those details had serious doubts about that too given the politically contentious nature of the issues that would need to be resolved and the lurking question of Northern Ireland's status, which would hang over any vote on the deal in Congress. But Brexit enthusiasts in the Trump administration could at least throw enough fairy dust in people's eyes to suggest a deal might happen, in an explicit contrast with Obama's statement in the lead-up to the referendum that the UK would be "at the back of the queue."[18]

Brexit politics went beyond the need to sustain the narrative that the country wouldn't pay an economic price for its departure from the EU. The UK was going to be on its own now. It was leaving its most important economic and political partnership behind at just the moment where economics, technology and trade had become highly securitized and brutally competitive, a situation now vastly accelerated by the COVID-19 pandemic. The less wild-eyed Brexiteers knew very well that this would necessitate tightened relationships with other like-minded partners, with the United States as the *sine qua non*. Many of them belonged to the strand in British thinking that said that the country should never have cast its lot in with the shifty continental Europeans in the first place but rather rooted its identity in the Anglosphere. Regardless of any free-trade agreements or populist Brexit/Trump mutual boosterism, the UK could not realistically chart a solo course after leaving the world's largest trade bloc, and the transatlantic partnership would be the essential foundation of whatever came afterwards. But the message coming from Washington was increasingly sharp: choosing Huawei will come at a real cost to the alliance.

For many in the British government who had been buried in Brexit issues for the past couple of years, the inclination was to see all this as more Trumpian bluster. They thought they could ride it out. Maybe there would be a period on the naughty step.

The anyway-difficult FTA might be threatened, they would be shouted at for a while and *in extremis* there might be some punitive-but-reversible steps on defense or intelligence cooperation. But then the US would learn to live with the new reality. There was the chance that elections in November 2020 might bring to power a new administration that would go softer on Huawei, UK officials privately suggested.

They were being told by their telecoms firms that the 5G rollout would be delayed if they listened to the Americans, putting at risk the plans to turn the country into a science, technology and advanced industrial hub that was supposed to be part of its post-Brexit rebirth. And the Chinese ambassador to the UK was stark about the implications for the bilateral relationship, stating in public later that year that Britain would "bear the consequences" if it treats China as a "hostile" country over its Huawei decision and that it was "not in the UK's interest" to make an enemy of Beijing.[19]

The UK Treasury fretted again about what this meant for the country's delicate economic situation, which—for all the public bluster from Conservative ministers—they knew would be squeezed harder once the withdrawal from the EU was complete. So, in January, NCSC duly issued its second remarkably-close-to-the-political-consensus finding that Huawei should be permitted in UK networks but—in a concession to the Americans—restricted to 35 percent of the radio access network.[20] On 28 January, the UK National Security Council signed it off. Huawei evinced satisfaction that London had reached an "evidence-based decision" that "will result in a more advanced, more secure and more cost-effective telecoms infrastructure that is fit for the future."[21]

In private, the reaction in the United States was apocalyptic. Matt Pottinger, newly installed as the deputy national security advisor, had led a delegation two weeks earlier to try to persuade the British government to change its mind. In public remarks earlier that month, he would comment: "Can you imagine [Ronald] Reagan and [Margaret] Thatcher having a conversation in the 1980s saying, 'Let's have the KGB build our telecommunications systems, because they're giving us a great discount'?" Trump had weighed in directly and angrily with Boris Johnson.[22] Pompeo had scheduled a visit the week following the decision. There were furious discussions among US officials about what steps to take to show that the UK would not get away with calling the US bluff. Public warnings from US senators over reviewing intelligence-sharing arrangements with the UK, as well as the perennial question of the FTA, were only a couple of the most obvious options. The Trump administration official who had been in charge of the National Defense Strategy openly speculated that "sucker-punching" the US on an "absolutely key issue" at a "critical juncture" should result in the use of US F-35s being placed on the table, and even Trident cooperation, the British nuclear deterrent that depends on the United States in a host of different areas.[23]

But most officials in the Trump administration wanted to hold their fire. One US official described the post-Brexit UK as a "wounded animal" in a fragile economic and political position. No-one wanted China to pull off the additional success of a rift between the United States and its closest defense and intelligence partner. That wasn't the only reason to hold fire though. US officials were considering steps that would nearly cripple Huawei's capacity to provide 5G networks altogether, by denying it access to the essential US technologies on which it still relied. And the one thing that was always true with 5G politics was that no decision was ever quite final. Having drawn a blank with intelligence counterparts and Boris Johnson himself, there was still hope that the decision could be reversed if another politically influential grouping was willing to step up again: the very Conservative

Brexiteers that had led the country to such a fragile situation in the first place.

A few months after Johnson took over the reins as prime minister, the Conservative Party had been re-elected with an increased majority, a sharp contrast to the disastrous decision to call early elections by his predecessor, which left the government's majority on a knife edge. Given the stakes and the divisions—far from neatly partisan—over Brexit, this resulted in a year of parliamentary rebellions that saw some of the largest defeats for a governing party in the country's history. This should have come to an end after December following the resounding Conservative victory. But the habit of rebellion had become entrenched. And the original rebels were the party's euroskeptic right. These included the former Brexit negotiator, David Davies, the former leader of the party, Iain Duncan Smith, and a cluster of less senior backbench MPs. Many of them had their own channels to the Republican administration and to their counterparts in Congress, who were also asking increasingly vociferously why the Brits had gone wobbly.

Many of the Brexiteers, as well as right-wing senators such as Tom Cotton, started to link the issue to Brexit itself. Why, they asked, should we shuck off our dependence on Brussels only to end up beholden to the Chinese? Indeed, some of them suggested that it was the same globalist "Remainer" establishment that was conning the country into the decision to give Huawei the green light. But if it had only been the serial rebels and Tory right that were up in arms, the government might still have expected to prevail given the size of its majority. In fact, the concerns went deeper.

Early that year, after the latest Huawei decision had broken, I received a message from an old school buddy who wanted to reconnect me with his friend, a Conservative MP, whom I'd met at university more than twenty years earlier. Neil O'Brien was an

MP of a different caliber than many of the other rebels. After running the UK's most influential euroskeptic and center-right think-tanks, he had gone into government as former Chancellor George Osborne's advisor during the peak of the "Golden Era," ended up in Downing Street and landed a safe seat soon afterwards. The *Financial Times* described him as "one of the central figures" in the new generation of modernizing Conservative MPs who had entered parliament in recent years. He wanted to chat about a new initiative he and his colleague were putting together, modeled on the European Research Group, a network in the Conservative Party that had acted as the locus of the hardline Brexit parliamentary rebellions. This one would have a different focus: China.

His colleague was Tom Tugendhat, Röttgen's counterpart as chair of the House of Commons' Foreign Affairs Committee, a former army intelligence officer who speaks fluent Arabic and had served in Afghanistan and Iraq. Both of them were examples of the liberal, internationalist, moderate, rising talents in the party rather than the "mad, swivel-eyed loons" who were riding the Brexit populist wave. Like members of the Bundestag, however, they could see the radical changes in both the salience of the China question and the politics around it. While O'Brien would occupy a less visible role on China, Tugendhat would become the sharpest and most visible voice on the 5G question in the months that followed.

The Brexiteers and the modernizers were not natural bedfellows, and some of the resentments would play out in the competition over which MPs should be seen as the leading parliamentary voices on the China question. But on the substance, there was little disagreement. One Conservative peer drew up an extensive delineation of the groups in the Conservative Party that were coalescing on the China issue: pro-Brexit Atlanticists who identified with the US position and didn't want a Huawei deal to jeopardize a free-trade agreement, senior former ministers who thought that China has failed to abide by its agreements, younger liberal internationalists, civil libertarians, religious freedom and human rights advocates, opponents of Chinese trade practices, globalization critics and many MPs who overlapped between multiple categories.[24]

Meanwhile, much like the SPD, the Labour Party was staking out a position on China that was even tougher on human rights and values issues than the Conservatives. And so as in Germany, the decision on Huawei would sit in limbo. The government knew it risked defeat if it brought a bill to parliament. It had already received warning shots with amendments on other unrelated bills. The combined forces of the Labour Party, the Brexiteers and the moderate Tory rebels were sufficiently potent to run the votes close even when they weren't trying very hard. So Johnson waited and hoped that something might change that would make it easier to pursue the preferred course of action. Of course, something did come along in the months that followed, which would have precisely the opposite effect: a potent virus from Wuhan that would tilt the political balance even more sharply.

* * *

The UK was one of the major economies hit hardest by the COVID-19 pandemic. By May of 2020, it had become the worst-affected country in Europe, surpassing Italy. While much of this reflected flaws in the government's response, it induced considerable concern about the level of dependence the UK had demonstrated on China for vital medical supplies and other strategic imports. It resulted in a set of civil service efforts called "Project Defend" that were intended to identify Britain's main economic vulnerabilities to potentially hostile foreign governments. It would put an even bigger question-mark over Huawei as a result. Then at the end of June 2020, China passed its long-rumored

National Security Law for Hong Kong, the provisions of which had been kept secret until China's rubber stamp assembly approved the legislation. Protests had already been roiling the city for the last year over a new extradition law, but the National Security Law went even further, representing the de facto end of the "one country, two systems" model that had been the treaty-founded basis for the handover of Hong Kong in the first place.

The UK bore special responsibility for the fate of the citizens it gave to Chinese rule under the guarantee that Beijing would maintain the principle. This sense of responsibility was even more acute—even tinged with guilt—among Conservative MPs. It was during their party's time in government that the agreement with Beijing on Hong Kong's future was negotiated, signed and agreed. The deep immersion of so many British companies and families in Hong Kong made it seem far closer than for most other countries. As one official put it: "It just feels different—being frank, the situation in Xinjiang was bad already and has got much worse. But Hong Kong is the first case that looks like a real rollback of freedom in an international city that is so familiar to us."

If the political climate was already looking icily bleak for Huawei, the United States helped to deal the killer blow, a face-saving one for the Brits as it happened. On 15 May, the US Department of Commerce amended a little-known tool, the "Foreign-Produced Direct Product Rule." The effects were seismic. It prevented

> the transfer to Huawei entities of any items produced or developed by Huawei and which are "direct products" of controlled US technology or software, and transfer to Huawei entities of any items that are both produced by manufacturing equipment that is the "direct product" of controlled US technology or software.[25]

It effectively meant that any use of US technologies by Huawei would require licensing, imperiling the capacity of the firm to roll out its 5G networks. Above all, this meant semiconductors.

Despite claiming to have stockpiled chips, there was simply no way to guarantee it would be able to deliver and sustain its equipment over time. It gave NCSC the grounds to write a whole new opinion, described with British understatement as "[modifying] the scope of its security mitigation strategy for Huawei." It has "significantly changed the risk to the UK, causing the NCSC to review our previous advice on Huawei from January 2020," the report stated: "It will be extremely challenging to gain confidence in Huawei's post-sanction equipment, and it may be impossible." Moreover, the measures pursued demonstrated

> a further hardening of the US position towards Huawei, setting an even clearer intent. Should this US action be ineffective, in particular if Huawei were to find a workaround, it is likely that the US government would continue to modify its approach until it had successfully had its desired effect on the company.[26]

As one US official at the time said with a shrug of the shoulders: "We had warned them that a company subjected to US sanctions already may not be a reliable supplier."

The legislation would have to be changed again. The last iteration had not yet been brought to the vote that they may have lost even before the US decision. The government ordered the complete removal of the company's kit from the entire 5G network by 2027. The UK's culture secretary, who—in a departmental quirk—had authority over the telecoms sector, came to the House of Commons where he had been repeatedly mauled by MPs from his own party to make a less tortured announcement: "This has not been an easy decision, but it is the right one for the UK's telecoms networks, for our national security and our economy both now and indeed in the long run."[27] He would go on to lay out a "clear path for the complete removal of high risk vendors from our 5G networks ... This will be done through new and unprecedented powers to identify and ban telecoms equipment which poses a threat to our national security."[28] There was still some wiggle room—the vain hope that things might change in the United States in November—but for Huawei in the UK, the journey that had kickstarted their rise in the advanced economies of the world was effectively over.

The process in Germany took nearly a further year to reach a still-preliminary conclusion. The result was more ambiguous than the UK's plan for the removal of Huawei kit. All elements of the implementation were kicked to the next government to resolve, and in the meantime the telecoms firms could not only get away with keeping the existing Huawei equipment but also continue quietly to roll out Chinese kit in the new 5G infrastructure. While the interior ministry now had the ability to restrict "untrustworthy" suppliers, the battle was not over. "Companies that are under the control of authoritarian states are considered to be untrustworthy," one CDU parliamentarian contended in the debate.[29] If it lacked the stark finality of the declarations in London, it was at least clear that the political tide for Huawei had turned, and not just in Europe.

New Delhi, April 2018

I was sitting in the lobby of the Taj Palace Hotel in New Delhi waiting for a meeting with Subrahmanyam Jaishankar, not knowing for sure whether he would arrive. He was too discreet to say so, but it appeared that Jaishankar had been pulled in urgently to see India's prime minister, Narendra Modi. The meeting had overrun, and evidently he could not send me emails about the delay. I was eager to speak, though, however briefly. He was in what proved to be a short window between leaving his position as foreign secretary and going back into government again as foreign minister, and I knew it was an opportunity for him to be maximally candid. The last time we had more than a brief exchange was back in Beijing, over gin and tonics in the embassy, while he was serving as ambassador there.

He was graciously apologetic when he arrived, but time was now very short indeed. In the minutes we had, he laid out a strikingly intense vision of how the rivalry with China would play out for India in the region. A deal had just been reached after their confrontation at the contested border, but his comments formed a sharp counterpoint to the ostensible stabilization of ties that the end of the recent crisis in the Himalayas was supposed to portend. Mike Pillsbury, who had recently achieved heightened prominence as Trump's favorite China analyst, joined us and poked fun at my assiduous notetaking. When we headed to the airport together the next day, Pillsbury would spend much of the drive complaining about India's unwillingness to sign a series of foundational agreements that would allow for closer communications, sharing of geospatial intelligence, and logistical cooperation with the US military.

India's tradition of non-alignment runs deep, and as foreign minister, Jaishankar went on to valorize a sophisticated version of it. In his years at the Ministry of External Affairs, few figures did more to tighten ties with the United States, whether as ambassador in Washington or his role in navigating the breakthrough India-US civil nuclear deal. But there was always a clear appreciation of where the lines needed to be drawn. Now, with the Trump administration straining traditional alliances to breaking point and tearing up trade agreements at will, India's nimbleness and greater self-reliance looked like the better path. Unlike anxious allies terrified at the withdrawal of US security commitments, India was confident in its autonomy. Since Indian power was itself an asset to the United States in the Indo-Pacific, there was no need to compromise much when it came to its economic and military ties with the states that were on Washington's bad side, Iran and Russia. It would win its exemptions from the US government for energy deals with the former and arms purchases from the latter. Nor did India need to sign the binding FTAs that smaller economies rely on. The "Make in India" agenda, the plan to build up its indigenous industries, worked better without them, so the argument went. Democracy too was an asset for India but nothing that should limit Indian foreign policy excessively, any more than it ultimately limited those of any other great power when relations with authoritarians serve a strategic purpose.

Meanwhile, for all that India was dealing with a military build-up from China on its border, and fierce competition in its traditional South Asian sphere of influence, it seemed that the two sides could still deal with each other judiciously when they needed to. Long-established bilateral mechanisms helped navigate flare-ups in the Himalayas without recourse to violence. There was a modus vivendi that held, however strained it seemed at times. Then in 2020, everything unraveled.

After years of worsening tensions, events during the pandemic took a stark turn. The border mechanisms that India had counted on for so long, and the restraint that had still characterized China's approach, was seemingly over. Following a huge Chinese mobilization at the border, a clash in Ladakh's Galwan Valley saw the first casualties there since 1975. Twenty Indian soldiers died in a high-altitude altercation that involved stones, clubs and sticks rather than guns, and an indeterminate number of Chinese soldiers too. The old norms no longer held. Beijing seemed intent on taking and fortifying positions on India's side of the line of actual control, which had demarcated the two sides' informal territorial writ for decades. One month later, Chinese officials and media also made claims to a large tract of territory in Bhutan, an area that had not featured in previous border negotiations.

Much as European politicians were baffled by China's behavior during the pandemic, the response in India was one of shock. As a former senior Indian official, who had been closely involved in handling the bilateral relationship, commented at the time:

The build-up was premeditated; we had never seen such a build-up. Whether the incident itself was planned is another matter but there is a complete loss of trust as a result. Despite all the channels we'd developed, they can't work if one or other party is not trustworthy. It's broken. There will be fundamental shift in India's policy towards China as a result.

Neither the sophisticated China handlers in the system nor the outright China hawks had seen it coming. There needed to be a deep rethink of India's approach, including the question of whether India's ties with major partners needed to be tightened further in the shadow of Chinese power. In the multidimensional spirit of the new policy environment, one of the first actions India took was a ban on Chinese apps, denying Chinese tech firms their single most promising overseas market with a stroke of the pen. Huawei and ZTE would be barred from participating in the upcoming 5G trials too. But it also set off a flurry of other activities. Indian backing for a leaders meeting among the "Quad", the quadrilateral security dialogue between India, the United States, Japan and Australia that China viewed as a democratic containment coalition. Expansive proposals to cooperate with the Europeans on financing alternatives to the Belt and Road. And Mike Pillsbury was happy: the last of the foundational agreements he was complaining about were quickly signed. India's "autonomy" would remain on vivid display during the Russian invasion of Ukraine two years later, when it refused to swing in behind the G7 position. But the need to align ever-more closely with the emerging counter-China coalition if India's interests were going to be secured was now becoming impossible to resist.

* * *

As the cases of Europe and India illustrate—and they are far from the only examples—it was not the COVID cover-up that was the main source of tension with China for most of the world in 2020. It was its level of belligerence at precisely the moment when everyone was reeling from the economic, security and political implications of a pandemic that Beijing's mishandling—or worse—had failed to contain.

If China's initial prickliness at a moment of political vulnerability was at least understandable, it soon morphed into a profoundly ideological campaign, a pushback against the entire democratic order. The new mode of Chinese foreign policy was neatly summarized by China's ambassador to Sweden, Gui Congyou: "We treat our friends with fine wine, but for our enemies we have shotguns," a line taken from a song eulogizing China's war with the United States on the Korean Peninsula in the 1950s.[30] But if the "shotgun" treatment was transforming the China policies of states across the world, the "fine wine" was not always appreciated by its recipients either. Beijing's behavior—increasingly rigid, hubristic and ideological—would also make it unnecessarily difficult when it came to a task that was starting to assume greater urgency. If democracies across the Atlantic and the Indo-Pacific were starting to coalesce in their concerns about Chinese power, Beijing needed a countervailing coalition of its own.

6

CAN'T BUY ME LOVE

CHINA'S TROUBLED COALITION-BUILDING CAMPAIGN

Karachi, December 2016

I WALKED ACROSS THE tarmac at Mehran naval air station to a small military aircraft, my eyes ineluctably drawn to the vast black and white mural in English at the opposite end of the runway: "Every opportunity in my life begins with a take-off." Joining me on the ninety-minute flight from Karachi was most of the Pakistani navy's high command, who engaged in cerebral geopolitical debates across the four-seater tables while a less voluble group of senior Chinese Party officials and diplomats listened quietly behind us. The destination was a fabled port city looking out onto the Arabian sea in Pakistan's restive Balochistan region: Gwadar.

Many experts working on Chinese foreign policy over the last decade have found themselves spending an unusual amount of time in and around ports. From Hambantota to Haifa, Piraeus to Palermo, I have wangled my way past reluctant security guards, peered down at old US navy submarines next to newly built Chinese facilities and sat through grindingly long loading procedures waiting for ships to leave. But perhaps no location on the map of China's maritime influence and military power had been as mythologized as Gwadar.

My previous attempt to pay a visit by way of a drive down the Makran coastal highway was blocked at the last minute by the Pakistani security services, who sensibly judged the trip to be wildly unsafe, though the officer responsible mused that with my pakol, shalwar kameez and reddish beard I might have got away with the risky journey by passing as a Pashtun. Now I was able to visit as the legitimate guest of the Pakistani navy as they launched a new protective taskforce for the port, their own contribution to the biggest story in the country: the China–Pakistan Economic Corridor (CPEC).

At the time of my visit in 2016, where I would provide part of the intellectual adornment at a conference that would launch the new taskforce, CPEC-mania was in full flow. Tens of billions of dollars in new Chinese investment were planned, and Gwadar was the symbolic, if seemingly highly impractical, heart of the plans. The notion that this moonscape at the edge of volatile Balochistan could be transformed into the locus point of an economically viable transit route seemed fanciful. But many of the Pakistani politicians and admirals who were mingling at the Pearl Continental Hotel, which looks down over the hammerhead-shaped peninsula jutting out into the Indian Ocean that is Gwadar's extraordinary natural harbor, had been going to China over the decades and had seen the improbable happening there too. We sat through presentations about the new airport, the expressway, the special economic zone, the logistics facilities, the housing projects, the desalination plants and the power supplies that were still so painfully inadequate. At one of the tea breaks, the chairman of the port authority pulled me aside to tell me not to bother returning for at least the next couple of years—this would all take some time to execute—but that when I did, the place would be unrecognizable.

His cautious but convinced optimism was common among sections of the Pakistani elite at the time. For all the legitimate criticism that CPEC attracted even then about its opacity and the less-than-generous contract terms that China negotiated, there was a period of hope. The notion of a Chinese-style developmental transformation seemed appealing to many in Pakistan after years of economic struggles, suicide bombings and an insurgency that had lapped uncomfortably close to the capital. Having been stuck as an appendage to the war in Afghanistan next door, the very idea of CPEC changed the narrative about the country. Not that the threats had disappeared. Military forces were posted at regular intervals along the roadside all the way through the city as our convoy drove from the airport to the hotel. The nervous executives from China's largest shipping firm, COSCO, that I chatted with over dinner on one of the Pakistani navy's frigates had never left their intimidating security bubble the whole time they'd been in the country. Gwadar's hinterland was Pakistan's most underdeveloped and insurgency-plagued province, not Karachi or Lahore, let alone Shanghai or Hong Kong. In the years that followed, the hotel we were staying in would be stormed by armed gunmen, and one of the Chinese shipping executive's colleagues would be shot dead by a hired assassin in another attack.

But for all its symbolism and mythology, CPEC's success was not contingent on Gwadar nor on the abating of security risks in Balochistan. If anything, there were points where the international fixation on the port and its potential value as a future Chinese military base felt like a distraction from what Beijing was really attempting in Pakistan. Prodigious energy was being channeled into plans for projects that would span the whole country, from power stations to industrial zones. "All of Pakistan is a corridor," as one Chinese official in Pakistan put it when disputes about the planning of the road construction were at their peak. Something far bigger than a future logistical option for the Chinese PLA Navy or a truck route from Xinjiang was being set in motion.

It had been so many years since anyone was willing to imagine the possibility of Pakistan as a real emerging market—and back it up with money—that even for many of those with reservations it seemed better at least to play along for a while. CPEC was appealing to American officials in the country too. Having long encouraged China to assume greater responsibility for helping

Pakistan to deal with its endemic problems, US diplomats were not going to object if Beijing started to shift the balance of its support towards railway lines and hydro electric dams rather than fighter jets and nuclear weapons. They wondered if Chinese officials fully understood what they were taking on. But most American policymakers were quietly happy to see Beijing make the attempt. President Obama, in a more exasperated moment, had even joked about washing US hands of Pakistan entirely and leaving the mess for China to clean up. It was clear, either way, that Beijing was serious about what it was doing. Its plans for CPEC were supposed to resonate well beyond South Asia.

* * *

When I first came to Pakistan in 2009, it was in a search for the answer to a seemingly simple question—how does China deal with its friends? The US alliance network was one of Washington's critical means of power projection, an edge over China that the Chinese then had almost no hope of replicating. For decades, this was not even a contest in which Beijing was engaged. Non-alignment gave more room for maneuver. Economic partnerships without a political and security overlay could be developed with virtually everyone. China explicitly denied any intention to build overseas military bases and spoke vehemently against the very principle of alliances. Institutions like NATO were deemed outdated "Cold War thinking." The one formal military alliance Beijing itself had, with North Korea, was treated as a bit of an embarrassment, a leftover from another era. The PLA made contingency plans in case the North Korean regime collapsed but conducted no joint exercises that envisaged rushing to Pyongyang's defense if it was threatened.

Nonetheless, there was a core of countries that had a special status for China. In some cases, these were governments with which it shared a distinct historic relationship of some kind, like

Robert Mugabe's ruling ZANU-PF party in Zimbabwe, which had been backed and trained by the PLA while it was still a guerrilla movement. In others, like Myanmar, China was the government's principal political protector and economic lifeline. The relatively short list of Chinese partners was a rather motley crew though. Where US allies were the industrial, technological and military powerhouses of Europe and Asia, the "friends of China" largely comprised the authoritarians who had found themselves politically on the wrong side of the West and were stuck with few places to turn.

This imposed considerable limitations on what China could actually do with most of these countries. Long-term plans were inherently fragile: if China was dependent on the survival of a frail regime for the future of an overseas military facility, it could hardly be relied on as a fixture of the PLA's global posture. If it leaned too hard into any of the relationships, Beijing also risked putting itself in the US crosshairs. Energy investments from Iran to Sudan were subject to sanction, and Beijing was episodically embroiled in diplomatic hand-to-hand combat at the UN Security Council attempting simultaneously to protect its friends and coax them into making deals with the other P5 powers. This didn't even guarantee gratitude. Countries backed into a corner and excessively dependent on Beijing were liable to chafe at their situation. Myanmar's opening to the West in 2011 came as a shock to Chinese officials, while North Korean truculence was a near-constant headache.

In the late 2000s, a new set of debates about these issues started bubbling up in China. Many of the same Chinese strategists who advocated a more assertive foreign policy and the shucking off of old hang-ups about China's international posture also wrestled with the question of how to put this shift into effect. Accomplices, partners and even allies were an unavoidable part of that story. Global power projection without them is impossible. But non-alignment had been such a central pillar of Chinese foreign policy in the last few decades that it would require not just a wrestling with new theories but new practices in dealing with the countries that might fall into this category. Was there a model for the sort of relationship that Beijing should be developing? Should China build outright alliances? Quasi-alliances that didn't involve formal defensive treaty commitments? Were the potential target countries for these efforts likely to function more as liabilities than assets? How could this circle of friends be enlarged? Which of them could be relied on in a crisis? I spent the period from the mid-2000s looking at how China was taking on the more difficult cases, traveling from Harare to Havana, and Mandalay to Chongjin, as Beijing navigated Mugabe's ruinous currency policies, the Myanmar junta's crackdown on monks' protests, the Fidel–Raúl transition and Kim Jong-Il's limited moves towards economic reform. But there was one country that fell into a somewhat different category.

Pakistan was unusual in several regards. It was one of the only countries where China was actually popular with the wider public. All the major political parties were committed to the relationship, meaning that changes of government modulated rather than upended it. The country's dominant political force, the army, provided these ties with even deeper foundations. And for all of Pakistan's pathologies, it had always had something to offer China, whether its access to nuclear technologies, its capable military, its networks in the Islamic world or simply its vantage point in the Indian Ocean. With security ties of the most sensitive kind between China and Pakistan going back decades, there was no need for Chinese officials to persuade anyone that the PLA Navy should be able to make port calls there whenever it wished.

All of this was conditioned by the fact that the two sides shared a military opponent in India and had long continued to see mutual benefit in collaborating to deal with it, ensuring an underlying strategic alignment that transcended any political flux. Yet the lack of any treaty commitments meant that it never required China to become embroiled in any of Pakistan's often-rash military gambits in Kashmir. Despite its unique features, this template—a close security relationship that could hold over time, without any onerous formal responsibilities to spring to an ally's defense—was something Beijing hoped might be replicable.

CPEC potentially provided the means of convincing other countries of the virtues of that model. Putative partners of China were supposed to see the benefits that accrued to the very closest of friends, the transformative flow of resources, the economic take-off, the privileged ties that it offered to China's own prodigious growth story. As a bonus, if Beijing pulled the whole thing off, it would also tell a valorizing story about the political and economic path that the Chinese Communist Party had chosen, especially after the US model of support to Pakistan, of prodigious military aid and periodic bursts of development money, had achieved so little.

I kept coming back to Pakistan over the years, first to try to make sense of this unusual relationship, then to write a book about it, and afterwards to watch how this new role that the country now tentatively occupied in Chinese grand strategy would play out. As time went by, I noticed the shift in the kinds of visitors Pakistan attracted from China. Initially it was just the South Asia hands that I'd bump into, the people who had been managing the relationship for decades. Then a different crowd started showing up, the businesspeople and economic policy officials who had once disdained the country's prospects and were now supposed to put CPEC in motion. But I was most struck by the appearance of another influential little group—the grand strategists, the policy intellectuals I used to meet in Beijing and Shanghai more than a decade earlier to talk about

US–China relations and Chinese foreign policy ambitions, the sort of people who had never even paid attention to Pakistan, let alone set foot in the place. Some of them were soon speaking a different language about the China–Pakistan partnership as a "model to follow," about Pakistan as Beijing's "one real ally."[1] Yet it quickly became clear that CPEC was not going to prove what they had hoped.

Islamabad, September 2018

Nearly two years after my Gwadar trip, I was back on one of my more regular visits to Islamabad. The mania was over, and the whole venture had gone into suspended animation. The Pakistani government that China had counted on to deliver CPEC had been maneuvered out by the army that China counted on for almost everything else. The new government's greatest enthusiasm was for corruption inquiries, and it was hauling officials in for interrogations. Ministers spoke openly about pausing the entire initiative. The Pakistani politicians and Chinese officials that would once have met to regale me with their stories of progress were now avoiding my messages. I bumped into a couple of them instead at the garden party of a prominent television journalist. One of them was Zhao Lijian, the number two at the embassy.

Zhao would later become infamous, first for a series of inflammatory tweets about race in Washington, DC, pushed out to his massively followed feed, and later through assuming the role of Wolf-Warrior-in-Chief as the foreign ministry's conspiracy-theorizing spokesman back in Beijing during the COVID-19 pandemic. Zhao had always been very candid with me, however, when we'd met at the austere new Chinese embassy, giving me numbers and assessments that always checked out with other sources. He was frank again that evening. The new Pakistani government didn't have a policy on CPEC, he complained, it had as many different ones as there were ministers in the cabinet. It wasn't even clear who should be brought into full confidence on the venture yet. The governing party simply didn't understand how they could benefit from the influx of Chinese resources. If the Pakistanis had decided they no longer wanted mega-projects and preferred "peanut projects," they could have them, he said. But peanut projects were not China's forte.

Zhao did not need to list all the other problems that had cast a cloud over the venture. The payment shortfalls on the energy projects, the glacial progress on the special economic zones, the fact that Gwadar itself had barely moved forward since my trip, or the many unhappy constituencies who felt they hadn't had their fair share of the pie. Some of these were problems that might have been fixed in better circumstances. But with Pakistan's economic situation in a mess, and a new government in office that believed CPEC to have been a gambit by its predecessor to consolidate its political power, the appetite for fixing them was low. Zhao was incredulous. He knew that executing CPEC would be difficult. But this wasn't supposed to happen in the single country in the world where China had a near-sanctified status.

He soon disappeared into a huddle with the planning minister, Khusro Bakhtiar, a member of parliament from a landed South Punjabi family. I'd last met him to discuss CPEC at the polo club in Lahore. This time, however, Bakhtiar really didn't want to talk to me. As Zhao had observed, the government did not have its story on CPEC straight, and any time a minister said something amiss, the Chinese diplomat's boss would call on the army chief who would tell the minister to shut up. As a result, most of them decided it was better to say nothing at all or—as Bakhtiar did that evening—only the most careful of generalities. When I wandered inside a few minutes later to get some dessert, I heard him opening a sentence to one of the other guests with:

"The problem with China is ..." He stopped dead when he saw my ears prick up and stalked out of the house, wearily exclaiming "I'm supposed to be off duty tonight!"

The tensions on show that evening were illustrative of a deeper problem. CPEC could at least be semi-fixed, put back on a track that would show that the whole venture was still moving forward. Yet that wasn't the bar. CPEC was supposed to have a demonstration effect. It would cement a deeper set of ties between the two sides, a success story that would encourage others to join the "friends of China" club. It had special billing. For Xi Jinping's globe-spanning, trillion-dollar Belt and Road Initiative, it was the flagship. The comparison that Chinese officials endlessly disavowed in public, thereby putting it at the top of people's minds, was the Marshall Plan. Beijing was going to flood the developing world with the finance that others wouldn't provide, to pay for the priorities—such as traditional infrastructure-building—that the West was telling these countries they shouldn't even want. And Chinese companies would occupy the central role in turning these dreams into reality on the ground. The repeated claims that this had no ideological quality to it never fully rang true. In Pakistan's case, evidently no-one expected the replication of China's unique system. But CPEC was always imbued with a strong sense that it wasn't only fellow Communist states that should learn from China's experience.

The belief on the part of Chinese officials that their development model had resonance beyond its borders long pre-dated the Belt and Road. From Kim Jong-Il to Fidel Castro, foreign leaders passing through China would routinely be subjected to lectures on why the Chinese reform and opening path was the right one for them to take. But it was one thing giving lectures to poor fellow-Leninists about how to preserve their systems, quite another to be exporting elements of your model to vast swathes of the developing world with hundreds of billions of dollars in financing behind it. When I used to discuss the plans with Zhao at the embassy, he rarely spoke of classic development or economic theory. His reference point was invariably Deng Xiaoping's "reform and opening" process and the bracing effect of foreign presence in special economic zones on the competitiveness of Chinese business.

CPEC was the first place where this was attempted at scale. The frustrations about what Chinese officials saw as the Pakistani elites' failure to take these lectures on board amounted to more than just a disappointment about CPEC itself. It was a question of whether the most ambitious goals of the entire strategy that the BRI embodied could ever really succeed.

Laamu Atoll, February 2020

In early 2020, I was paying a visit to a port that only ever existed on paper, if at all. In the Maldives' southern atoll, where speculation about China's investment plans abutting a major Indian Ocean sea-route had once raged, there used to be a striking juxtaposition. The island of Gaadhoo, near the One and a Half Degree Channel, where many of the shipping routes back and forth to Asia pass, become the subject of intense conjecture as the habitation there was evacuated and rumors swirled that a Chinese port or surveillance facility was planned. Chinese workers had been there on neighboring Laamu in force, building the Maldives' longest road, which ran handily from the airport to the most convenient spot for transit to the potential facility. At the same time, India had a military helicopter at the nearby Maldivian air-force base attached to the airport. And facing Gaadhoo was a US-run sea cucumber farm, believed with total conviction by various Maldivian officials to be a CIA facility.

It was the new Cold War in the Indian Ocean in microcosm, replete with rumors that often substantially outran reality. I headed down in early 2020 to take a look. Two of the elements were still very much alive and kicking. The Indian helicopter was now manned by an even larger group of its military personnel. The US sea cucumber facility was in full flow, its staff a little exasperated at being seen as CIA agents. The Chinese workers, however, who had been sticking around under the previous government to perform "maintenance," had all gone, leaving only the incongruous road and a little of their construction debris behind. Across the water, the island where the port was once envisaged now stood entirely empty of its residents.

CPEC and Gaadhoo were far from the only projects that were running into problems. Indeed, 2018 was an annus horribilis for the entire initiative. One of the most reputationally damaging cases was Malaysia, which competed with Pakistan for the sheer financial scale of the projects that were being pursued. The ninety-two-year-old Mahathir Mohamad's return to power in May had seen China subjected to the same vituperation that he used to reserve for the Western powers. Unlike the Pakistanis, who needed to manage the relationship carefully in public, the veteran leader pulled no punches in stating that tens of billions of dollars in infrastructure plans would be canceled outright.

The change in government saw the emergence of a series of shocking stories about how China had secured the contracts in the first place. Leaked minutes from the Malaysian government revealed Beijing's willingness to bail out the scandal-ridden 1MDB fund, the mammoth state-run strategic development company whose assets were siphoned off into Prime Minister Najib Razak's bank account and the playboy lifestyle of its mastermind, Jho Low.[2] They also promised to press other countries to stop their probe into the corrupt venture, to finance projects at massively plussed-up levels in order to generate additional sources of money to skim off, and to bug the *Wall Street Journal* reporters investigating the 1MDB corruption case. It was so manifestly egregious that, as one of the Malaysian officials involved in the negotiations told me later that year, when the new government laid out what they knew and demanded huge slashes to the project costs as a result, Chinese officials didn't even attempt to push back.

At least Pakistan and Malaysia were weighty enough actors to fend for themselves. The accusation directed increasingly tellingly at China was that its financing practices left smaller countries so beholden to Beijing that a change in government made little difference. In early 2018, I was paying a visit to perhaps the most emblematic example of this, Sri Lanka, for a tour of some of China's infamous white elephant projects there: Hambantota's barely functioning port, the fully staffed airport without any flights, and the oversized cricket stadium, all constructed in the former president's home constituency as ostentatious political spoils with his name affixed to them.

Although these projects pre-dated the Belt and Road, the ramifications would last well afterwards. The defeat of the China-friendly Rajapaksa government in 2015 had seen its critically minded successor, in economically straitened conditions, agree a ninety-nine-year lease with Chinese companies for the port in return for some breathing room on its wider debt situation. India and the Western powers had encouraged and embraced Rajapaksa's fall and then pretty much left Sri Lanka to it. The cost to China's image was acute, with Hambantota cited almost endlessly as a precautionary tale. But the implication of the whole episode was still that, in the end, there was no alternative to Chinese money.

A few hundred miles further out in the Indian Ocean, a story was unfolding that suggested that events were about to repeat themselves. Colombo, Sri Lanka's capital, was the base for the Maldivian opposition, where a childhood friend, Paul, worked as an advisor to the former president, Mohamed Nasheed. Through

his work with Nasheed, I had followed the Maldivian opposition
from their days as a forlorn-looking protest movement in exile,
standing with cardboard signs outside luxury hotel conventions
in London discouraging unethical investments in the country's
resorts, to their sweep into office in 2008 at the expense of the
country's longstanding dictator. Barely three years later, they
were forced out again in a soft coup.

Paul told the story in blow-by-blow detail to the international
press from a bathroom in the president's office while soldiers
marched through the building. It sent the democratic opposition
back into exile. Nasheed, recently released from his second stint
in a Maldivian prison, lived in a modest apartment in Colombo,
and I was dropping by to discuss a subject that had shifted from
a peripheral issue when he was last in office to his number one
problem now: China.

Whiteboards in Nasheed's makeshift office mapped out the
flows of Chinese money to the authoritarian president who had
taken his place, with bank account numbers and shadowy
Chinese entities forming a complex puzzle that his staff were
trying to disentangle. Nasheed was aware that this went beyond
corruption on the projects themselves. In the Sri Lankan elections three years earlier, China had dropped the pretense of non-
interference to provide outright slush money to the Rajapaksa
campaign.[3] With the Maldivian government under mounting
international pressure to hold elections itself later in 2018, the
concern was that it would be carried back into office on a tidal
wave of Chinese cash.

At the time of the coup that forced him out several years
earlier, Nasheed's deposal was treated with a degree of indiffer-
ence by India and the United States. He was spiky and independent and not very deferential to bigger powers that expected the
little Maldives to get in line. Ironically, one of the issues that
New Delhi held against him was the supposedly excessive level

of openness to China that Nasheed had exhibited as president, allowing Beijing to open an embassy and accepting small sums of Chinese financing for a housing project.

Nasheed was a fierce democrat and had little enthusiasm for dealing with the Chinese Communist Party. He would take obvious pleasure in standing up to Wen Jiabao at the 2009 Copenhagen climate summit. It was the Maldivian delegation that fed out the critical information to the international media about how China had tanked the talks. But Nasheed had promised to build housing in his election campaign and struggled to find the modest sums of money required from other sources. This nonetheless counted as a black mark against him in India. If another pliable autocrat from the family of the old regime held the reins of power in the Maldives again, did it really matter?

It turned out that it mattered quite a lot. As time went on, Yameen, his successor as president, led the country into a vastly greater economic embrace of China. Indian companies were thrown off the construction of the airport, huge sums were sunk into bridges, roads and islands in sensitive locations. A free-trade agreement with China was rammed through parliament without the opposition even having the opportunity to look at the text.

By early 2018, Beijing was the only friend that Yameen had left. His increasingly authoritarian behavior had seen the Maldives effectively frozen out of the Commonwealth, and the United States, India and the major European states started to exert a growing squeeze on him ahead of the elections that were nominally due to take place later that year. In February, everything was coming to a head. There was a febrile level of conjecture that China was moving naval vessels in to protect him. Nasheed called outright for an Indian military intervention to restore democracy in the country. At a conference we both attended in Bangalore, Nasheed would be prominently photographed meeting with the Indian defense minister, a pointed warning to China that his intervention request was not being dismissed out of hand. "There is a new Cold War in South Asia, and we have to choose sides," Nasheed stated baldly in his remarks there. He accused China of pushing the country into extremes of debt, in lockstep with the corrupt President Yameen, who was now single-handedly being propped up by Chinese money as virtually every other country deserted him.

In fact, India had calculated that—whether or not it was advisable—no military intervention would even be required. As Washington, New Delhi and European capitals exerted their squeeze, Yameen—under threat of further sanction—ended up holding the scheduled elections later that year and miscalculating his prospects in a campaign where he had banned most opposition leaders from running. A final gambit, which involved using electronic tablets from China to tabulate the election results, failed when they all mysteriously crashed on Election Day and the tallies had to be undertaken with pen and paper instead. Nasheed's ally, Ibrahim Solih, won the presidency comfortably. When I next met Nasheed himself again in the densely populated Maldivian capital, he was Speaker of the House.

I watched him at the Democratic Party's headquarters preparing candidates for the parliamentary elections they would storm the following month. Ministers were poring over the details of the Chinese contracts, digging out any indication of corrupt practices. The free-trade agreement with China sat unsigned in a corner of the president's office and was the subject of running jokes from his advisors. Money flowed in from India and its partners to shore up the debt-ridden economy, and while the new president trod more carefully in his language on China, Nasheed continued his denunciations and engaged in regular public spats with the Chinese ambassador. "We're happy to pay them back fairly," he told me during a quick chat as another batch of candidates trooped in for his pep talk: "But only the real price, not all the inflated mark-ups too." Needless to say, there was no more talk of Chinese listening facilities in the southern atoll.

The Maldives was one of a number of countries that were supposed to become part of the circle of Chinese friends. The sums of money at stake for a country with a GDP of $5.6 billion and a population of 500,000 were not large, and there were ways in which a well-crafted economic package there could have landed well with the opposition too. There was no intrinsic reason for the fevered political back and forth that would come with each election. But it was also very clear that there was no chance for the country to become a reliable military partner unless Beijing could consolidate an authoritarian regime in place there over the long term.

Pakistan meanwhile was the closest thing politically for Beijing to an open goal, a country where criticism of China, the so-called "all-weather friend," had once not just been muted but seen as virtually unconscionable. Building a national consensus behind CPEC was hardly an insurmountable reach. Failure here was even more painful.

The story of Chinese investments in Pakistan, the Maldives, Malaysia and many other locations certainly did not come to an end in 2018. Slimmed down versions of some of the ventures have still been moving ahead. As Nasheed's remarks illustrate, even China's fiercest critics did not wish to abjure an economic relationship with Beijing altogether. But politically, the whole venture had become a reputational headache, in many countries achieving precisely the opposite of its intended strategic effect. China itself was under no illusions about what it meant. The Belt and Road Forum in Beijing the following year saw an uncharacteristically chastened-looking Xi Jinping explaining how in future everything would look different. There was talk of a BRI 2.0—a more consultative approach, more judicious about political and economic risk, better attuned to standards, more focused on quality and less focused on speed and scale. This, however, was the path that Xi had already rejected. Indeed, one of the most effective critiques of the BRI came from within the Chinese system itself, before the venture was even fully launched. The road not taken was that of Jin Liqun.

* * *

At first glance, Jin's profile looks unusual—a former Red Guard who would go on to chair a Chinese investment bank, translate a classic history of J. P. Morgan and modern finance, and move fluidly between senior roles at the Chinese Ministry of Finance, its sovereign wealth fund, the World Bank and the Asia Development Bank (ADB). But for all that he was personally exceptional, the world of Chinese economics and finance had a number of other similarly brilliant characters. Many embodied the insider–outsider quality that would see them steeped in classical economic theory, trained in the West, deeply familiar with the workings of the existing international institutions, yet viewing it all from a perspective rooted in their own lives and experiences in China.

For decades, the most important role that people like Jin had played was at home—the economists doing the heavy lifting work in China's domestic reform efforts, acting as bridges between the Chinese system and the multilateral development banks that played a critical role in China's economic transformation. They saw the deficiencies of Chinese institutions and practices and wanted to apply and tailor the best of international thinking and experiences to fixing them. But in the aftermath of the 2008 global financial crisis, something changed.

The nature of the moment is still best captured by Wang Qishan, then the Chinese vice-premier, and himself one of the most internationalized, financially literate figures at the top of the Chinese system. His remarks to US Treasury Secretary Hank Paulson as the crisis unfolded—"You were my teacher but look at your system, Hank, we aren't sure we should be learning from you any more"—became emblematic of the mindset shift among Chinese elites.[4] China's relative resilience through the crisis, and the catastrophic failure of the various US "masters of the universe" to manage and regulate the financial and economic architecture they had built, had a number of profound effects on attitudes in Beijing.

One was an end to deference about how parts of that architecture worked. The longstanding CPC ideological critique, which objected to the priority accorded to human rights versus economic development, was certainly emboldened. But there were also those who thought the international financial and development institutions were doing an inadequate job and that China could change things. In 2014, this critique started to be expressed more forcefully and plans to address it set in motion: the focus was infrastructure, and Jin was the man taking on the task. The embryonic institution that would become the vehicle for this was the AIIB.

In late 2014, Jin was in Washington, DC in an attempt to persuade US officials and the wider policy community that the United States should not set itself against the new institution that he would go on to lead. In his rounds at the DC think-tanks, Jin would blitz through presentations of his case. He knew the failings of the World Bank and the ADB from the inside out and could also translate the implications to ground-level examples in Afghanistan and myriad other developing countries. The basic argument was that there was a tremendous infrastructure deficit in the developing world that the banks' own reports acknowledged—the ADB put the figure for infrastructure needs alone at nearly $1.7 trillion dollars a year[5]—but that their structures and practices did not allow it to be addressed with the urgency required. They were too fixed in their ways to change. The entire development community had turned hostile to big infrastructure projects long ago. So China would develop its own institution—to complement rather than rival the other multilateral development banks—that would be nimbler and more ambitious at tackling the problem.

Multilateralizing the effort would help China too, and Jin was frank about what this amounted to. If Beijing channeled its financial firepower bilaterally, not only did the Chinese policy banks have little experience doing serious economic development work outside their borders but they would also be subjected to the familiar pressures to favor Chinese companies and make corrupt deals. Much of China's money would end up wasted. The AIIB would, in essence, help keep China honest. The slogan that Jin later adopted for the bank was that it should be lean, clean and green.

I caught up with a friend in the State Department after Jin's visit—knowing that he had been making the same case to US officials—and noted that it was an impressive performance and a compelling case. He laughed—"Yes, that's exactly what we're afraid of!" Jin was making considerable headway around the world with his preliminary talks. The Europeans were eager to sign up. Even India saw the benefits. This was the vision of China stepping up that everyone had hoped for. It left the United States in an invidious position. For all that some senior Obama administration economic policy officials believed that it undercut the existing institutions, that allies should be discouraged from joining it and were understandably disturbed at the alacrity with which they did, other officials on the China side of the house saw this as a very dubious fight to take on. It felt and looked like it was primacy rather than principle at stake. It wasn't a fight that the United States was likely to win anyway. And of all the fronts on which the United States and China were in competition with each other, multilaterally financed development aid didn't seem like one to elevate.

Ostensibly, the AIIB episode was characterized by rifts between the United States and its allies, most of whom—with the exception of Japan—ended up joining the bank anyway. But for all the juicily angry quotes in the *Financial Times* from senior White House officials, the administration's heart wasn't in it. When the AIIB eventually launched in 2014, the United States would raise no objections to the elaborate web of partnerships that Jin established with the World Bank, the ADB and the European Bank for Reconstruction and Development. The attitude was the same as I saw from US officials in Pakistan in the years that followed—skepticism, yes, but if China could pull off what they proposed, good luck to them.

Meanwhile, much of the rest of the world—including the Europeans—pursued a smother-with-love approach, sending politicians and officials to staff Jin's already highly international team, and crafting the AIIB's statutes and rules in ways that everyone could find acceptable. The aim was not to dilute but to ensure that it became what Jin claimed he wanted—a Chinese-created bank that was genuinely multilateral rather than a wholly Chinese-run bank with a bit of international window dressing. Beijing got the kudos of building a new institution and a vastly greater say in the decisions than in the existing ones, yet the whole thing was tempered by the goals and preferences of others, all of whom had been consulted meticulously at every stage in the act of creation.

The AIIB was often conflated with the Belt and Road, but Jin's vision for his bank was informed by just as much awareness of how China needed to be saved from itself as the failings of the international system. The Belt and Road itself would operate in precisely the opposite fashion. The rigidity, the ideological paranoia and the need to instrumentalize economic power to serve political and security goals that had become the hallmark of Xi Jinping's approach would prevail instead. The AIIB would only attract a tiny fraction of the resources that Beijing ended up funneling through its own direct Belt and Road lending. It was clear where Xi's priorities lay. The changes that took place were mostly in speed and scale after Xi's chastened summit, not in substance. The pandemic would only deepen the debt crises that a raft of countries were experiencing. Contracts published in 2021 revealed they were under stringent restrictions too, both not to reveal the terms and to accord China privileged status that would mean it would be paid back ahead of other creditors.[6] The contracts functioned as a drag on the entirety of the debt renegotiations across the developing world.

But even before this, the Belt and Road—from its flagship in Pakistan to the tiny Maldives—was tarnished. If the free-market democracies were able to do a better job of offering alternatives, the opportunity for pushback was there, even with trillions of dollars in play on the Chinese side. As the West had already demonstrated in another country in the neighborhood, vast sums of finance were no guarantee of success.

Kabul, July 2010

I had been sitting outside the US embassy in Kabul for half an hour and was growing apprehensive. It was the summer of 2010. My meeting with the ambassador had been confirmed and reconfirmed and my vehicle information placed carefully in the system, but it wasn't showing up. I was half-wondering whether the meeting would happen and half-nervous about the vulnerable location, too green to the ways of the city to be fully at ease. That Karl Eikenberry was willing to see me at all was surprising. The US was at the peak of its powers there and the war was the single biggest national security priority for the Obama administration. The sense that the eyes of the world were on Afghanistan was tangible from the big-name foreign correspondents thronging in the gardens of the Gandamack Lodge.

But Eikenberry was a Sinologist, more aware than most how large China would loom over the future of the country and willing to spare a little time for a visitor who was trying to puzzle it out. When I finally made it inside, he shared with me his personal efforts to coax the Chinese into doing a little bit more at least to help out with the economic stabilization of the country. The Chinese had acquired the copper mine at Aynak, which—despite the corrupt circumstances around the deal—would have ensured as much as a third of the government's revenue, but they seemed in no hurry to extract anything from it. The Chinese ambassador, Zheng Qingdian, was friendly, willing to entertain some modest joint projects, but Eikenberry's suggestions that the two visit those projects—or indeed do anything visibly together in public—were always rebuffed.

Within the year, that had changed. The Chinese assessment had been that the US wanted to stick it out in Afghanistan and consolidate its position in China's western periphery as part of a broader containment strategy. When Afghan officials met with their Chinese counterparts, they would be subjected to assiduous queries about the utility of specific military bases that the Chinese would point out on maps. But Obama's 2011 speech signaling both a surge and a drawdown was interpreted, after some internal debate, to be more about the latter than the former. Beijing was happy to help the Americans leave, as long as they did so in the right manner. Joint-ness was no longer a problem, and soon no longer were meetings with the Taliban. Beijing was not going to do anything with the copper mine, as the violence in the country intensified, but it would pull out the stops to try to get a peace process underway between the Afghan government, the Americans, and their military opponents.

These talks proceeded in fits and starts. At points, the US was not serious about them, at times the Afghan government was not serious about them, and at points the Taliban would not show up. China hosted meetings in Beijing, meetings in Xinjiang, joint meetings with the Americans and the Pakistanis, meetings with the Taliban alone. The discomfort was still evident to participants in those meetings: "They would watch the Taliban and Afghan government delegations greet each other warmly and look utterly confused. They had no feel for the people or the relationships ... In the end they mostly defaulted to backing up the Pakistanis," as one participant noted. China was a host, or at best a facilitator. This mattered at times, given how hard it was to get the parties to the table. But it was never a real mediator.

The Chinese official who had been one of the Taliban's handlers for their first visit to Beijing a couple of decades earlier was still struck by the slightly alien nature of the whole experience: "They brought their own bread, they wouldn't eat our food, they wouldn't leave their rooms except for the formal meetings program." It was never a comfortable relationship. A fundamentalist movement that swept into power with the backing of China's Pakistani friends had been looking to Beijing for protection from UN sanctions, economic assistance and recognition of their Islamic Emirate as the legitimate government of Afghanistan. In 2021, they wanted exactly the same things. But for all the meetings that had taken place between the two sides over the preceding decades, Chinese officials were no more at ease with the Taliban than they had been at the turn of the millennium. Yet again, they were ready to deal pragmatically with them. Yet again, that would prove even harder than they had hoped.

In principle, this was now a worldlier and savvier Taliban than the Kandaharis the Chinese had sent their intelligence agents to meet back in 2000. When I asked a member of that preparatory mission what he had made of Mullah Omar, he paused and chose his words carefully: "Very ambitious." It was the ambition that still troubled them. They were used to handling all manner of regimes and largely untroubled by what they chose to do within their own borders. Parts of the Taliban sought to convince their Chinese interlocutors that they were really a nationally minded political grouping that just wanted the Americans out and the rest of the world to leave them in peace. This was reassuring. One Chinese academic, Wang Yiwei, even wrote an article implausibly claiming that the Taliban were "Afghanistan's People's Liberation Army," for whom "studying Mao Zedong thought takes precedence over reciting the Quran."[7] But China was well aware of the transnational agenda of much of the movement and the groups that found haven with them, fought with them and pledged allegiance to them. Beijing cared about one of them over all others: the Turkistan Islamic Party (TIP).

"There is no way to separate Al Qaeda and the Taliban from the TIP." I was in Shanghai talking to a former Chinese security official who was now running a center on Big Data and Terrorism. He had a team working with open-source tools that had traced the name and location of virtually every Uyghur fighter in Syria and Afghanistan, the bank accounts of Turkish and Saudi funders, the arms that had been transferred to them, the passports provided to help them make their way to Istanbul. "The Turkish government is a little bit stupid, you cannot leave so many traces. How do they expect that the Chinese government and any other government cannot identify their involvement if even outside researchers can find this?" He was explaining the changing fortunes of the group that the Chinese government still called the East Turkistan Islamic Movement (ETIM), the name by which it had been designated as a terrorist entity at the UN:

> They were very weak when they formed ETIM in the 1990s. The Islamic Movement of Uzbekistan [IMU] helped them to join Al Qaeda. Now the IMU has been destroyed. The TIP emir is a member of Al Qaeda's shura. They negotiated with the IMU on behalf of the Taliban and Al Qaeda when the IMU affiliated to Islamic State. They fought with the Taliban against the Afghan government.

The tangled story of their affiliations was difficult for most non-specialists on militant groups across Central Asia and the

Middle East to follow, but it pointed to the fact that the TIP was now a less disposable partner to the Taliban than it had been in the 1990s, and a more capable one too. It was the track record of the TIP in Syria that worried many of the Chinese counter-terrorism experts who were assessing what might happen if more of them came back to the region and were given a free hand again by the Taliban:

> They're like special forces, the most capable, fearless fighters, indoctrinated intensively, they get their political and religious training from Saudi imams. Their job is fighting—we see them like victims, like cannon fodder, but they're very skillful: they coordinate well, attack points with suicide vehicles, then flood in their fighters.

When Lu Shulin, the Chinese ambassador to Pakistan, had gone to meet the Taliban's elusive leader, Mullah Omar, in the year 2000, he had highlighted China's concerns about rumors that the Islamic Emirate of Afghanistan was assisting "the Muslims in Xinjiang," receiving the reassurance from Omar that "Afghanistan never had any interest or wish to interfere in China's domestic issues and affairs, nor would Afghanistan allow any group to use its territory to conduct any such operations or support one to that end."[8] The guarantees sounded convincing, but in practice ETIM members were simply sent to operate under slightly more straitened conditions in IMU camps, as the Big Data expert had noted.

Relations between China and the Taliban back then had hardly blossomed. While Beijing started to provide some limited economic support to the embattled government in Kabul—including Huawei and ZTE going in to set up phone lines—the Taliban's decision to destroy the Bamiyan Buddhas set relations back to such an extent that visiting Taliban delegations had arrived in China after the incident to find all their meetings canceled. By the time a major economic delegation from China went back to sign up to a more expansive package of activities, it was on the eve of the 9/11 attacks.

After the US invasion, Chinese officials never dropped their contacts with the Taliban, continuing to meet with them in Pakistan after they had regrouped. As one former Chinese diplomat put it: "We were the only ones aside from the Pakistanis to maintain continuous contacts with the group." The Pakistanis had told them that the retreat from Afghanistan was not permanent, and that the relationship was worth keeping alive. In the meantime, China still wanted to make sure that they stuck to their pledge. It provided money and arms as the Taliban's insurgency resumed, though it dialed down the support after complaints from the British and US governments about the volume of weapons they were encountering on the battlefield.

There was a subtle but important distinction that the Chinese drew, as their interactions with the Taliban continued. The Pakistanis were keenest that Beijing deal with their people, which usually meant the Haqqani network. The Haqqanis comprised much of the Taliban's military leadership and would go on to dominate the Taliban government when they ultimately took over. While the Chinese would find ways of doing business with the Haqqanis, they had been skeptical of them, not least given their proclivity for hosting TIP members in their camps. Beijing was more positively disposed to some of the original crowd around Mullah Omar, whom it saw as more pragmatic, and who would comprise much of the Taliban's international representation. This was the group that sought peace talks with the Afghan government. The most prominent of them was Mullah Baradar, Omar's right-hand man.

* * *

Baradar's early efforts in 2010 to push for talks with the Afghan government, without the blessing of the Pakistanis, saw him detained after a joint ISI–CIA operation. He would spend the next eight years in a Pakistani prison, released only in the later stages of the talks. But for the final stages of the process, someone of his political weight was essential. He had been close to Mullah Omar, setting up a religious school with him, married to his sister, and would go on to occupy a number of political and military roles in the first Islamic Emirate. Having Baradar as head of the negotiating team was a very different proposition from the foreign policy spokesperson types who were staffing the office in Qatar.

The agreement ultimately reached between the Taliban and the United States was little more than a force protection agreement, the Taliban being more than happy to facilitate the US exit. All the difficult questions over political power balance in the country were left unresolved, in principle for the ongoing intra-Afghan negotiations, in reality to be determined by military force alone as the Taliban's advances continued. For a long time, Beijing had watched the war in Afghanistan and wanted neither side to win. It was becoming increasingly clear, though, that China needed to prepare to deal with the aftermath of a Taliban victory. On 29 July 2021, it pressed ahead with an eyebrow-raising meeting in the northern port city of Tianjin. For all the meetings with the Taliban that had taken place before this, most of them were behind closed doors, avoiding the images of Chinese ministers or even officials appearing alongside leading Taliban figures. Now Baradar would be received in the style that one might expect from a leader-in-waiting.

There was a neat symmetry to the occasion. In the aftermath of 9/11, Wang Yi, then an assistant foreign minister, had been dispatched on mission to figure out what concessions the Pakistani army chief, Pervez Musharraf, had granted the Americans as they prepared for war in Afghanistan. There had been no time for exchanges or consultations with the Chinese when Pakistan was being threatened with being "bombed back to the Stone Age" by US officials, who had a lengthy list of demands—from breaking ties with the Taliban to an extensive array of military and intelligence cooperation—almost all of which Musharraf accepted.[9] Wang not only "clarified the Pakistani position that under no circumstances would Pakistan allow its cooperation with the US to undermine Chinese strategic interests" but suggested that Pakistan might put forward a timeframe for the United States to leave Afghanistan.[10] Twenty years later, Wang was standing with one of the Taliban's top leaders as they prepared to take power again.

Beijing's hope was still that the endgame in Afghanistan would see an agreement reached that could shore up a lasting political framework in the country. The Taliban would dominate now, the power realities demanded that, but the Chinese still wanted to see at least a fig-leaf of accommodation to the countries' other political forces. Short of that, any longer-term investment plans or scope to contain security threats in the wider region would look very fragile. They already had warning signs. A couple of weeks before Baradar arrived in Tianjin, China had experienced the worst terrorist attack in the history of its involvement in Pakistan. A bus bombing sent a bus carrying Chinese engineers in the northwest of the country toppling into a ravine, killing nine Chinese and four Pakistanis. The situation in Balochistan had grown so bad that most Chinese workers were pulled out of Gwadar. Beijing's fear was that after the Taliban's takeover, the situation would only worsen, whatever the promises Baradar and others made.

* * *

As the chaos of the US withdrawal played out in 2021, Beijing sought to use it as part of the messaging on its most important political front. This proved that you can't rely on the Americans, China contended in a litany of statements and propaganda material. Elites like those in Afghanistan who had bet their future on relations with Washington should understand that in time, they would be stuck dealing with the long-term resident power in the region whether they liked it or not. As one Chinese op-ed put it:

> Many people cannot help but recall how the Vietnam War ended in 1975: The US abandoned its allies in South Vietnam; Saigon was taken over; then the US evacuated almost all its citizens in Saigon. And in 2019, US troops withdrew from northern Syria and abruptly abandoned their allies, the Kurds. Some historians also point out that abandoning allies to protect US interests is an inherent flaw that has been deeply rooted in the US since the founding of the country.[11]

This was unsubtly directed at Taipei, in particular, even if analogizing itself as the Taliban in what Chinese propaganda outlets described as an "omen of Taiwan's future" was not exactly designed to win hearts and minds among the Taiwanese.[12]

Behind the aggressive messaging, China was extremely concerned. This was precisely the kind of withdrawal it had feared. Chaotic, rapid, leaving no settlement behind and a Taliban that felt entirely victorious and beholden to no-one. As a number of international commentators pronounced this a great victory for China, providing new opportunities to access Afghan minerals, most Chinese commentators were deeply skeptical. "If the resources are so useful, why didn't the Americans or the Russians get them when they were actually running the country?," one Chinese resource specialist noted.

Indeed, many of them warned that the whole situation was a trap: a lively paper by Zhang Jiadong listed the various economic and strategic dimensions of that trap, even a "Clash of Civilizations Trap": "Once directly involved in the internal affairs of Afghanistan ... no matter which faction you support, there will always be people who oppose it, and opposition from either faction will eventually develop into a conflict with the wider Muslim community."[13] A Chinese analyst affiliated to the Ministry of Commerce, Mei Xinyu, published an exceptionally blunt article "Do Not Blindly Revel in the Post-American Afghan Economy"—China should not fall for a "fool's dream," he wrote:

> Wake up! Learn about the history of this country! Afghanistan has been turbulent for the past two hundred years ... it has never been able to build a sustainable economy that can keep up with the pace of modern society ... claims that Afghanistan is a "crossroads of civilization" and how important it is to the "Belt and Road" are nothing more than fantasies.[14]

Soon, it would be clear that things were worse than the Chinese feared. Far from reaching an accommodation with other political forces in the country, it was not even fully clear that there was an accommodation within the Taliban. China's least-worst option, Mullah Baradar, would not win the top job, virtually all of the most important of which were instead swept up by the Haqqanis and other sections of the Taliban's military leadership. There were stories of an outright confrontation between Baradar and Khalil ur-Rahman Haqqani in the presidential palace, while their supporters brawled. Meanwhile, the situation with the TIP was shaping up to be exactly as the Chinese government had foreseen. Restrictions were placed on their activities, but there would be none of the expulsions, detentions or extraditions that Beijing typically expects of most of its neighbors, far less even than it had received from the elected Afghan government that the Taliban had overthrown. The TIP was a standing bargaining chip for the Taliban—we will restrain them, but we expect your help.

Skeptical Chinese companies went in to explore the economic prospects under the new government. The Ministry of Mines was open for business, and by late 2021 the Chinese companies were soon back in talks on the modalities of resuming work on their old projects, the copper mine at Aynak and its oil investments in the north. One visitor to the Serena Hotel in Kabul noted Chinese company representatives playing snooker very badly at the table there, among the few foreign guests coming through town. The negotiations moved ahead in detail.

Much of the country was secure now, even if the Chinese were not sure for how long, and trips to the mine at Logar were no longer hair-raisingly risky. Even if the Chinese had not retained employees at the facility, they had cameras there, enabling them to monitor closely what was going on as the Taliban took charge. The copper price was at its highest level on record. It was at least worth looking into what it would take to move ahead with production at the mine. But Chinese experts would complain that the Taliban lacked technical capacity, despite its attempts to hold on to most of the existing employees at the ministries. The task of getting the rest of the infrastructure in the country up-and-running seemed painfully difficult even at the best of times. Yet the country was still under stringent financial sanctions, a reflection of the fact that so many members of the new leadership were still listed as international terrorists.

For the Taliban, China represented even more of a hope than it had back at the turn of the millennium. Soon after taking control of the country, their spokesman would describe Beijing as the Taliban's "main partner."[15] It was, they believed, the only power with the resources to allow them to operate without being beholden to the West's demands. Yet some of the things the West wanted, China wanted too: a government that could achieve the bare minimum of international legitimacy, enough of a political accommodation that it could survive over the long-term, a pulling back of support to some of the militant groups that threatened to destabilize the neighborhood.

The Taliban had made clear that they had little interest in acquiescing to these demands. As far as they were concerned, they had secured the country, had demonstrated their capacity to exercise effective military power and political discipline, and there was no reason for the Chinese to hold back from extracting minerals just because a few corrupt members of the former government weren't given roles. The composition of the new administration was their business, and Beijing was supposed to believe in "non-interference." What were they waiting for? Casting Beijing's lot in fully with the Taliban in these circumstances would be a wild gamble rather than a calculated risk. But China also had to do enough to keep the relationship on good terms, which meant some level of economic commitment, at least enough to funnel money to its friends in Kabul. China was determined not to fall into the trap. But every incremental decision drew the Chinese closer to it.

* * *

Each of the cases in China's western neighborhood exemplified a different problem for Chinese strategy. Pakistan was a reliable military partner, but Beijing's hopes of building the relationship into a comprehensive strategic and economic model for others to follow had collided hard with political realities in the country. The Maldives was a reminder of how fragile China's gambles on "friendly" governments could be, that those bets themselves could even prove politically costly for those governments once China's activities came under scrutiny. Afghanistan was yet another on a long list of pariah governments turning to Beijing for help, where all but the most starry-eyed Chinese officials and analysts could see that the upsides of providing it on a meaningful scale were extremely limited. It was the usual difficulty that Chinese advocates of coalition-building efforts kept running into once it came to listing the countries themselves rather than general principles about the value of Chinese alliances.

In 2021 though, Beijing was facing a Biden administration that was starting to make real headway in assembling a network of partners to work on the China challenge together. Chinese behavior throughout the pandemic had made that task far easier. But there appeared to be no sense on Xi Jinping's part that he might recalibrate the approach that was proving so alienating: China's coercion tactics would only intensify. Beijing would instead cast its lot in with the one heavyweight partner that could represent a real asset for its geo-strategic position if, as it seemed Xi believed, China was now engaged in an all-out struggle with the West.

7

NO LIMIT

CHINA, RUSSIA AND THE WAR WITH THE WEST

Washington, DC, November 2019

THE GATHERING WAS A regular one in the sitting room of Michael Schiffer's house in Adams Morgan, where Michael's expansive array of spirits, wines and other stray drinks was put at everyone's disposal, while his cat patrolled languidly. An initially disconsolate gang had started convening in the early days of the Trump administration under the guiding eye of Michael and Mira Rapp-Hooper, both leading Asia hands in the Democratic Party. With the exception of the odd foreign outsider like me, the group would have collectively comprised the Asia staff of an incoming Hillary Clinton administration. Instead, they were stuck licking their wounds, comparing notes on policy developments and biding their time.

By late 2019, the point in the election cycle had arrived when everyone was picking their candidates, slotting in to write campaign strategy papers and positioning themselves for what might happen after the November 2020 elections. The discussions started to sharpen up over what a new administration's Asia policy should look like. As a periodic attendee of the group, I had at times been struck by how much of an adjustment to the shifting landscape on China some of the "Asia Dems" still had to go through. The distinctions between the economic, technological and security lanes that most of them once happily occupied as trade experts or military strategists had virtually collapsed in the intervening period. The gap between the China policy world of 2019 and 2016 felt far larger than the whole of the preceding decade.

The mainstream view among the Democratic Asia hands was that intense competition with China was the new normal. But some of the correctives to the Trump administration's approach—be nicer to allies, be more multilateral, show up in Asia—felt like the easy pieces of the puzzle, not wrestling with the harder choices at stake.

Yet there were also a number of policy experts whose thinking went beyond even the cutting-edge officials in the Trump administration. That particular evening in November 2019, it was one of the younger academics working with the Warren campaign who was laying out a picture of what a Democratic administration's China strategy might look like. Cooperating on climate, stabilizing relations, working with allies were the familiar elements of the story. But the more interesting part lay in how this might fit together with the wider domestic policy agenda.

The issues that this wing of the Democratic Party wanted to take on ran from tech regulation to clampdowns on dirty money flows to the revival of antitrust policy. Ostensibly this had little to do with China. In fact, it had everything to do with whether the system China was looking to challenge had the capacity to renew itself. While Warren failed to secure the Democratic nomination, many of the voices that would once have been deemed the left of the party would find themselves in prominent roles in the Biden administration. And this mode of thinking extended well beyond the Warren wing too, whether or not those advisors, like our speaker that evening, actually took jobs at the White House.

Anyone looking down the list of early Biden China appointees would note that most of them were not classic China handlers. Some were not Sinologists at all: many of them had spent more of their time dealing with allies than with Chinese officials. Even the China experts were steeped less in bilateral relationship management and more in strategizing about how to compete. Also notable was how many of them had been think-ing about elements of the wider domestic agenda, from technol-ogy strategy to the green transition. This was not really a "left" agenda anymore. It rather reflected the sense that the stakes in the China challenge merited a grand strategy, not a regional one nor even a national security strategy alone. Indeed, one of the first voices to call for a new US industrial policy in 2019, once a virtually heretical notion for free-marketeers, was Republican Senator Marco Rubio.[1] The ground had already shifted radically during the Trump administration, but there was still much fur-ther to go.

Foreign policy hands dabbling outside their area of expertise can sometimes sound ludicrous: policy wonks steeped in theories about nuclear issues in East Asia earnestly explaining that the only way of truly taking on the China challenge is to ensure that the United States becomes the exemplar of a democratic and egalitarian society, heals racial divisions, overcomes partisanship and re-engineers every area of domestic policy are liable to be laughed out of the room. Equally, the idea that bitter rifts can be healed with the soothing balm of "competition with China" or that China should be the determining factor in deciding every-thing from privacy laws to immigration policy is a stretch. Yet the notion that China should recondition choices in most of these areas is not. And neither is the idea that China makes the wider task of adapting and rebuilding faith in the way democracy and free markets work even more urgent.

It was an argument that one of the figures most central to the new administration's approach had absorbed. As the top Biden jobs were being lined up, it was not clear that Jake Sullivan would assume the role of national security advisor, the position he had been slated for under Hillary Clinton four years earlier. For much of the preceding period, he had been absorbed with domestic affairs, and many observers expected him to pop up in another guise. But much of the agenda he was exploring was really a fusion of the two. Rethinking how the economy operates "is a geopolitical imperative as well as an economic one," as he wrote in an article with Jennifer Harris, who would join him in the White House. "Shifts in grand strategy have from time to time necessitated a shift in economic philosophy and national security arguments have proved critical to securing that change."[2] Sullivan and a number of other figures in the administration had been closely involved in devising the "foreign policy for the middle class" effort that looked at how US policy had to be justified with reference to a "middle class in crisis" in Colorado, Nebraska and Ohio rather than the traditional precepts of US strategy.[3]

While there had been "a marked shift in the debate on issues including worker power, the taxation of capital, anti-monopoly policy, and the scope of public investment," this had not yet been fully integrated by foreign policy thinkers, who still clung on to a very traditional view of what international economic policy should look like. Market access and traditional free-trade agreements were still at the core of the ingrained old sense of US priorities. Officials during the Trump administration wrestled seriously with the question of how far the objectives of major US firms really overlapped with wider US strategic interests. But the actual content of the deal-making with China—including the negotiations on a trade deal that took up so much of the administration's agenda—was very traditional boilerplate from US lobby groups looking to expand their firms' position in the Chinese market. The shift signaled as the Biden administration took office would be pithily summarized in Sullivan's line that "our priority is not to get access for Goldman Sachs in China,"[4] implicitly a principal negotiating objective in US trade policy for decades. Financialization, light-touch regulation, inversions and self-policing platforms all felt like they were part of the era that had serially pushed the system to the point of crisis.

Privately, officials on both sides of the Atlantic had become increasingly scathing about the behavior of many of their firms. From Washington, DC to Berlin, it was common to hear talk of the China market as a "drug"—for the short-term revenue hit they were willing to transfer their technology voluntarily and lobby their own governments to weaken their stance on other areas of policy. All the while, they would refuse to provide their own officials with the market-relevant data they needed to mount cases to protect their own industrial sector from Chinese predation. As one US official put it:

> We need blocking statutes. People need to go to jail. We need to stop them taking the candy. They've just got used to the fact that you can do it. They only come to us now if the shit hits the fan and their entire business is going to be tanked. But it's a mess they've made for themselves.

A senior European industry association representative was equally stark: "Some of our major firms are addicts. And they just want us to make it easier for them to get their fix." When I caught up with a number of Biden administration officials in late 2021, there was no topic that elicited more colorful language than the efforts from parts of US industry to maintain their commercial ties with China at the expense of US national security, and the US government officials who advocated for them.

* * *

In October 2019, there was a speech that ran precisely the opposite case to Sullivan's. Mark Zuckerberg was in Washington, DC to announce that he had gone through a Damascene conversion after years of trying to penetrate the Chinese market. He would now pivot hard in the opposite direction:

> I wanted our services in China because I believe in connecting the whole world and I thought we might help create a more open society

... But we could never come to agreement on what it would take for us to operate there, and they never let us in. And now we have more freedom to speak out and stand up for the values we believe in and fight for free expression around the world.

This required American companies to prevail in the battle that was playing out among global platforms:

China is building its own internet focused on very different values, and is now exporting their vision of the internet to other countries. Until recently, the internet in almost every country outside China has been defined by American platforms with strong free expression values. There's no guarantee these values will win out.

So far so true, yet the subtext of the entire Zuckerberg argument was that this was precisely why Facebook and the other Silicon Valley giants should not be tied down by unhelpful proposals for content regulation, let alone the "break up Big Tech" agenda. "This question of which nation's values will determine what speech is allowed for decades to come really puts into perspective our debates about the content issues of the day," he pointedly noted.[5]

The embattled US tech industry's turn to the China argument mirrored the push on the other side of the Atlantic for "European champions." Some leading European firms and their advocates contended that what was really required now was a relaxation of competition rules and a healthy dose of subsidies. Just as China is acting as one of the catalysts for a more serious look at how the system works, there is a countervailing argument that the contest should, in essence, play out on the terrain that the Chinese Communist Party has defined.

Rather than antitrust authorities going after Chinese behemoths, they should allow home behemoths to grow untrammeled. Rather than going after Chinese subsidies, governments should ramp up financial backing to firms at home. There was a significant part of the China-conditioned political agenda that simply pushed sovereign control—funding European firms to take on their US counterparts and vice versa, re-shoring supply chains, domestic control of data, and "Buy American."

It is an approach that is at best modestly troubling to China in the short term. A contest of sheer scale and nationally driven economic competition is one that China is likely to win in the long run. Indeed, much of Beijing's self-confidence has stemmed from its view that it was not taking on a functioning system at all anymore. It was challenging a fading set of powers that were incapable of pulling together.

When either Europe or the United States have talked about system competition, the system they implicitly meant was often their own. For all the language around authoritarianism versus democracy and free markets versus state-dominated economies, the major democracies and free markets have still been at least as absorbed by the distinctions between each other's models as shoring up the wider framework they inhabit.

In Europe's case, the Trump years only accentuated this tendency, with the continent shocked into discovering the need to be able to act more autonomously. In the process was the risk of heading down the road towards a vision of Europe standing apart—what has sometimes been dubbed a Gaullist Europe—rather than Jean Monnet's Europe. Monnet saw European strength bolstered in an Atlanticist context and the allies pulling closer together—economically as well as militarily—when faced with a common threat. This was not lazy, reflexive Atlanticism, an excuse to avoid Europe taking responsibility for its own affairs, but an acceptance of power realities—that there are junctures when neither the United States nor Europe is strong enough to take on certain challenges alone. The Trump era—and fears about the long-term direction of US democracy—certainly bolstered the rival argument, however: those in Europe that said that you could not trust the United States, and that Europe needed to differentiate itself, taking on the role of a balancing power rather than a full US partner. This was precisely what China counted on with its clunky praise for European "strategic autonomy" and the consistent private messages it conveyed to European leaders—we can live with most of what you do, as long as you don't team up with the Americans. As one European official put it:

> I'm not so concerned now about our analysis on China, that's heading in the right direction. But we still can't define our relationship with the United States. There is a group of virtually slavish Atlanticists, there is one country that basically doesn't want to work with the US on the big issues at all, and we have not been able to reconcile it.

Washington, DC, November 2021

Late in 2021, I was in Washington, DC to run through a stock-take on how the first year of the Biden administration's efforts to build a new coalition to take on the China challenge was faring. It had started badly. Even before the new administration had taken office, China had made a series of concessions in negotiations with the EU over an investment deal that Angela Merkel, in her last year in office, proceeded to jam through despite considerable reluctance among other EU member states.

After years of stalling, Beijing had timed the concessions to land during the window between Biden's election and inauguration, when the incoming administration was in purdah, restricted in its contacts with foreign governments. It was specifically designed to spike the Biden administration's new coalition-building efforts, and the Europeans were told that the concessions were only on offer if they agreed to the terms now. Jake Sullivan had been reduced to plaintively tweeting that he hoped the Europeans would wait until there was a chance for the two sides to consult. They did not. The mood in Berlin, Paris and Brussels was still anxious and defensive. One German official explained to me that they had been told to be wary even of moving forward on areas where they agreed with their US counterparts. "There are plenty of individual areas where we are cooperating—such as the talks on dual-use exports or the attribution of cyber-crimes. But the Chancellery will also say—the Americans are dragging us, on all these little projects, into a different approach to China from the one we want." The sense of threat had not gone away:

> We don't know what the tipping point is with Beijing—which provocation is it where they'll decide that they no longer see a difference between us and Washington? So even when we agree in substance, we are still hesitant ... We need to be able to present whatever we do as "European sovereignty" in order to deal with the costs that these actions have with the Chinese. We are also wary of being pulled into an all-fronts confrontation. The width and depth of it isn't in our interest. There is a consensus on containment in Washington and we're not on the same page.

European officials in the early talks with the Americans on China were struck by how far instructions they had once expected to receive only from Paris—lean back, don't be too eager to cooperate—were coming from Berlin too.

Merkel seemed to be on a mission to preserve a vision for the EU–China relationship that most officials even in Germany thought no longer corresponded to reality. At the Munich Security Conference in February 2021, Biden's rallying call for cooperation among democracies in the long-term strategic competition with China was barely referenced in the remarks that followed by France's president and Germany's chancellor. Macron had already claimed earlier in the month that to "join together all against China" is a "scenario of the highest possible conflictuality" and "counterproductive."[6] He used similar distancing language at the G7 and NATO summits in June, stating that "China isn't part of the Atlantic geography"[7] and that the G7 is "not a club hostile to China."[8] Meanwhile, Merkel stressed the need for "balance," arguing that China is "our partner in many aspects."[9] As one official put it: "The chancellery still gets migraines when you say 'partner, competitor, rival'; they still don't buy into that even though it's been European policy now for two years."

There was also an explosive blow-up over US plans to push ahead with plans for a new agreement with Australia and the UK to supply Canberra with nuclear submarines, at the expense of an existing French deal. The strength of the French reaction to being blindsided caught the US off-guard, as their ambassador was recalled amid angry denunciations about a "stab in the back." "Totally over-the-top," one US official working on Asia was still complaining months later, shaking his head: some of the "Asia Dems" who had been driving the decision were politically damaged by the experience, and still bitter about the French handling of the affair.

Yet by November 2021, things were looking up. The elections in Germany had brought to office a government that was set to be far tougher on China than its predecessor, with striking references to "systemic competition" at the very start of the coalition treaty that the parties had agreed, while Taiwan, Xinjiang and transatlantic coordination on China were explicitly enshrined in the text. On each of the areas where Merkel had sought to lean back, it leaned forward. It seemed to embody something closer to the consensus that spanned the BDI and the preponderance of the Berlin policy community rather than the inertia of the Merkel years. The new Green foreign minister, Annalena Baerbock, had so troubled Chinese officials with her positions that they had lodged undiplomatic questions, ahead of her taking office, about whether she was appropriate for the job. In one early interaction with Wang Yi, in which he boasted about the approval ratings for Xi Jinping and the Chinese Communist Party, she drily remarked that her constituency in East Germany used to return similar numbers before the fall of the GDR.

Beijing's decision to slap expensive counter-sanctions on European lawmakers, officials and think-tanks after a rather modest package of EU sanctions on some of the officials responsible for Chinese repression in Xinjiang soon derailed the China-EU investment agreement that Merkel had pushed so hard. Europe and the United States had also buried their differences on a number of longstanding irritants, from the Boeing–Airbus dispute to the Trump administration's steel tariffs.

A new EU–US trade and technology council had just been established, where officials from the two sides thrashed out coordinated approaches on areas that included export controls, investment screening, global trade challenges, "misuse of technology threatening security and human rights," ICT security and competitiveness, secure supply chains, climate and clean tech, and technology standards, virtually an entirely China-driven agenda.[10] The EU was moving forward with an ambitious new package of financing that could support alternatives to the Belt and Road. "For any country that has a digital package on offer from China, we want to be able to say: here's what we can offer instead, and here's the money to pay for it. We were never able to do that before," as one senior European development official put it.

The Quad had held its first leaders' meeting, a grouping that had once been held back by Indian or Australian caution now elevated to the highest levels of government. The mood was cautiously optimistic that the democratic allies were starting to pull together, doing the patient negotiation work on tech alliances, carbon clubs, Indo-Pacific security cooperation, infrastructure financing and other building blocks of a new coalition.

One State Department official I saw in early November, who was working on broader US strategy for the next twelve months, was less so. "Next year is going to be bad." Cooperation in dealing with China was inching forward, yes, but he warned that the whole agenda was about to be eclipsed by a looming crisis about which few in Europe or Asia were yet fully aware. It would have a significant impact on China's strategic position too.

Vilnius, March 2022

Vilnius is a city on the front lines of a new geopolitical and geo-economic divide. Walking through the old city a few weeks after Russia's invasion of Ukraine and you would, like in much of Europe, find yourself surrounded by images of yellow and blue, but it is that much more present and every threat that much closer. The Belarusian opposition rallying outside the town hall is less than 200 miles from the border. Putin has made repeatedly clear that Lithuania should never have been allowed to be a NATO member. Sophisticated cyber-attacks are almost routine. The Suwałki corridor—which separates Belarus from the Russian territory of Kaliningrad—cuts across Lithuanian territory and would prevent land access for NATO to the Baltic states altogether if Russia decided to target it. Everyone was preparing for a more explicit set of military threats if the invasion succeeded. As Ukraine's president, Volodymyr Zelensky, put it: "If we are no more, then God forbid, Latvia, Lithuania and Estonia will be next."[11] A state of emergency was declared on the day of the invasion. Sales of guns and tinned goods mushroomed. "We now look like West Berlin during the Cold War, we are in a particular geopolitical surrounding," noted the chairman of the Foreign Affairs Committee.[12]

Yet the front line is not with Russia alone. Unlike many other ostensibly more powerful states, Lithuania had decided that it would refuse to be pushed around by Beijing too, and as a result was subjected to a set of coercive economic and diplomatic measures more expansive than any other state had experienced. "It was like they tried to erase us," as one official put it. The Lithuanian foreign minister, Gabrielius Landsbergis, grandson of the country's first post-independence leader, was one of the principal movers behind a sequence of events that would infuriate China, leading Beijing to train the full might of its economic powers on the Baltic state, putting vast pressure on it to back down.

But this was before the Russian invasion of Ukraine, and China's announcement of a "no limits" partnership with Putin barely weeks before it took place. Now Lithuania was feeling emboldened. Its efforts to stand up against all forms of pressure from authoritarian states were starting to look like a painful but necessary step that others would need to follow too, especially now that those states were increasingly acting in concert. "We had to send the message that we are not overwhelmed by taking on Russia and China simultaneously. It's the same principles that apply in both cases," said one senior Lithuanian politician:

> China thought that Lithuania was too small to matter. But now basic principles are under attack. Even if we have nothing to offer but our willingness to fight for those principles, we can still bring together a strong coalition to support them ... It is literally about defending ourselves.

As one Lithuanian official put it: "We came to the realization that with most countries, there are differences that can be overcome. But there are systemic differences that can't, differences that more fundamentally affect how countries relate to each other."

* * *

Lithuania thought it was familiar with what Chinese retribution looked like. Like many other European states, a meeting between Lithuania's president and the Dalai Lama in 2013 had led to a year in which the bilateral relationship was placed on ice. But back then, China was unusually desperate to warm it up again. It was two years into the 16+1 process, and Beijing wanted to make sure it had the full sweep of Central and Eastern European leaders in attendance. The next summit in late 2014 was due to be held in Serbia, and as it crept closer, Chinese officials started appearing with increasingly urgent draft letters for the patching-up quasi-apology that typically ends Beijing's Dalai Lama-related punishments. "We want your Prime Minister in Belgrade in December," it was made clear, and, after a little textual to-and-fro, China accepted a low-key resolution, a letter from Lithuania's ambassador.

The two PMs met in Belgrade, with no mention of the troubling incident. But that was not the end of the Dalai Lama's visits. Indeed, he was a regular guest of the Baltic states. A consecration ceremony for Russian Buddhists in Latvia took place annually, and the traffic to Lithuania continued. Then in May 2019 the prime minister of the Tibetan government-in-exile, Lobsang Sangay, had a trip scheduled. It was sufficiently public that he even had a lecture arranged at the Vilnius Institute for Policy Analysis on the "Geopolitics of China in Europe." The Chinese ambassador, Shen Zhifei, didn't appear to have clocked it until Lobsang Sangay's plane was about to touch down. "He was making desperate calls everywhere to try to stop him from landing," as one official put it. It was to no avail. Shen would be personally and visibly involved in the incident that came next.

On 23 August 2019, a thirtieth anniversary rally to commemorate the Baltic Way was taking place in Cathedral Square. In 1989, 2 million people had formed a human chain between the three Baltic capitals on the fiftieth anniversary of the Molotov–Ribbentrop pact, the Nazi–Soviet agreement that foreshadowed the Baltics' annexation by the Soviet Union. The peaceful protest had been a charter moment in their campaign for independence, and 23 August was a day of remembrance in Europe for the victims of totalitarian regimes. As part of the anniversary event, a small group of demonstrators was there to show support for the protests in Hong Kong, then at their high-water mark. It would be met by a violent counter-protest, ostensibly from the Chinese diaspora.

If the notion of being physically attacked by Chinese nationals for a legal, peaceful demonstration on a day dedicated to such anti-totalitarian rallies was already shocking to Lithuanians, the bigger one was the blatancy of the Chinese embassy's involvement. The ambassador, the deputy and several others were sitting a few meters away under the trees, with no attempt even to conceal what they were doing. The flags and banners for the counter-protestors were openly delivered in an embassy car, with diplomatic license plates, and distributed outside a hotel on the south side of the square. The deputy defense attaché was known to have been instrumental in putting the violent protest together. The lead-up had seen a visit to Vilnius from a United Front group—which has the mobilization of overseas Chinese as one of its tasks—a new diaspora-registered organization, and the embassy putting the word out through channels such as the Confucius Institute. Having initially claimed that the diaspora protests were "spontaneous," the ambassador then claimed that he was there "to protect their nationals" and "celebrate the Baltic Way." Since it was the first such incident, the Lithuanian government decided that a strongly worded protest note would be sufficient to deter the Chinese government from repeating this behavior. It was not.

Barely a few weeks later, the embassy had planned a firework display in the middle of the city, celebrating the seventieth anniversary of the People's Republic of China. Just as with the protest in Cathedral Square, the embassy decided not to go to the trouble of registering their plans and getting permission from the local authorities. It magnified the sense that Chinese officials had started to feel entitled to do as they wish without troubling themselves with such niceties as local laws. They had gone to the trouble, however, of booking large banners in the center of Vilnius with an advertising agency, publicizing the celebration of the Communists' taking power in Beijing, eliciting vehement public reaction. "It's a communist tyranny which now has over a million of its citizens in concentration camps ... what is there to celebrate?" one MP wrote;[13] another stated that celebrating the establishment of the People's Republic of China would be akin to celebrating Lithuania's incorporation into the Soviet Union. The outcry would see the mayor stepping in to refuse the go-ahead for the firework display and ensuring the banners were taken down.

The incident that followed in December was uglier. The Hill of Crosses, in northern Lithuania, had been a place of pilgrimage since Soviet times, where hundreds of thousands of crosses were laid out by visitors, many with short prayers and messages about freedom written on them. By some accounts, it traced its origins back to the mourning relatives of victims of revolts against the Russian regime from as early as 1831. The Soviet authorities had made several attempts to destroy the site, but the Lithuanians kept rebuilding it. Pope John Paul II had visited in 1993, the crucifix he left there becoming a focal point for pilgrims. It fused the sacred and the tradition of peaceful resistance. Chinese tourists also paid a visit to the pilgrimage site, on what seemed to be a mission of desecration. Scouring the hill, they located crosses on which "pray for Hong Kong" or "free Hong Kong" had been written, destroyed them, filmed it and put the video and images on social media. "Just throw it there, get lost!" one woman is filmed saying: "We've done a good thing today. Our Motherland is great!" Another cross was graffitied with "Hope all the protester cockroaches soon rest in peace."[14]

Lithuanian officials believed that the vandalism was as "spontaneous" as the Cathedral Square protest. Without knowledge of who had gone there before, the chances of being able to locate the Hong Kong crosses on the vast site were slim. There was uproar yet again. "Every month we had something. It explains why the public here woke so early. People are touchy about some of the allergies relating to our past." The Chinese government seemed intent on inflaming them.

Beijing, 2020

Normally when a new ambassador arrives in China, as in other countries, it is a process of seamless ease. There is a VIP channel. Entry procedures are specially facilitated. Protocol receives you. When Lithuania's new ambassador, Diana Mickevičienė, entered the country in 2020, it was another era. She arrived alone at an empty airport, COVID-tested for the third time, with only a few hazmat-besuited Chinese airport staff for company. Her luggage was sprayed and dumped to one side of the terminal. She was spirited off to a cellophane-covered quarantine hotel, after a few hours of the entry routines, to wait for test results. When these were delayed and she was informed that she going to have to stay overnight, she was told that no food had been booked for her. Chinese officials relented and provided a packet of instant noodles and sausage at 11pm, her first ambassadorial dinner. Unlike much of what would follow, this was not a special punishment relating to the worsening bilateral relationship, this was simply the life of a newly-arriving ambassador in China in COVID times.

Worse was when she returned with her son. China had a rule that infected minors were to be taken to hospitals and quarantined separately from adults. One Dutch-Belgian family had their three-year-old taken away, with only half an hour of online contact with his mother a day. The Chinese foreign minister ultimately relented here too, telling a gathering of European ambassadors that if everyone kept quiet, the rule wouldn't be applied to diplomats. But before then, any return to the capital involved an anxiety-riddled three-week process of testing where any positive result would see the two separated. The Lithuanian ambassador ran this gauntlet twice, for the sake of only the briefest of stays, before she was forced out of the country even more unceremoniously than the manner in which she arrived.

In December 2020, the Chinese government made a bemusing set of proposals to the 17+1 states, of which Lithuania was one, suggesting that they might explore a separate FTA with China. It was, as Chinese officials were quickly informed, not just unacceptable in substance but in spirit. The EU was the only actor that could negotiate any such agreements for members of the trading bloc, as the Chinese side knew well.

Early in the new year, the Central and Eastern European states were bounced again. After a series of relatively friendly conversations about figuring out an appropriate time for the next 17+1 summit, they were suddenly informed by Chinese officials that it would take place on 9 February. A letter was received in Vilnius simply stating that China had decided the day. The question of summit-hosting had already become fraught as the whole initiative had grown more and more contentious, culminating in a summit in Dubrovnik in 2019 when no-one agreed to host the next one. "The 16+1 had once been a shiny balloon. By then we realized it was a shriveled empty sack," as one official put it. The Chinese—out of cycle—said they would host it themselves and upgrade it from prime ministerial level to Xi Jinping himself. The Visegrád Group, the Czech Republic, Hungary, Poland, and Slovakia, already had an anniversary summit for the group arranged on that date, in person, in Poland, between all four leaders. Warsaw was pressed to accommodate a video call with Xi. In addition to simply announcing the date and corralling everyone into attending, the Chinese side had taken to picking which political leaders they wished to attend the summits. Invitations depended on which figure was the more powerful or the more China-friendly, rather than following protocol.

The Lithuanians decided that enough was enough. The new government would not join the summit they had been summoned to attend. They informed the Chinese government. Then the pressure began. On Friday night, ahead of the summit, the embassy in Beijing received a request to come to the foreign ministry urgently. The Estonians, who were in the same boat, were instructed to come in too. They were "scolded" by the vice-minister, Qin Gang, for the decision to decline the invitation. The level of desperation soon became clear though. "Just connect for 15 minutes," they were asked. Qin had sought to revive the format, and it was turning into a disaster. At this stage, five countries were not sending "suitable" attendance. By the Monday, the pleading was for them to send any minister at all. The Lithuanians relented, but only by sending the minister of transportation. It didn't go down well. But they were finished with the whole affair. In the aftermath, they decided to withdraw from the 17+1 process altogether. There were numerous discussions about whether to pull out with others, who were equally fed up. But Lithuania moved alone.

They informed the Chinese side that they were leaving. There were attempts by Vilnius to make it discreet, even to cast it as Beijing's decision if it helped: "Just don't invite us," they suggested. Instead, the Chinese ramped up the 17+1-related invitations to a host of other actors beyond the government, from mayors to media representatives. The Lithuanians would even find that at 17+1 meetings they were no longer attending, their flag was still on display, with a Chinese person sitting behind it rather than a Lithuanian official. Meanwhile, the real Lithuanian officials were excluded from all bilateral meetings with the Chinese as a result of their actions.

Landsbergis decided that the time to be "discreet" was over: "There is no such thing as 17+1 anymore, as for practical purposes Lithuania is out," he told Politico in May 2021.[15] "From our perspective, it is high time for the EU to move from a dividing 16+1 format to a more uniting and therefore much more efficient 27+1," Landsbergis said: "The EU is strongest when all 27 member states act together along with EU institutions." Things were about to get a lot worse.

In August, discussions that had been underway for several months came to fruition: Taiwan would open a representative office in Vilnius, and Lithuania would open an office in Taipei. This was not unusual in its own right, since Taiwan had 112 diplomatic missions, even if only sixteen of them have official status. What was unusual was the name. While most of these representations reference "Taipei," including the unofficial embassy in Washington, DC, the Taipei Economic and Cultural Representative Office in the United States, this one would have "Taiwanese" as a formal part of the title. While there were later attempts to claim that this was a translation snafu—that in Lithuanian it meant the "Taiwanese people"—no-one was very convinced, and certainly not the Chinese government.

The retaliation was swift. China's ambassador was recalled. They demanded the withdrawal of Lithuania's ambassador to Beijing. And the embassy itself was unilaterally downgraded to the "Office of the Chargé d'Affaires." Within a day, the new name was already in the Chinese taxi apps. All Lithuanian diplomatic IDs were revoked. Even getting the remaining possessions out of China proved to be difficult. Moving companies in Beijing made clear that they were not keen on handling Lithuanian goods. Chinese propaganda outlets published contemptuous Russian opinion pieces declaring that Lithuania "is not a country but a geographical destination with a very limited sovereignty and almost no place in the international competitive environment,"[16] while Chinese pundits dismissed it as a "US running dog,"[17] a "crazy, tiny country full of geopolitical fears," "a small country, whose population is less than a district of one of China's first-tier cities."[18] "It is like we are swatting a fly," one column dismissively pronounced,[19] though the level and volume of invective suggested that the "fly" had troubled them far more than they wished to pretend. "Small countries" were not supposed to stand up to Beijing. They were supposed to roll over.

In September, the Lithuanian defense ministry warned that consumers should stop using Chinese phones. "Our recommendation is to not buy new Chinese phones, and to get rid of those already purchased as fast as reasonably possible," said Deputy Defense Minister Margiris Abukevičius.[20] Xiaomi's flagship 5G phone was found to have software that could detect and censor terms including "Free Tibet," "Taiwan independence" and "democracy movement," while Huawei's 5G phone, they assessed, put users at risk of cyber-security breaches. Lithuania had already decided against Chinese firms taking a role in future 5G networks. Now it was warning everyone that Chinese consumer products, too, may be means of importing censorship and exfiltrating data.

When Taiwan's representation office opened in November, Beijing escalated its efforts. A "normal" level of retaliation might have seen a de facto block on certain parts of Lithuania's trade with China, a variant on the "Dalai Lama effect." But Lithuania found itself simply erased. The country's name was removed from the customs declaration system altogether, making it impossible for Lithuania's exporters to move their goods through Chinese ports. Following pressure from the EU, the Chinese reinstated it, claiming that the incident was a "glitch." Other measures to achieve the same effect followed, often using the same pretense that the problem was only a technical one. Even when the name Lithuania reappeared in the index, the system would get stuck when anyone chose it. The effect was a 95 percent decline in exports to China, a near-total breakdown, while China also made sure that—while continuing to ship consumer goods—any raw materials that Lithuania might need for its production processes were cut off too. But this was only the start.

The problem Beijing faced was that trade relations between the two countries were minimal. Lithuanian politicians had calculated that they could live with the economic consequences of Chinese retribution far better than most other states and were ready to deal with the damage. So the Chinese government tried another tactic. It would not only go after Lithuanian firms, it would also start exerting pressure on other firms with Lithuanian suppliers. Swedish, French and German companies, including the car parts giant Continental, were told that if they used Lithuanian parts they would no longer be able to sell to or receive supplies from China. This was a real economic threat. If major investors in Lithuania could no longer include factories there as part of their supply chain, it could have a devastating effect on economic confidence. To stand up against the pressure, Vilnius would need the backing of its other European partners. And much of the rest of the EU was not happy.

"Of course we have to swing in behind them," one official put it, "but they should have consulted us first. They were talking to the Americans for weeks before it happened but then they expect the rest of their European partners to give them support." This was the milder version—EU trade officials in private were vituperative. Lithuanian officials note that they did, in fact, put a call in to the EEAS from their Permanent Representation about the matter ahead of time, but this did not allay the sense in various European capitals that they had been bounced. Public opinion in Lithuania was wobbling too. A poll commissioned by the foreign ministry, who had driven the Taiwan initiative, found that only 13 percent fully backed the government's approach, with 60 percent negatively disposed.[21] By February, there were mutterings that even US officials were suggesting that changing the name might not be a bad idea.

The EU initiated a dispute complaint at the WTO, making it clear to China that an attack on the EU single market was unacceptable. It also expedited plans for a new anti-coercion instrument, which would allow the European Commission to take retaliatory measures against similar actions in future. But Lithuania itself would not be a beneficiary of any such measures for now, which would potentially take years to move through the EU legislative process. The United States was offering an export credit finance line. Taiwan would make an even more significant offer of turning the country into a focal point for its semiconductor cooperation in Europe, and immediately set up a $200 million investment fund. Nonetheless, Lithuania looked as if it was very much out on a limb, the pressure building to find a face-saving way to de-escalate the issue: "It was like China was running an experiment on us, to try out every single measure simultaneously and see what happens." It almost worked.

Then in February 2022, Russia's invasion of Ukraine turned everything on its head. When I saw one of the main figures behind Lithuania's pivot on China, Deputy Foreign Minister Mantas Adomėnas, in March, the situation looked radically different. A Cambridge-trained classicist (I later bumped into him in a coffee shop outside the foreign ministry talking one of his students through Petronius texts), he had been closely involved in supporting the Hong Kong democrats from his previous vantage point in parliament. He was one of the organizers of the protest in Cathedral Square that the Chinese embassy had tried to attack. "Public opinion has turned," he acknowledged, but ruefully rather than with any relish. These were not the circumstances in which he would have wished it to happen.

* * *

For Chinese strategists thinking about alliance-building, Russia was by far the greatest prize. Cerebral foreign policy theorists explained how a different quality of relations between the two sides could transform China's international position. Hawks like Hu Xijin, the former editor of China's firebrand *Global Times* newspaper, would colorfully summarize it: "Corralling a few dogs, even a pack, is easier with two lions than with one."[22] But as prizes went, it was an elusive one. Although the two sides happily coordinated at the UN Security Council to thwart American initiatives and traded tips on domestic repression techniques, when it came to the moves that would really have made a difference to China, Russia kept holding back. Pipeline deals were always just out of reach. Advanced weapons sales, such as the S-400 missile defense system and the Su-35 fighter jets, were not forthcoming. The Russian market was essentially closed to Chinese investment.

Even when the top leaders seemed to see eye to eye, the willingness to take each other into confidence over strategic issues was virtually non-existent. The Chinese side had been shocked by Russia's willingness to allow the United States access to military supply lines for Afghanistan after the 9/11 attacks. Hu Jintao would then be notably embarrassed when Russia staged its invasion of Georgia on the same day as the opening ceremony of the 2008 Beijing Olympics. As one US official at the time put it: China "didn't just reject it, they almost organized the opposition to it" in Central Asia, as Russia sought to drum up legitimizing support.[23]

For a long time, mistrust between the two sides substantially exceeded any common authoritarian affinity. The legacy of the Sino-Soviet split ran deep, and ran until remarkably recently. In the 1980s, China had been integrally involved in the campaign to hit Soviet targets in Afghanistan, supplying prodigious volumes of arms to the mujahideen and even backing the targeting of military officers and officials inside Russia itself. If the collapse of the Soviet Union was, in Putin's eyes, the greatest geopolitical disaster of the twentieth century, it was one that China had actively helped bring about. While relations were already on a different footing by the time of Gorbachev's ill-fated visit at the peak of the protests in Tiananmen Square, Chinese officials would hold what they saw as his weak leadership to blame for the "fall of Communism," and the Yeltsin era as the embodiment of the chaos that China should seek to avoid.

Putin was a different matter. He functioned as a kind of dark counterpoint to Chinese leaders, showing them up, horrifying them and fascinating them at the same time. He was bold where they were cautious. Polling of Chinese netizens, whatever its flaws, fairly credibly seemed to find Putin by some way the most popular international leader. For some Chinese strategists, this was a function of their relative positions: China was augmenting its power every year. Patience worked to its advantage. Russia could not count on that. It only had the military card and the energy card to play. China had many more. But Putin's behavior was also a sort of temptation—he seemed to keep getting away with things Chinese leaders would rather like to get away with themselves.

When I met Chinese military and foreign policy experts after every further Russian gambit, their enthusiasm continued to rise. The 2014 annexation of Crimea was seen as a daring and successful maneuver, even if they had some doubts about Russia's subsequent activities in Eastern Ukraine. So intrigued were some in the PLA by the Russian intervention in Syria the following year that they debated whether they should they should find a way to engage in joint counter-terrorism missions there—primarily for the sake of combat experience that could prove more useful elsewhere. This was a practice they saw as one of the main US motivations for its otherwise inexplicable wars in the Middle East.

While regional experts and logisticians in the Chinese system curbed this particular flight of fancy, the overall appeal was undimmed: China had something to learn from Russia, especially a military that had not been put to the test since its intervention in Vietnam in 1979.

But it was Xi Jinping himself who would make the bigger difference. He evinced a personal obsession of his own with the Soviet Union. This was hardly unusual in the Chinese Communist Party, which analyzed the subject almost endlessly. As one official commentary in October 2013 noted: "Today, the Soviet Union, with its history of 74 years, has been gone for 22 years. For more than two decades, China has never stopped reflecting on how the communist party and nation were lost by the Soviet Communists."[24] But Xi's conclusions led him in a very different direction from the man who had set China's course in the aftermath of the Soviet collapse. Deng Xiaoping's view was that the Party should double down on the path of economic reform to avoid the same fate: the failures of the Soviet economic system should not be repeated. In his famous Southern Tour of 1992, when he reaffirmed the importance of this course after a post-Tiananmen period of retrenchment, he made the point plainly:

> Had it not been for the achievements of the reform and the open policy, we could not have weathered June 4th. And if we had failed that test, there would have been chaos and civil war ... Why was it that our country could remain stable after the June 4th Incident? It was precisely because we had carried out the reform and the open policy, which have promoted economic growth and raised living standards.[25]

Xi's analysis was different. As president of the Central Party School in 2009, he had commissioned yet another study on the subject. He would lay out some of his conclusions during an infamous leaked speech, soon after becoming leader of the Party. His trip was to the same locations as Deng, twenty years later, another southern tour to Shenzhen, Zhuhai, and Guangzhou. In public, the story was about the continued importance of market reforms, perhaps even a revival of the stalled process after slow-going during the Hu–Wen era. In private, it was most memorable for a blistering set of remarks:

> Why did the Soviet Union disintegrate? Why did the Soviet Communist Party collapse? An important reason was that their ideals and beliefs had been shaken. In the end, "the ruler's flag over the city tower" changed overnight. It's a profound lesson for us! To dismiss the history of the Soviet Union and the Soviet Communist Party, to dismiss Lenin and Stalin, and to dismiss everything else is to engage in historic nihilism, and it confuses our thoughts and undermines the Party's organizations on all levels.[26]

For Xi, ideology and Party dominance were at the core:

> Why must we unwaveringly assert our party's control over the military? ... Because this is the lesson the Soviet collapse teaches. The Soviet Red Army was depoliticized and departyized, becoming a national institution, and so the Soviet Communist Party surrendered its weapons. When those who wished to save the Soviet Union did step forward, the instrument of dictatorship had already slipped from their grasp.

Xi made his own sense of mission very clear, in his scathing view of the last Soviet general secretary: "Finally, all it took was one quiet word from Gorbachev to declare the dissolution of the Soviet Communist Party, and a great party was gone. In the end, nobody was a real man. Nobody came out to resist."[27]

But it was clear that Xi thought Putin was a "real man" too, with a view of history that he found congenial. He was not going be stuck dealing with a Khrushchev, a Gorbachev or a Yeltsin but someone that the CPC leaders saw as like-minded in important ways. "We are similar in character," Xi would tell Putin in 2013.[28] Putin's post-Crimea speech lamenting the "historical

injustice" visited on a Russia that had been "incapable of protect-
ing its own interests," fulminating against Western-led "color
revolutions" and "containment," and demanding "respect"
reflected the private thoughts of many Chinese leaders.[29]

And while the absurdly long list of Russian literature that Xi
claimed to have studied struck most analysts as over-compensat-
ing, it did seem to have featured in the limited reading he was
able to undertake during the Cultural Revolution. The enthusiasm would spill over during his visits and meetings with Putin,
of which he would rack up a remarkable number. Xi's very first
overseas trip was pointedly to Moscow. At the time, there was no
personal bond between the two leaders. But that would soon
change. Another bold Russian move was about to effect a dramatic transformation in the relationship.

* * *

When Russian troops crossed the border with Ukraine in
February 2014, there was no suspicion in the West that Xi
Jinping had given a quiet nod and a wink to Moscow's actions.
Barely a couple of weeks after the formal incorporation of Crimea
as a Russian federal subject, Xi was due to embark on a visit to
Europe that would become acutely awkward. Desperate to avoid
alienating either side, Xi would limit himself to incredibly
oblique statements about the topic. The Chinese foreign ministry's line that "there are reasons that the Ukrainian situation is
what it is today"[30] was topped by Xi's own statement that the
situation "seems to be accidental but has the elements of the
inevitable," which at least gave some clues about where his sym-
pathies lay.[31]

The real action would come later. The sanctions imposed by the
United States and Europe represented the first occasion that the
advanced toolkit drawn up to go after first North Korea and then
Iran was deployed on an economy of Russia's size and economic

interconnectedness. Unlike traditional sanctions, they relied on a cascade effect of private sector actors—particularly in the financial sector—reducing their exposure to any of the targeted entities, lest they be frozen out of the international financial system altogether. It was a model that involved compliance departments at major banks doing more of the heavy-lifting than US officials. An ostensibly modest set of sanctions induced a panic effect, with vast outflows of funds from the Russian economy.

The only state that could plausibly cushion the impact was China. But for that to happen, Russia would have to unblock at least some of the areas where economic flows between the two sides were in stasis. It would evidently not be an advantageous moment to do so. Beijing knew perfectly well that Moscow was only giving the green light because its back was against the wall. Negotiators for Chinese enterprises are notorious for driving an exceptionally hard bargain, to such a pronounced extent that in sanctions-wracked countries such as Iran, the sense that Chinese energy firms were exploiting the vulnerability left a deep residue of mistrust. Xi Jinping staged a direct political intervention. This was too big an opportunity to risk being undercut by a few over-eager Chinese enterprises. He instructed the Chinese firms going into negotiations with their Russian counterparts not to act as if this was a moment of weakness for Moscow, not to allow any perception that they were taking advantage of the situation. The economic relationship with China in these conditions should feel like a partnership, not like a foreclosure sale.

In the months following the Crimea annexation, Moscow lifted each of the most important restrictions that had constrained ties between the two sides. The long-stalled pipeline deal, Power of Siberia, was finally agreed. Russia permitted sales of its most advanced fighter aircraft and missile defense systems, with tangible benefits for Chinese capacity to project airpower over Taiwan and the South China Sea. Chinese investors in Russia were no longer treated as pariahs.

Most importantly, it prompted a more protracted reassessment of the deeper-rooted myths and truisms that had led to these obstacles in the first place. Russian policymakers concluded that Chinese population flows did not really pose a threat to its Far East. Advances in PLA capabilities meant that it was preferable for the Russian military industrial complex to cash in on its continued edge in sectors such as aircraft and missiles while that edge still existed rather than worrying that China would reverse-engineer them. The two sides' interests in Central Asia were sufficiently congruent on the fundamentals that their differences could be managed. There would be no more claims that: "We understand this Chinese initiative"—the Belt and Road—"as just another attempt to steal Central Asia from us," as one senior Russian official put it in an interview with the Russian China scholar, Alexander Gabuev.[32] Moreover, the dynamics in all areas, not just military kit, continued to shift in China's favor. Better to lock in the terms of a partnership at today's prices.

There were steps that China was not willing to take. Its commercial banks still ran scared of Western sanctions, with some Russian officials complaining that they were even more prone to over-interpreting some of the restrictions than their Western counterparts. More ambitious plans to circumvent Western payment systems would only proceed slowly: the internationalization of China's currency was still constrained by the deep anxiety about what the consequences would be if China's capital account was liberalized. A panic in the Chinese stock market early in Xi's tenure, coupled with his attempts to ensure that money was not funneled out of the country to escape the anti-corruption crackdown, meant that any political interest in this from Beijing was further away than ever.

But in addition to the energy and arms contracts, China would make sure that its more-sanctions-proofed state-run policy banks—EXIM Bank and China Development Bank—had financing on offer for deals that involved members of Putin's inner circle. Politburo Standing Committee members would also start involving themselves more deeply in Russian economic ventures. The long-term direction of travel was also clear. Both sides needed to be resilient against Western financial pressures if they wanted real freedom to act.

When Xi arrived in Moscow in May 2015 to attend the Victory Day parade commemorating the Allied victory in World War Two, any angst about China usurping Russia's role in trans-Eurasian trade had largely abated. Officials from both sides had been working to figure out how to stitch their two schemes together, the Silk Road Economic Belt and the Eurasian Economic Union. Relieving the economic pressure on Russia itself was only part of the picture. Moscow's invasion of Ukraine had been precipitated not by the looming prospect of NATO enlargement, which had been off the table for years, but the "threat" of Kyiv signing an economic partnership agreement with the EU. Russia could use outright military force if it had to, but for all its oil and gas reserves, it could not function as an alternative economic center of gravity that might pull neighbors into its orbit.

The long-term trajectory for many of the states where Moscow wanted to retain control still looked ultimately like one of convergence with the Western, liberal democratic free-market system. There was one alternative, though. Pursued in conjunction with China, a rival economic and ideological order, which could continue to underpin that sphere of influence, was at least possible. China's economic heft would give it the ascendant role, but that was the lesser of the two evils, and Beijing—including Xi Jinping personally—was making that choice seem as painless as possible. At the victory celebrations, he was flexible, solicitous and publicly gushing. "In the past six years, we have met nearly 30 times. Russia is the country that I have visited the most times, and President Putin is my best friend and colleague," he told the press with unusual effusiveness.[33] At the time, this still outran the reality lower down the food chain. In both the Chinese and the Russian systems, there was still considerable skepticism and resistance. In the past, that had often proved decisive, regardless of what the men at the top wanted. But the geopolitical circumstances had shifted. And there were now two leaders in place who were near the peak of their powers.

The bureaucracies swung into gear. When I was in Moscow later that year to talk about the Belt and Road, I was struck by the sheer level of logistical detail in the discussions. The relative cost advantages of various Chinese transit routes, customs obstacles in the Caucasus and shipping times across the Caspian Sea were bandied about not just by specialist government officials but by outside analysts. Some of the Russian China hands quietly lamented that the Kremlin was venturing into this closer embrace not out of a clear-eyed sense of any long-term goals with Beijing but as a byproduct of its westward-facing agenda. The intervening years would strip away a number of illusions about what was and was not possible between the two sides. But with the overall direction so clearly set, this would only make things easier when the next phase of the confrontation with the West began in earnest.

* * *

As the build-up to Russia's invasion of Ukraine in 2022 accelerated, China might have been expected to drop off the radar screen in Western capitals, much as it did in 2014. But Xi Jinping seemed determined to tie Beijing's fate as closely and visibly to Russia's as possible. US officials briefed their Chinese counterparts on Moscow's plans, only to find the details of those briefings shared extensively with the Kremlin, alongside the reassurance that Washington's machinations would not get between them. Intelligence reports suggested that Chinese officials had requested that any military intervention be delayed until after the Winter Olympics were out the way, to avoid a repeat of 2008. European officials quietly encouraged China to repeat the performance of neutrality it had exhibited over Crimea in 2014, which would at least mean that Beijing did not provide active support or encouragement to Russia. Instead, Xi received Putin in Beijing and signed a joint statement of dizzying breadth.

The 2022 statement looked like China shucking off its remaining foreign policy inhibitions to lay out the contours of a global entente. Alongside Xi's vision of an ideological alignment with Moscow, areas that had once been out of bounds, such as Beijing backing the Russian position on the European security order, were plainly spelled out there in China's support for two Russian draft treaties that demanded a rollback of NATO military presence in all the states that had joined the alliance since German reunification. For its part, Russia would stand against US alliance-building efforts in China's backyard, including Beijing's biggest bugbears, AUKUS and the Quad.

One prominent Russian foreign policy expert described the statement as taking the relationship "to the level of a common front to push back against US pressure on Russia and China in Europe, Asia, and globally."[34] Coming at the very peak of Western anxieties about a looming invasion, it was an extraordinary signal for Beijing to send, seeming to reflect not only a confidence in Moscow's strategy but a dismissiveness about the reactions it was likely to induce in European capitals. Russia had got away with its lightning annexation of Crimea before, why should this be any different? The material consequences were soon clear: Russia reduced its troop levels at the borders with China and Mongolia to its lowest levels since the 1920s and moved them west to prepare for the invasion.

* * *

"The biggest surprise for China was that Russia totally mis-judged its own power. We thought that Russia would win a very fast war," the Chinese expert explained ruefully, a few weeks after the invasion. It was not the official line, which was then in the phase of intense attempts to persuade global audiences that Beijing had no idea what was coming. But it was a better reflection of Chinese foreign policy thinking than either playing innocent or repeating ad nauseam that the invasion of Ukraine was the responsibility of the United States and NATO pushing a big power against the wall. One of the main reasons behind Beijing's resistance to such entanglements in the past was not because partners and allies weren't useful but because the countries in question risked dragging China down with their mistakes. The "Pakistan model," which China had been touting, was conditioned by exactly this experience: Beijing didn't want to get stuck defending every Pakistani intervention in Kashmir or inadvertently drawn into a conflict with India, so it confined itself to providing the capabilities its friend needed and then staying above the fray. Russia was not the first Chinese partner to believe it would win a very fast war and found itself in a hole; but China wasn't usually pulled into it with them.

The problem Beijing faced in 2022 was that in crucial areas, it was still too soon to make a break with the West. China remained dependent on the US dollar system. For all the speculation about renminbi internationalization, Chinese payment systems, and its new digital currency, China was barely any closer to constructing a resilient alternative financial architecture than it had been in 2014. The technology story was equally problematic: despite the massive push to build its own semiconductor industry, Chinese firms were still painfully reliant on US intellectual property. This left many of its companies exposed if they continued to do business in Russia, much like any other sanctioned entity. It was Huawei's and ZTE's sanctions-busting dealings in Iran that had risked decimating the two firms once the United States had the legal justification to go after them with full force. Now articles entitled "Is Russia the New Huawei?" were popping up, as the United States applied the same Foreign Direct Product Rule restrictions to the entire Russian tech sector that had been the final blow for Huawei's 5G plans in the UK. Circumvent them, and those Chinese firms could kiss goodbye to their advanced semiconductors. The net effect was that from banks to telecoms, most of the companies that might have wished to take advantage of the newly opened vacuum in the Russian market instead faced even greater limitations on their activities.

Almost as bad for China, the narrative about a West divided and in decline was becoming harder to sustain, to the extent that its propaganda outlets stopped trying to advance it at all. Beijing had been able to make considerable hay with Trump, COVID, Brexit, the US withdrawal from Afghanistan and much else in recent years. But now it was confronted with a different picture. The sanctions put in place by the United States, Europe, Japan, and a healthy array of other states in Asia were not the thin gruel of 2014 but far more potent in their effect—and disturbingly replicable for China too. Central bank sanctions threatened China's $3 trillion foreign reserves war-chest, prompting emergency meetings between Chinese regulators and banks to discuss how to protect China's overseas assets from comparable measures. The new US-led plurilateral grouping established on Russian export controls, comprising countries wielding more than half of the world's GDP, could deny China critical components and technologies too. It was the first such effort on this scale since the entity that did the job during the Cold War—the Coordinating Committee for Multilateral Export Controls, more widely known as COCOM—was retired in favor of a multilateral regime in its aftermath.

In addition, Beijing watched companies simply writing off tens of billions of dollars of assets in Russia as they fled for the exits, going well beyond any formal requirements by Western governments. It undercut one of China's most important hedges: Xi had personally laid out plans to tighten international firms' dependence on China in order to form "a powerful countermeasure and deterrent capability against foreigners."[35] That countermeasure and deterrent now looked a great deal less effective. Surveys of sentiment among international investors in China, which had held up during the early stages of the pandemic, weakened sharply. The combined effect of investors' anxiety about being swept up in the Russia sanctions directly, and a repricing of risk in light of fears that China could go through a repeat of the Russia experience itself, was one factor. As the FBI director, Christopher Wray, noted in a speech: "There were a lot of Western companies that had their fingers still in that door when it slammed shut. If China does invade Taiwan, we could see the same thing again, at a much larger scale. Just as in Russia, Western investments built over years could become hostages, capital stranded, supply chains and relationships disrupted."[36]

Xi's continued pursuit of a zero-COVID policy, rendering global supply chains increasingly dysfunctional after two years of strict lockdowns in coastal economic hubs, had even greater immediacy for firms' bottom line. Nearly a quarter of European companies surveyed in April 2022 said they were now considering moving out altogether.[37] As the head of the EU Chamber of Commerce there, Jörg Wuttke, put it:

> Western companies are grappling with the scenario that they would have to leave China—just as they are now leaving Russia—if China tried to forcibly integrate Taiwan. And it doesn't help, of course, that China is adopting Russia's aggressive rhetoric. The effect is the same as from the COVID policy: foreign companies are hitting the pause button. New investments are suspended for the moment ... The

president has maneuvered himself into two dead ends at once: He can't change his COVID policy, and he can't change anything about his friendship with Vladimir Putin.[38]

The China risk was being priced differently now. The military picture was also troubling to Chinese policymakers. Backed with Western training, arms and intelligence support, the domestic will to resist, and a public opinion climate in the West that saw the war in starkly black and white terms, Ukraine was proving far more resilient than China had anticipated, even without direct NATO military involvement. The read-across to Taiwan was not reassuring: what would already be an extremely difficult military operation for a PLA inexperienced at real warfighting—potentially involving a complex amphibious assault, and the intervention of both the United States and Japan—now looked even more daunting, especially once the wider strategic context was taken into account. As one widely circulated analysis document by a group of influential Chinese think-tankers argued:

> The changing nature of warfare dictates that Putin cannot win in the true sense of the word ... The war is being updated in real time on social media, the impact of the war is expanding from the maritime to land to air transport and gradually affecting regional trade links; transnational capital is being withdrawn and projects are being stalled. War is no longer simply a military conflict but a broad economic war. The issue of territorial borders is no longer the most important aspect. Even if Putin wins militarily, he will not win the war.[39]

China's bet was that the world's liberal democracies were on the wane, incapable of collective mobilization in the face of a common challenge. Instead, Beijing was watching the country that was supposed to be its great strategic asset helping to bring about precisely the coalitions and instruments of economic warfare it had sought to prevent. Western policymakers had failed to deter

Russia, surprising even themselves with the breadth of the financial measures taken. An economy based on commodity exports could always find buyers too, blunting at least the short-term effectiveness of any efforts to place Moscow under a constrictive squeeze. Yet China could not afford to be sanguine about the consequences for its own situation if the liberal democracies delivered a like-for-like response to a future case of Chinese belligerence. The factors that made Beijing vastly more capable as a strategic competitor than Moscow—the breadth, scale and sophistication of its integration into the global economy—also made it more vulnerable if international banks, insurers, software companies and semiconductor manufacturers suddenly cut it off.

Western policymakers and firms were also starting to work backwards from some of these worst-case scenarios—which would be immensely costly for them too—to look at how to mitigate their own vulnerabilities. Re-shoring, near-shoring, friend-shoring, diversification and a host of other phrases had moved from the fringes to the mainstream and into firms' operational planning. Even for those who wanted to keep some version of globalization alive, it no longer had China at the center. As one European policymaker remarked soon after the invasion: "Everything we had been talking about doing during COVID was still a choice; now it's a necessity."

EPILOGUE

Guangzhou, 1999

I CLIMBED UP THE DINGY stairwell to reach the dormitory room belonging to my former students. It was another monstrously humid summer in China's southern capital, and I was on a visit to the academy where I had once been a teacher. A little group of them was anxious to tell me the story of their involvement in an incident that had taken place at the US consulate a couple of months earlier, so I perched on one of the cramped beds and listened.

NATO's bombing of the Chinese embassy in Belgrade in May 1999 had set off an eruption of protests, which saw US diplomatic facilities attacked by tens of thousands of young Chinese carrying placards and throwing rocks. The protests, then Vice-President Hu Jintao said, "fully reflect the Chinese people's great fury at the atrocity of the embassy attacks by NATO, and the Chinese people's strong patriotism."[1] Among them were the teenagers who had been eagerly learning English in my classes the year before.

I had expected there to be residual anger, or at least a few questions. Their jaundiced response to a TV documentary on the Opium Wars that they had to sit through was indicative of that generation's more skeptical view of nationalist propaganda. But it would not have been unreasonable for the US story about erroneous maps to have prompted a great deal of skepticism too. In fact, they just wanted to reassure me.

They had no animus directed at the West and hadn't much wanted to be there at all. The government had sent buses to the school the day after the incident and supplied the materials. The students were instructed to head to the consulate and put on a show. It was the same theater as their wearying early morning patriotic exercises. They admitted that it had proved to be an entertaining day out for them, but they wanted to stress that I shouldn't mistake the images I had seen for any deeper underlying sentiment.

Aside from organizing such ineffectual "spontaneous" protests, which were less fervent in spirit than they appeared, the Chinese government was largely impotent. The US military advantage was intimidatingly complete even when it came to China's greatest national security concern. Beijing's missile tests during Taiwan's elections a couple of years earlier led the United States to lay on the biggest show of military power in Asia in decades, a forceful demonstration that any Chinese attempts at coercion would fail. The United States had the preponderance of economic power, and the model of free markets and democratic governance was advancing seemingly remorselessly, understood almost universally as the single path to success.

Chinese officials were well aware that it was often the embrace of the market that preceded any democratic transition. Yet notwithstanding the risk, they were desperate to become an embedded part of the global free-market system, even if it necessitated a serious domestic economic overhaul. China was still in negotiation over the stringent terms of its WTO accession, without which trading relationships with its major markets remained fragile.

The gap with the United States was comprehensive, let alone with the G7 as a whole. As the next technological revolution rippled out from Silicon Valley, with American firms occupying virtually every leading position among the industries of the future, it appeared that each dimension of US power was mutually reinforcing. This was economic, military, technological, political and ideological dominance, not just "edge." China was in distant catch-up mode. Most Chinese still saw themselves living in a world that was being shaped mostly by forces from elsewhere, whether as students of Western economic theory or the victims of US missile strikes.

In the years that followed, every pillar of that seemingly impregnable strength came under strain. The material dimension of this was important in its own right. China's economic catch-up, the advance in its military capabilities, its technological prowess and the expansion in its political influence evidently had their effect. But there was more to it than that. I watched much of the drama of the subsequent two decades unfolding through the eyes of friends, colleagues and acquaintances in China: Afghanistan, Iraq, Lehman Brothers, Greece, Crimea, Brexit and Trump.

First there was the eroding potency of US military power. Most Chinese officials came to see Iraq and Afghanistan as colossal resource-drains, the kind of trap they should ensure they didn't fall into themselves. But they also saw a US military transforming itself into a force that was focused mostly on low-grade opponents, against whom they were seemingly unable to deliver victory to boot. And they saw a political class that appeared to be losing its sense of belief in the use of conventional military power. Where Moscow staged short, sharp interventions to achieve its political goals, in a manner that—until 2022—continued to impress their Chinese counterparts, the United States seemed to oscillate between excess and excessive caution, with targeted killings becoming the military measure of first resort instead.

Then there was the global financial crisis, and the obliteration of the notion that the United States and Western bankers were the responsible "grown-ups" in the international economic system. China's state-led stimulus and investment package, for all its egregiously distorting effects, provided one of the few sources of stability in the global economic order, while the financialized model of capitalism, which many Chinese economists had seen as the ultimate goal for their own system, now looked hopelessly volatile.

The last straw was the political shift of 2016, the turmoil induced by the dual populist upsurges of Brexit and the election of Donald Trump. The sense that the old order was under threat had already been apparent in Europe, where the rise to power of assorted parties of right and left promised to sweep it all away. Then from June 2016 on, the very pillars of the system started to look fragile. It was not just the uncertainties posed to the US alliance network by a president who barely distinguished between friends and foes or the unique act of disintegration represented by the UK withdrawing from the European single market that it had such a central role in forging. It also went beyond the diminished governing capacity in both countries, the questioning of whether the very core of the Western democratic political system was even up to running itself capably anymore, let alone the rest of the world.

It was the sense that consent had been withdrawn. That a critical mass among the supposed beneficiaries of the system, the Western publics, no longer seemed to believe that it was delivering for them, and no longer believed that the political, economic and cultural trend lines were heading in the right direction, that the future was on their side. Even if many of those voting knew that most of the charlatans and confidence artists that they backed to take over were ill-equipped to do anything more than run that system into the ground, this act of self-harm itself at least sent a signal to the technocratic managers of the order they rejected.

It also sent a signal to Chinese policymakers. Whether or not the precise narrative they told themselves about Western decline was accurate, it was clear that the West was heading in a troubled, insecure, internally conflicted direction, and—as their Russian friends had demonstrated—that all these fissures were ripe for exploitation. Beijing had been and remained paranoid about Western political influence. Now it appeared that the supposed manipulators could themselves be maneuvered into various forms of self-destruction. If this was system competition, China now saw itself competing with a system that was losing faith in itself and could be encouraged to do so even more deeply.

By the time the Chinese government decided to take that task on openly, it had vastly different means from twenty years earlier. Its economy was at parity to both the United States and the European Union. And Chinese technology was now feared for its capacity to supersede Western efforts in a number of essential sectors, not mocked for lagging hopelessly behind. Yet as the Chinese government's growing self-confidence has bled into hubris, and as the polished, pragmatic heirs of Zhou Enlai have made way for diplomatic thugs, the clarity of the challenge posed by China has sharpened. David Rennie of the *Economist* characterized it as a "Bond villain blunder" on Xi's part.[2] Just as at the moment when a Blofeld or a Goldfinger have James Bond exactly where they want him, they decide that now is not the time to kill him on the spot but instead to lay out their scheme for conquering the world, leaving the opportunity open for Bond to escape and thwart their plans.

From the Belt and Road to Made in China 2025, from Wolf Warrior diplomacy to Lithuania's "erasure," what had once been approached by Chinese policymakers with a degree of subtlety, discretion and deniability was now openly, and often crudely declaimed. After the many years in which other crises were invariably more urgent in Western capitals, the sheer political barrage from Beijing finally made it impossible to ignore. In this sense, the dawning realization among the world's leading democracies was the moment of waking up, like 007, strapped to a table with a laser beam moving inexorably—but still rather slowly—towards one's vital assets. It is not clear that even this will be enough though. For all that the Russian invasion of Ukraine has only heightened the sense of not wanting to make the same mistake again with China, Vladmir Putin's almost-caricatured villainy also demonstrated that making chillingly clear what you plan to do to your neighbors is still no guarantee of a spur to action when wishful thinking, self-deception and short-term commercial imperatives have a sufficiently distorting effect on political judgment. As one China expert put it, "every few months, I'm asked: 'is this the moment that really changes everything?' 5G, COVID, Hong Kong, Russia. But then nothing changes quite as much as it should."

* * *

I had received another WhatsApp message from my friend Desmond in the spring of 2021. He wanted to talk about the rollout plans for his own book. It was something he could never have written while still in China or if he had any hopes of continuing to profit from the Party further down the line. We had sat down to discuss it a couple of times, but he had always been cautious. The material from within that system was incendiary. The shocking quotes from the likes of Deng Xiaoping's granddaughter lionizing the number of Chinese killed by the Party as a badge of honor, the ins-and-outs of how corruption was really practiced by its most skilled exponents at the top of the pile, and much else that had been talked about in hushed terms over drinks in Beijing would now, he told me in the message, be on sale in every airport in America in a few months' time.

He would be a marked man, his family would be at risk and his motives and choices would be judged and dissected by hundreds of thousands of unknown readers. But as conditions deteriorated even in his old bolt-hole of Hong Kong, he started to feel he had no choice. When we met in London at the peak of the protest movement, he showed me pictures of how even some of the wealthiest Hong Kongers had shuttled injured protestors away from the scene in their sports cars. This was not the voice he had imagined for himself back in the early 2000s, when his resources were being funneled into helping the Chinese government craft a smarter economic and foreign policy. But now there was an even more essential task. The rest of the world had to understand fully the nature of the system it was taking on. And there was no longer any time to spare.

The sense of a gap between the urgency of the challenge and the relatively slow-moving nature of the measures pursued in response is common in the China policy field. As this book has explained, the rethink on China was driven not by hostile know-nothings who wanted to see the country fail but by many of the people who had been closest to it, and the most personally invested in its success. Businesspeople who had spent decades in Hong Kong and were shocked at the scale of the political crackdown. Technology experts who had been enthusiasts for the blistering dynamism of the Chinese start-up scene and now saw Beijing squeezing its own private sector, hardening its model of the surveillance state, and starting to replicate it overseas. Economists who had worked in close collaboration with their Chinese counterparts who now saw vast industrial policy plans underway that would pose a grave threat to the competitiveness of their industries at home. The tipping points varied, person by person, whether it was the detention of a million Uyghurs or the detention of a single friend. But there was a uniform appreciation that something was fundamentally different now. Some of them characterized it intellectually: the transition from an authoritarian system to a totalitarian one. Others more viscerally. As one businessman put it: "I don't feel safe there anymore. It's spooky. The feel has changed: a wall that was not there before."

Yet if there is a pervasive concern among many China hands in and close to governments in Western capitals, it is that the "feel" is still lacking among most of the politicians who are charged with putting the essential changes in motion. Some continue to fall back on the mantras that had long provided their shorthand for making sense of a complex and seemingly alien power—about how the Chinese Communist Party "will not risk domestic economic growth" or is "pragmatic rather than ideological"—even when they have long been eclipsed by reality. Others are convinced in theory that China represents the biggest challenge to the international system but are simply not personally seized with the task.

For generations of politicians, China has been a relatively distant and peripheral matter, lacking the vital immediacy of the transatlantic relationship, Russia, terrorism, peace in the Middle East, Afghanistan, Iran or any number of other topics. Now, when they are suddenly being asked to re-shape crucial elements of their own economic model or make difficult trade-offs over how technology and security ties with friends and allies need to be re-forged, the impetus is so often missing.

Grand plans to compete with China on infrastructure finance fizzle quietly when bits of the aid bureaucracy pick them apart, ensuring that their traditional priorities are left intact. Lobbyists for tech firms make sure that their exports to China are carefully exempted from restrictions. Military and diplomatic resource re-allocations to the Indo-Pacific are low-balled. Attempts to open industrial policy schemes to international partners are blocked by local interests. Or attention can simply drift: US officials who once made the security of Europe's 5G networks a priority are told to focus instead on pushing an initiative backed by US telecoms firms that is years away from being viable and demonstrably less secure. German politicians who fought to win what they believed to be the big 5G decision fail to notice that their telecoms firms have quietly used the gap between legislation and implementation to include significant Huawei presence in their 5G rollout. Given the scale and complexity of what renewing the system and making it more resilient will require, the risk is that the joint response to China falls far short, hobbled not by the full-frontal opposition of years past but by inertia, inattention, a desire for the path of least resistance, a death by a thousand cuts.

Even if the collective energies of Europe, the United States and a handful of the advanced economies in Asia are mobilized, this is also far from sufficient. For much of the world, the Western-dominated version of global order was not appealing, and their experience of the "system" was often as an imposition. The chafing at restrictive IMF programs, aid programs constructed around shifting donor priorities, unevenly tilted trade agreements and condescending outside experts telling them how to run their economies are among the reasons why China's arrival was initially so refreshing. If the rise of the United States as a global power with its own anti-imperial experience was a fundamental redressing of the balance in the world that expedited the dismantling of the old European empires, China's ascent promised something else: a still-developing, non-Western power with serious resources to deploy. If was there was one commonplace in speaking about China with African officials and ministers in the mid-2000s, it was a sense of relief at being treated as a partner in doing business rather than a benighted subject of Western "help."

The coming decades bring with them the prospect that the top ranks of global power will look radically different, no longer dominated by a small cluster of capitals that have been running much of the world between themselves for the last few hundred years. When the Chinese government attacks "small cliques" representing a tiny share of the global population and yet still expecting to set norms for everyone, the fact that it comes from such a problematic messenger doesn't mean that the claim itself is without resonance. In the fallout from the Russian invasion of Ukraine, this is the pitch that Beijing has been falling back on. Chinese leaders are gradually relinquishing hopes of salvaging relations with the liberal democratic powers, but still see the opportunity to rally a large, non-aligned group of states across the developing world against being pushed around by the West. The growing sense is that this will be the battleground that ultimately matters in deciding what political, security, economic and technological rules and norms will prevail in the world in the century to come.

This is the very challenge that excited me and so many others who were watching the earlier phase of China's takeoff. The integration of Beijing into the global system, into its old councils of power and its economic decision-making processes and structures was never just about China adopting that system's norms wholesale. In its best version, it was about the system adapting too. Jin Liqun's critique was exactly the kind of shock it needed to do better, to change its priorities, to build real global consent of a sort that it had never actually managed to achieve. This was not just a fantasy. All of us who have been lucky enough to be regular visitors to China over recent decades have countless friends, colleagues, teachers and acquaintances who have reshaped our understanding of the disciplines and regions we think about. Even in the often-stultifying shadow of the Chinese Communist Party, the thinkers, the artists, the writers—and many of the government officials and Party members too—were bringing to the table refreshingly different ways of taking on global problems, of wrestling with questions of justice, equality, distribution, legitimacy, democracy as well as the more immediate, practical matters of how to bring peace to Afghanistan or stabilize the international financial architecture.

As the years have passed, those voices, which should have grown louder and ever-greater in number, have instead become quieter and dwindled to an ever-smaller band. It has become harder to see old friends and contacts in China, and they have grown more circumspect, while shrill, nationalist, doctrinaire voices are given platforms and projected by the Party as "China's" voice in the world. Some of the country's most talented diplomats spend their time stripping out funds for human rights monitors in UN peacekeeping forces, mobilizing shabby counter-demonstrations against Chinese dissidents, penning comically crude denunciations of the West's wrongs and issuing gangster-like threats to their host countries for a bewilderingly expansive array of perceived slights. Every now and then there is another flash of what the alternative might represent. The Chinese whistleblower doctors at the outset of the COVID-19 pandemic and the brief window when investigative journalists were given the space to take on the question of why the country was convulsed by a devastating virus. The explosion of Chinese voices on the social media site, Clubhouse, debating Hong Kong, Taiwan, Xinjiang and other controversial matters in no-holds barred fashion, without CPC orthodoxies to constrain them. But for the most part, we are no longer dealing with China's rise, in its totality, but a narrow, distorted version of what that should really mean.

For all its failures, the longstanding push to embrace and integrate China was characterized in part by the hope that, since its ambitions for wealth, influence and power were realizable within the system, the Chinese Communist Party could accommodate itself to it and that some of the other faces of China would still be a part of that process. Understandably, there has been great reluctance to give up on that bet. It is not only that undoing elements of the integration effort will result in an outcome that is in important respects worse than if it had come off. Fracturing global trade will certainly come at a cost, as will the loss of the technological advances that would have been possible if Beijing, Berlin, Silicon Valley, Shenzhen, Tel Aviv and Taipei were all seamlessly intertwined innovation hubs. Beyond the damaging elements of the security, political and ideological competition that we already see, it represents a whole model of the global economy coming to an end. But for those who have spent so much of their lives immersed in China, it also feels painfully like acceptance that a curtain is descending, that vast swathes of humanity are going to be separated by a growing series of barriers. There is already the sense that we are experiencing a human decoupling as much as an economic or political one. It came gradually, then suddenly. Even those who are following developments closely have not yet fully adjusted, let alone those whose exposure to China is more limited.

Yet most of the China hands who have been transformed from cautiously optimistic, somewhat detached analysts into activists, trying to make sure that policymakers understand the nature of the challenge that confronts them, have at least come to terms with the fact that this is no longer our choice to make. That the Chinese Communist Party is clearer than ever that it is engaged in an ideological struggle with the West, whether we choose to describe it that way or not. That the Chinese Communist Party is set on a hardening self-reliance drive, whether we "believe" in decoupling or not. That the interactions we still wish to have with Chinese society are being closed down. That what we think is "in China's rational interest" is not the same analysis that Xi Jinping shares. That when we think that Beijing is "making a mistake" in alienating so many of even its sympathizers, the relevant decision-makers in the Chinese system neither agree nor think the "mistake" should be corrected.

None of this has changed the China experts I know into advocates for a closed, Western club. At a minimum, it has certainly made them more careful about trying to ensure that what was once healthy openness does not turn into defenselessness when a powerful authoritarian state, which long benefited from unfettered access to that liberal-democratic system, sees its very way of operating as a threat.

More ambitiously, as the final chapter of the book explained, some of them see in this moment an opportunity to establish a set of economic, political and security arrangements that a wider global constituency, the silenced voices in China among them, can live with too. Because the competitive challenge posed by China will not only impose costs. If saving and revitalizing the system is understood to be a precondition for prevailing in the battle for the future, it presents the elusive possibility of defining a new consensus amid a bitterly divided politics.

It has become clear that taking the Chinese technological, industrial, military and ideological agenda seriously provides one of the very few prospects of bringing together political coalitions that range from conservative US Republicans to German Greens around a few shared precepts. It is no coincidence that China-related bills have been among the rare legislation to pass the US Congress or that the political groupings that came together in Europe over 5G were so ideologically diverse. Where the global financial crisis proved insufficient to transform the nature of Western capitalism and the role of the state, and three decades of the post-Cold War era saw the vitality waning among some of the core parts of the democratic alliance network, China has started to act as a very different kind of galvanizing force. The shock of the Sino-Russian collective challenge has only magnified its effects.

The response that will be required is not just about defense expenditure, military posture in the Indo-Pacific, counter-disinformation efforts or restrictions on Chinese firms' presence in critical infrastructure. The political agenda that China is already reshaping spans issues that include strengthened democratic control over the activities of major multinationals, bolstered privacy laws and platform regulation, transparency of financial flows, greater levels of investment in advanced technologies, more resilient supply chains and better-crafted economic offers to the developing world, to name only a few examples. It is as much about how we deal with ourselves and each other as how we deal with the Chinese system itself. Much of the agenda stands on its own merits, while each element of it is subject to its own contentious debates in which China plays only a partial role. Yet the entire landscape looks different with the specter of the Chinese party-state looming over it. It is certainly not happening in the way I had hoped when I moved to a Beijing in intellectual ferment in the early 2000s. But China is now changing the balance in the battle of ideas as much as it is changing the balance of power.

NOTES

INTRODUCTION

1. "State Councilor and Foreign Minister Wang Yi: China Wins International Respect and Recognition with Efforts and Sacrifice," Embassy of the People's Republic of China in the United Kingdom of Sweden, Press Release, 15 Feb. 2020.
2. Bob Woodward, *Rage*, New York: Simon & Schuster, 2021, p. 20.
3. David Barboza, "Billions in Hidden Riches for Family of Chinese Leader," *New York Times*, 25 Oct. 2012, https://www.nytimes. com/2012/10/26/business/global/family-of-wen-jiabao-holds-a-hid-den-fortune-in-china.html?searchResult Position=4, last accessed 8 July 2022.
4. Hubert Védrine, "Les États-Unis: Hyperpuissance ou empire?," *Cités*, vol. 20, no. 4 (Apr. 2004), https://www.cairn.info/revue-cites-2004-4-page-139.htm, last accessed 8 July 2022.
5. Robert B. Zoellick, "Whither China: From Membership to Responsibility?," remarks to National Committee on U.S.–China Relations, 21 Sept. 2005, available at https://2001-2009.state.gov/s/d/former/zoellick/rem/53682.htm, last accessed 8 July 2022.
6. "State Councilor and Foreign Minister Wang Yi Meets WHO Director General Tedros Adhanom Ghebreyesus," Embassy of the People's Republic of China in the Republic of Fiji, Press Release, 15 Feb. 2020.

7. Michael R. Pence, remarks at the 2019 Munich Security Conference, 16 Feb. 2019, available at https://www.presidency.ucsb.edu/documents/remarks-the-vice-president-the-2019-munich-security-conference-munich-germany, last accessed 8 July 2022.

8. Nancy Pelosi, remarks at the 2020 Munich Security Conference, 14 Feb. 2020, available at https://www.speaker.gov/newsroom/21420–1, last accessed 8 July 2022.

9. Laura Silver, Kat Devlin and Christine Huang, "Unfavorable Views of China Reach Historic Highs in Many Countries," Pew Research Center, 6 Oct. 2020, https://www.pewresearch.org/global/2020/10/06/unfavorable-views-of-china-reach-historic-highs-in-many-countries, last accessed 12 July 2022.

10. Joe Biden, remarks at the 2021 Virtual Munich Security Conference, 19 Feb. 2021, available at https://www.whitehouse.gov/briefing-room/speeches-remarks/2021/02/19/remarks-by-president-biden-at-the-2021-virtual-munich-security-conference, last accessed 8 July 2022.

1. WHEN DOVES CRY:
HOW THE UNITED STATES AND EUROPE
WOKE UP TO CHINA

1. John Kerry, speech at lunch for Chinese President Xi Jinping along with Vice-President Joe Biden, 25 Sept. 2015, available at https://2009-2017.state.gov/secretary/remarks/2015/09/247326.htm, last accessed 8 July 2022.

2. Apple, 2015 Annual Report, p. 30, https://www.annualreports.com/HostedData/AnnualReportArchive/a/NASDAQ_AAPL_2015.pdf, last accessed 8 July 2022.

3. United States Department of Defense, "Summary of the 2018 National Defense Strategy of the United States of America: Sharpening the American Military's Competitive Edge" (United States Department of Defense, 2018), https://dod.defense.gov/Portals/1/Documents/pubs/2018-National-Defense-Strategy-Summary.pdf, last accessed 8 July 2022.

4. Robert Work, "Remarks by Deputy Secretary Work on Third Offset Strategy," 28 Apr. 2016, available at https://www.defense.gov/News/Speeches/Speech/Article/753482/remarks-by-deputy-secretary-work-on-third-offset-strategy, last accessed 8 July 2022.

5. Tom Blackwell, "Exclusive: Did Huawei bring down Nortel? Corporate espionage, theft, and the parallel rise and fall of two telecom giants", *National Post*, February 20, 2020, https://national-post.com/news/exclusive-did-huawei-bring-down-nortel-corporate-espionage-theft-and-the-parallel-rise-and-fall-of-two-telecom-giants, last accessed: July 11, 2022.

6. Michael Brown and Pavneet Singh, "China's Technology Transfer Strategy: How Chinese Investments in Emerging Technology Enable a Strategic Competitor to Access the Crown Jewels of U.S. Innovation" (Defense Innovation Unit Experimental (DIUx), 2018), https://nationalsecurity.gmu.edu/wp-content/uploads/2020/02/DIUX-China-Tech-Transfer-Study-Selected-Readings.pdf, last accessed 8 July 2022.

7. Chris Buckley, "China Takes Aim at Western Ideas," *New York Times*, 20 Aug. 2013, https://www.nytimes.com/2013/08/20/world/asia/chinas-new-leadership-takes-hard-line-in-secret-memo.html, last accessed 8 July 2022.

8. European Commission and HR/VP, "EU–China: A Strategic Outlook" (France, European Commission and HR/VP, 2019), https://ec.europa.eu/info/sites/default/files/communication-eu-china-a-strategic-outlook.pdf, last accessed 8 July 2022.

9. Jean Monnet, *Memoirs*, London: Profile Books, 2015, p. 224.

10. Ibid.

11. National Cyber Power Index 2020, Belfer Center for Science and International Affairs, Harvard Kennedy School; comparative rankings on p. 8.

12. Magdaline Duncan, "Vestager: 'I do work with tax and I am a woman,'" Politico, 18 July 2018, https://www.politico.eu/article/margrethe-vestager-i-do-work-with-tax-and-i-am-a-woman-donald-trump-google, last accessed 8 July 2022.

2. NOBODY DOES IT BETTER:
BRITISH SPIES AND THE 5G QUESTION

1. Mike Burgess, "Then and Now: Coming Out from the Shadows," Director-General ASD speech to ASPI National Security Dinner, 29 Oct. 2018, available at https://www.asd.gov.au/publications/director-general-asd-speech-aspi-national-security-dinner, last accessed 8 July 2022.

2. Nicholas Eftimiades, "The Impact of Chinese Espionage on the United States," *The Diplomat*, 4 Dec. 2018, https://thediplomat.com/2018/12/the-impact-of-chinese-espionage-on-the-united-states, last accessed 8 July 2022.

3. Douglas Busvine, "Explainer: Germany, at Last, Launches 5G Spectrum Auction," Reuters, 18 Mar. 2019, https://www.reuters.com/article/us-germany-telecoms-explainer-idUSKCN1QZ1YN, last accessed 8 July 2022.

4. Chuin-Wei Yap, "State Support Helped Fuel Huawei's Global Rise," *Wall Street Journal*, 25 Dec. 2019, https://www.wsj.com/articles/state-support-helped-fuel-huaweis-global-rise-11577280736, last accessed 8 July 2022.

5. "The Company that Spooked the World," *The Economist*, 4 Aug. 2012, https://www.economist.com/briefing/2012/08/04/the-company-that-spooked-the-world, last accessed 8 July 2022.

6. "Suppliers, Network Operators and Academics Questioned on UK Telecommunications Infrastructure," United Kingdom Parliament, 10 June 2019, https://committees.parliament.uk/committee/135/science-and-technology-committee/news/100942/suppliers-network-operators-and-academics-questioned-on-uk-telecommunications-infrastructure, last accessed 8 July 2022.

7. "Huawei in Euro Initiative for Multi-domain Infrastructure for 5G Services," Huawei, 23 Nov. 2015, https://www.huawei.com/ch-en/news/2015/11/huawei%20in%20euro%20initiative%20for%20multi-domain%20infrastructure%20for%205g%20services, last accessed 8 July 2022.

8. "Czech Cyber Watchdog Calls Huawei, ZTE Products a Security Threat," Reuters, 17 Dec. 2018, https://www.reuters.com/article/us-czech-huawei/czech-cyber-watchdog-calls-huawei-zte-products-a-security-threat-idUSKBN1OG1Z3, last accessed 8 July 2022.
9. Richard Aldrich, *GCHQ: The Uncensored Story of Britain's Most Secret Intelligence Agency*, London: HarperPress, 2010, p. 56
10. Ibid.

3.TAINTED LOVE: TRUMP, MERKEL AND GERMANY'S CHINA PROBLEM

1. Chris Tomlinson, "Trump's Right Hand Man in Europe Rick Grenell Wants to 'Empower' European Conservatives," Breitbart, 3 June 2018, https://www.breitbart.com/europe/2018/06/03/trumps-right-hand-man-in-europe-wants-to-empower-european-anti-establishment-conservatives, last accessed 8 July 2022.
2. Deutsche Welle News, Twitter Post, 17 Feb. 2017, 12:36 PM, https://twitter.com/dwnews/status/832554253050863616?s=20&t=I4mVxjvFRrrEqZZ8MF0yUA, last accessed 11 July 2022.
3. Jonathan Swan, "Scoop: Trump Tells Macron the EU Is 'Worse' than China," Axios, 10 June 2018, https://www.axios.com/2018/06/10/donald-trump-emmanuel-macron-eu-worse-than-china-trade-tariffs, last accessed 12 July 2022.
4. Katrin Bennhold and Jack Ewing, "In Huawei Battle, China Threatens Germany 'Where It Hurts': Automakers," New York Times, 16 Jan. 2020, https://www.nytimes.com/2020/01/16/world/europe/huawei-germany-china-5g-automakers.html, last accessed 11 July 2022.
5. Norbert Röttgen et al., "Causa Huawei: Unionspolitiker stellen sich gegen Kanzlerin Angela Merkel," Handelsblatt, 22 Oct. 2019, https://www.handelsblatt.com/meinung/gastbeitraege/gastkommentar-zum-5g-ausbau-causa-huawei-unionspolitiker-stellen-sich-gegen-kanzlerin-angela-merkel/25137724.html, last accessed 11 July 2022.
6. Ma Si, "Huawei Secures 91 5G Commercial Contracts around the World," China Daily, 20 Feb. 2020, https://www.chinadaily.com

cn/a/202002/20/WS5e4e7c2aa31012821727914c.html, last accessed 11 July 2022.

7. Yuan Yang, "Is Huawei Compelled by Chinese Law to Help with Espionage?," Financial Times, 5 Mar. 2019, https://www.ft.com/content/282f8ca0-3be6-11e9-b72b-2c7f526ca5d0, last accessed 11 July 2022.

8. "Huawei Founder Says He Would Defy Chinese Law on Intelligence Gathering," CBS News, 20 Feb. 2019, https://www.cbsnews.com/news/huawei-president-ren-zhengfei-says-he-would-defy-chinese-law-on-intelligence-gathering, last accessed 11 July 2022.

9. Laurens Cerulus, "Europe's Huawei Plan Explained," Politico, 29 Jan. 2020, https://www.politico.eu/article/europe-eu-huawei-5g-china-cybersecurity-toolbox-explained, last accessed 11 July 2022.

4. BURNING DOWN THE HOUSE: CHINA'S SHOCK TO THE SYSTEM AND THE CRISES THAT MATTERED MORE

1. John Pomfret, "U.S. Takes a Tougher Tone with China," *Washington Post*, 30 July 2010, https://www.washingtonpost.com/wp-dyn/content/article/2010/07/29/AR2010072906416.html, last accessed 11 July 2022.

2. James Fallows, "What Happened in Copenhagen, #4," *The Atlantic*, 11 Jan. 2010, https://www.theatlantic.com/technology/archive/2010/01/what-happened-in-copenhagen-4/33266, last accessed 11 July 2022.

3. Andreas Fuchs and Nils-Hendrik Klann, "Paying a Visit: The Dalai Lama Effect on International Trade," *Journal of International Economics*, vol. 91, no. 1 (Sept. 2013).

4. Yoichi Funabashi, *The Peninsula Question: A Chronicle of the Second Korean Nuclear Crisis*, Washington, DC: Brookings Institution Press, 2007, p. 267.

5. Jehangir Pocha, "9/11 Reminds Chinese of America, Global Bully," *San Francisco Chronicle*, 9 Sept. 2003, https://www.sfgate.com/

politics/article/9-11-reminds-Chinese-of-America-global-bully-2558035.php, last accessed 12 July 2022.

6. Henry Paulson, *Dealing with China: An Insider Unmasks the New Economic Superpower*, New York: Grand Central Publishing, 2015, p. 225.

7. Ibid., p. 254.

8. Ibid., p. 260.

9. David H. Autor, David Dorn and Gordon H. Hanson, "The China Shock: Learning from Labor Market Adjustment to Large Changes in Trade," NBER Working Paper 21906, https://www.nber.org/system/files/working_papers/w21906/w21906.pdf, last accessed 11 July 2022.

10. Erik Kirschbaum, "Merkel, Li Call for End to EU–China Solar Trade Row," Reuters, 26 May 2013, https://www.reuters.com/article/cbusiness-us-china-eu-trade-merkel-idCA-BRE94P0CD20130526, last accessed 11 July 2022.

11. "Family Businesses in Italy," Associazione Italiana delle Aziende Familiari (AIDAF), https://www.aidaf.it/en/aidaf-3/1650–2, last accessed 11 July 2022.

12. Edoardo Nesi, *Story of My People: Essays and Social Criticism on Italy's Economy*, New York: Other Press, 2014.

13. Michele Geraci, "La Cina e il governo del cambiamento", Grillo Blog, 11 June 2018, https://beppegrillo.it/la-cina-e-il-governo-del-cambiamento/, last accessed 11 July 2022.

5. FEVER: THE POLITICS OF THE PANDEMIC

1. "Coronavirus: Chinese Aid to the EU Delivered to Italy," European Commission, Press Release, 6 Apr. 2020.

2. Rym Momtaz, "Inside Macron's Coronavirus War," Politico, 12 Apr. 2020, https://www.politico.eu/interactive/inside-emmanuel-macron-coronavirus-war, last accessed 11 July 2022.

3. Rym Momtaz, Hans von der Burchard and Barbara Moens, "Beijing Doubles Down in EU Propaganda Battle," Politico, 27 Apr. 2020,

https://www.politico.eu/article/beijing-doubles-down-in-eu-propaganda-battle, last accessed 11 July 2022.

4. Francesco Bechis and Gabriele Carrer, "How China Unleashed Twitter Bots to Spread COVID-19 Propaganda in Italy," Formiche, 31 Mar. 2020, https://formiche.net/2020/03/china-unleashed-twitter-bots-covid19-propaganda-italy, last accessed 11 July 2022.

5. Quartz Staff and Jane Li, "An Italian Doctor Is Now Key to China's Efforts to Sow Confusion over the Coronavirus's Origins," Quartz, 1 Apr. 2020, https://qz.com/1823417/italy-now-key-to-china-coronavirus-origin-propaganda-efforts, last accessed 11 July 2022.

6. Zhou Bo, "Why the US and Europe Need to Draw Closer to China and Drop the Hubris," *South China Morning Post*, 24 Apr. 2020, https://www.scmp.com/comment/opinion/article/3081079/why-us-and-europe-need-draw-closer-china-and-drop-hubris, last accessed 11 July 2022.

7. Valerie Hopkins, "Hungary to Keep Details of Beijing-Funded Rail Link Secret," *Financial Times*, 2 Apr. 2020, https://www.ft.com/content/251314b5-8d6a-4665-a14b-0110dd88754c, last accessed 11 July 2022.

8. Guy Faulconbridge, "UK Urged to Stop China Taking Control of Imagination Tech: Lawmaker," Reuters, 14 Apr. 2020, https://www.reuters.com/article/us-china-britain-imaginationtechnologies/uk-urged-to-stop-china-taking-control-of-imagination-tech-lawmaker-idUSKCN21W1FW, last accessed 11 July 2022.

9. Joakim Reiter, "5G after COVID-19," Lawfare, 16 Apr. 2020, https://www.lawfareblog.com/5g-after-covid-19, last accessed 11 July 2022.

10. Abraham Denmark, Charles Edel and Siddharth Mohandas, "Same As It Ever Was: China's Pandemic Opportunism on Its Periphery," War on the Rocks, 16 Apr. 2020, https://warontherocks.com/2020/04/same-as-it-ever-was-chinas-pandemic-opportunism-on-its-periphery, last accessed 11 July 2022.

11. "US Warned Not to Squeeze Huawei," *Global Times*, 11 Mar. 2020, https://www.globaltimes.cn/content/1182273.shtml, last accessed 11 July 2022.

12. "Netizens Call for Dutch Products Boycott, Halt to Medical Exports over Taiwan," *Global Times*, 28 Apr. 2020, https://www.globaltimes.cn/content/1186988.shtml, last accessed 11 July 2022.

13. Gerry Shih, "Bristling at Calls for Coronavirus Inquiry, China Cuts Australian Beef Imports," *Washington Post*, 12 May 2020, https://www.washingtonpost.com/world/asia_pacific/bristling-at-calls-for-coronavirus-inquiry-china-fires-trade-salvo-at-australia/2020/05/12/29c53058-93fe-11ea-87a3-22d324235636_story.html, last accessed 11 July 2022.

14. Josep Borrell, "The Coronavirus Pandemic and the New World It Is Creating," European External Action Service (EEAS), 24 Mar. 2020, available at https://www.eeas.europa.eu/eeas/eu-hrvp-josep-borrell-coronavirus-pandemic-and-new-world-it-creating_en, last accessed 11 July 2022.

15. John Irish, "Outraged French Lawmakers Demand Answers on 'Fake' Chinese Embassy Accusations," Reuters, 15 Apr. 2020, https://www.reuters.com/article/us-health-coronavirus-france-china/outraged-french-lawmakers-demand-answers-on-fake-chinese-embassy-accusations-idUSKCN21X30C, last accessed 11 July 2022.

16. "EEAS Special Report Update: Short Assessment of Narratives and Disinformation around the COVID-19/Coronavirus Pandemic (Updated 2–22 April)," EEAS, 27 Apr. 2022, https://www.eeas.europa.eu/delegations/un-geneva/eeas-special-report-update-short-assessment-narratives-and-disinformation_en, last accessed 11 July 2022.

17. Javier Espinoza, "Vestager Urges Stakebuilding to Block Chinese Takeovers," *Financial Times*, 12 Apr. 2022, https://www.ft.com/content/e14f24c7-e47a-4c22-8cf3-f629da62b0a7, last accessed 11 July 2022.

18. Anushka Asthana and Rowena Mason, "Barack Obama: Brexit Would Put UK 'back of the queue' for Trade Talks," *The Guardian*, 22 Apr. 2016, https://www.theguardian.com/politics/2016/apr/22/barack-obama-brexit-uk-back-of-queue-for-trade-talks, last accessed 11 July 2022.

19. "UK Will Face Consequences if it Rules China is a Hostile Country: Envoy," Reuters, 6 July 2020, https://www.reuters.com/article/us-britain-huawei-envoy-idINKBN24718V, last accessed 11 July 2022.

20. "Huawei to Be Removed from UK 5G Networks by 2027," Government of the United Kingdom, Press Release, 14 July 2020.

21. Kevin Liu, "With Decision on 5G Toolbox, EU Supports Huawei," Huawei, 10 Feb. 2020, https://www.huawei.com/en/voice-of-huawei-europe/eu-supports-huawei, last accessed 11 July 2022.

22. Raisina Dialogue, Twitter Post, 16 Jan. 2020, 03:23 PM, https://twitter.com/raisinadialogue/status/1217814743823466497, last accessed 11 July 2022.

23. Elbridge Colby, Twitter Post, 31 Jan. 2020, 12:39 PM, https://twitter.com/elbridgecolby/status/1223209251881017344, last accessed 11 July 2022.

24. Dean Godson: "How the Conservatives divide on policy towards China", Policy Exchange, May 1, 2020, https://policyexchange.org.uk/dean-godson-how-the-conservatives-divide-on-policy-towards-china/, last accessed 11 July 2022.

25. Bureau of Industry and Security, Commerce, "Addition of Huawei Non-U.S. Affiliates to the Entity List, the Removal of Temporary General License, and Amendments to General Prohibition Three (Foreign-Produced Direct Product Rule)," Federal Register of the United States of America, 20 Aug. 2020, available at https://www.govinfo.gov/content/pkg/FR-2020-08-20/pdf/2020-18213.pdf, last accessed 11 July 2022.

26. National Cyber Security Centre (NCSC), "Summary of the NCSC Analysis of May 2020 US Sanction," NCSC, 14 July 2020, https://

www.ncsc.gov.uk/report/summary-of-ncsc-analysis-of-us-may-2020-sanction, last accessed 11 July 2022.

27. Oliver Dowden, "Digital, Culture, Media and Sport Secretary's Statement on Telecoms," Government of the United Kingdom, 14 July 2020, available at https://www.gov.uk/government/speeches/digital-culture-media-and-sport-secretarys-statement-on-telecoms, last accessed 11 July 2022.

28. "Roadmap to Remove High Risk Vendors from Telecoms Network," Government of the United Kingdom, Press Release, 30 Nov. 2020.

29. Oliver Noyan, "EU Countries Keep Different Approaches to Huawei on 5G Rollout," Euractiv, 20 May 2021, https://www.euractiv.com/section/digital/news/eu-countries-keep-different-approaches-to-huawei-on-5g-rollout, last accessed 11 July 2022.

30. "How Sweden Copes with Chinese Bullying," *The Economist*, 20 Feb. 2020, https://www.economist.com/europe/2020/02/20/how-sweden-copes-with-chinese-bullying, last accessed 11 July 2022.

6. CAN'T BUY ME LOVE: CHINA'S TROUBLED COALITION-BUILDING CAMPAIGN

1. Yufan Huang, "Q. and A.: Yan Xuetong Urges China to Adopt a More Assertive Foreign Policy," *New York Times*, 9 Feb. 2016, https://www.nytimes.com/2016/02/10/world/asia/china-foreign-policy-yan-xuetong.html, last accessed 12 July 2022.

2. Tom Wright and Bradley Hope, "WSJ Investigation: China Offered to Bail Out Troubled Malaysian Fund in Return for Deals," *Wall Street Journal*, 7 Jan. 2019, https://www.wsj.com/articles/how-china-flexes-its-political-muscle-to-expand-power-overseas-11546890449, last accessed 11 July 2022.

3. Maria Abi-Habib, "How China Got Sri Lanka to Cough Up a Port", *New York Times*, June 25, 2018, https://www.nytimes.com/2018/06/25/world/asia/china-sri-lanka-port.html, last accessed: July 11, 2022

4. Paulson, Ibid. p240.

5. Asian Development Bank (ADB), "Meeting Asia's Infrastructure Needs" (Philippines: ADB, 2017), available at https://www.adb.org/sites/default/files/publication/227496/special-report-infrastructure.pdf, last accessed 12 July 2022.

6. Anna Gelpern et al., "How China Lends: A Rare Look into 100 Debt Contracts with Foreign Governments" (Peterson Institute for International Economics, Kiel Institute for the World Economy, Center for Global Development, and AidData at William & Mary, 2021), available at https://docs.aiddata.org/reports/how-china-lends.html, last accessed 12 July 2022.

7. Geremie R. Barmé, "The Fog of Words: Kabul 2021, Beijing 1949," SupChina, 25 Aug. 2021, available at https://supchina.com/2021/08/25/the-fog-of-words-kabul-2021-beijing-1949, last accessed 11 July 2022.

8. Abdul Salam Zaeef, *My Life with the Taliban*, New York: Columbia University Press, 2010, p. 135.

9. Suzanne Goldenberg, "Bush Threatened to Bomb Pakistan, Says Musharraf," *The Guardian*, 22 Sept. 2006, https://www.theguardian.com/world/2006/sep/22/pakistan.usa, last accessed 11 July 2022

10. Fazal-ur-Rahman, "Pakistan's Evolving Relations with China, Russia, and Central Asia," *Acta Slavica Iaponica*, no. 16 (25 June 2007), p. 215.

11. "Afghan Abandonment a Lesson for Taiwan's DPP: Global Times Editorial," *Global Times*, 16 Aug. 2021, https://www.globaltimes.cn/page/202108/1231636.shtml, last accessed 11 July 2022.

12. Ibid.

13. Zhang Jiadong, "U.S. Leaves 'Four' Traps in Afghanistan," China Academic Journal Electronic Publishing House, 10 Oct. 2021, https://kns.cnki.net/kcms/detail/detail.aspx?dbcode=CJFD&dbname=CJFDLAST2021&filename=JSDD202108014&uniplatform=NZKPT&v=R5r4pkxln18J9ATf4TT5HMMEjt4-

OhAjGZXNz0j9o52YyyCOiQjqD-5OEtyWxpEm, last accessed 12 July 2022.

14. Mei Xinyu, "Do Not Blindly Revel in the Post-American Afghan Economy," *Aisi Xiang*, 18 Aug. 2021, https://m.aisixiang.com/data/128108.html, last accessed 12 July 2022.

15. Barış Seçkin, "China Will Be Our Main Partner, Say Taliban," Anadolu Agency, 2 Sept. 2019, https://www.aa.com.tr/en/asia-pacific/china-will-be-our-main-partner-say-taliban/2353877, last accessed 11 July 2022.

7. NO LIMIT: CHINA, RUSSIA AND THE WAR WITH THE WEST

1. Marco Rubio, "American Industrial Policy and the Rise of China," speech at National Defense University (NDU), 10 Dec. 2019, available at https://www.rubio.senate.gov/public/_cache/files/5922cc54-2966-48a1-8e88-f7b51bbeca06/D0E7312 935012E45F20C67A3450DDAFD.ndu-china-industrial-policy.pdf, last accessed 11 July 2022.

2. Jennifer Harris and Jake Sullivan, "America Needs a New Economic Philosophy: Foreign Policy Experts Can Help," *Foreign Policy*, 7 Feb. 2020, https://foreignpolicy.com/2020/02/07/america-needs-a-new-economic-philosophy-foreign-policy-experts-can-help, last accessed 11 July 2022.

3. Salman Ahmed et al., "Making U.S. Foreign Policy Work Better for the Middle Class" (Carnegie Endowment for International Peace, 2020), available at https://carnegieendowment.org/files/USFP_FinalReport_final1.pdf, last accessed 11 July 2022.

4. Press Briefing by Press Secretary Jen Psaki and National Security Advisor Jake Sullivan, the White House, February 4, 2021, https://www.whitehouse.gov/briefing-room/press-briefings/2021/02/04/press-briefing-by-press-secretary-jen-psaki-and-national-security-advisor-jake-sullivan-february-4-2021/

5. Tony Romm, "Zuckerberg: Standing for Voice and Free Expression," *Washington Post*, 17 Oct. 2019, https://www.washingtonpost.com/

technology/2019/10/17/zuckerberg-standing-voice-free-expression, last accessed 11 July 2022.

6. Rym Momtaz, "Macron: EU Shouldn't Gang Up on China with US," Politico, 4 Feb. 2021, https://www.politico.eu/article/macron-eu-shouldnt-gang-up-on-china-with-u-s, last accessed 11 July 2022.

7. Ryan Heath, "G-7 Leaders Fighting on 2 Fronts," Politico, 12 June 2021, https://www.politico.com/news/2021/06/12/g7-leaders-fighting-brexit-beijing-china-493634, last accessed 11 July 2022.

8. "France's Macron Says G7 Is Not Hostile towards China," Reuters, 13 June 2021, https://www.reuters.com/article/g7-summit-macron-china-idUSP6N2IP00T, last accessed 11 July 2022.

9. Stephen Collinson, "Biden Pushes China Threat at G7 and NATO, But European Leaders Tread Carefully," CNN, 15 June 2021, https://edition.cnn.com/2021/06/14/world/meanwhile-in-america-june-15-intl/index.html, last accessed 11 July 2022.

10. "U.S.–EU Joint Statement of the Trade and Technology Council," European Commission, Press Release, 16 May 2022.

11. Katrin Bennhold, "Lithuania, a Vulnerable NATO Link, Readies for Putin", *New York Times*, March 14, 2022, https://www.nytimes.com/2022/03/14/world/europe/lithuania-russia-attack-ukraine-nato.html, last accessed July 11, 2022.

12. BNS, "'We're like West Berlin': Committee Chair Expects More US Troops in Lithuania," Lietuvos nacionalinis radijas ir televizija (LRT), 7 Feb. 2022, https://www.lrt.lt/en/news-in-english/19/1609259/we-re-like-west-berlin-committee-chair-expects-more-us-troops-in-lithuania#:~:text=%E2%80%9CWe%20now%20look%20like%20West,United%20States%2C%E2%80%9D%20he%20added, last accessed 11 July 2022.

13. "Vilnius Takes Down Ads after China Promotes Unsanctioned Commemoration—'It's a geopolitical provocation,' Says MP," LRT, 23 Sept. 2019, https://www.lrt.lt/en/news-in-english/19/1100141/vilnius-takes-down-ads-after-china-promotes-unsanctioned-com-

memoration-it-s-a-geopolitical-provocation-says-mp, last accessed 12 July 2022.

14. Lithuania to ban Chinese-speaker who vandalised pro-Hong Kong crosses—Lithuanian FM", LRT, January 14, 2020, https://www.lrt.lt/en/news-in-english/19/1133284/lithuania-to-ban-chinese-speaker-who-vandalised-pro-hong-kong-crosses-lithuanian-fm, last accessed July 11, 2022.

15. Stuart Lau, "Lithuania Pulls Out of China's '17+1' Bloc in Eastern Europe," Politico, 21 May 2021, https://www.politico.eu/article/lithuania-pulls-out-china-17-1-bloc-eastern-central-europe-foreign-minister-gabrielius-landsbergis, last accessed 12 July 2022.

16. Timofei Bordachev, "Lithuania Just Doesn't Behave Like a Sovereign, Independent State," *Global Times*, 25 Nov. 2021, https://www.globaltimes.cn/page/202111/1239893.shtml, last accessed 12 July 2022.

17. Hu Xijin, "Lithuania Will Pay the Price for Making Radical Moves on the Taiwan Question," *Global Times*, 10 Aug. 2021, https://www.globaltimes.cn/page/202108/1231087.shtml, last accessed 12 July 2022.

18. "Lithuania Risks Trouble with Geopolitical Move: Global Times Editorial," *Global Times*, 23 May 2021, https://www.globaltimes.cn/page/202105/1224253.shtml, last accessed 12 July 2022.

19. "Punishing Lithuania Like Swatting a Fly: Global Times Editorial," *Global Times*, 19 Nov. 2021, https://www.globaltimes.cn/page/202111/1239425.shtml, last accessed 12 July 2022.

20. Andrius Sytas, "Lithuania Says Throw Away Chinese Phones Due to Censorship Concerns," Reuters, 21 Sept. 2021, https://www.reuters.com/business/media-telecom/lithuania-says-throw-away-chinese-phones-due-censorship-concerns-2021-09-21, last accessed 12 July 2022.

21. "Most Lithuanians Critical of Vilnius' China Policy: Survey," LRT, 12 Jan. 2022, https://www.lrt.lt/en/news-in-english/

19/1586875/most-lithuanians-critical-of-vilnius-china-policy-survey,
last accessed 12 July 2022.

22. Hu Xijin, "Sino-Russian Solidarity Makes the US Uneasy:
Corralling a Few Dogs, Even a Pack, Is Easier with Two Lions than
with One," Guancha, 6 Feb. 2022, https://user.guancha.cn/main/
content?id=689062&s=zwyess, last accessed 12 July 2022.

23. Kaiser Kuo, "China Tries to 'Square a Circle' in Ukraine," SupChina,
9 Mar. 2022, https://supchina.com/2022/03/09/china-tries-to-
square-a-circle-in-ukraine, last accessed 12 July 2022.

24. Ren Zhongping, "Shouhu renmin zhengdang de shengmingxian,"
Renmin ribao, 14 Oct. 2013, http://opinion.people.com.
cn/n/2013/1014/c1003-23187114.htm, last accessed 13 July 2022.

25. Deng Xiaoping, excerpts from talks given in Wuchang, Shenzhen,
Zhuhai and Shanghai, 18 Jan.–21 Feb. 1992, available at https://
dengxiaopingworks.wordpress.com/2013/03/
18/excerpts-from-talks-given-in-wuchang-shenzhen-zhuhai-and-
shanghai, last accessed 12 July 2022.

26. Sophie Beach, "Leaked Speech Shows Xi Jinping's Opposition to
Reform," China Digital Times, 27 Jan. 2013, https://chinadigi-
taltimes.net/2013/01/leaked-speech-shows-xi-jinpings-opposition-
to-reform, last accessed 12 July 2022.

27. Ibid.

28. Josh Chin, "Endangered Tiger Released by Putin Escapes to China,"
Wall Street Journal, 9 Oct. 2014, https://www.wsj.com/articles/
BL-CJB-24412, last accessed 12 July 2022.

29. "Transcript: Putin Says Russia Will Protect the Rights of Russians
Abroad," *Washington Post*, 18 Mar. 2014, https://www.washington-
post.com/world/transcript-putin-says-russia-will-protect-the-rights-
of-russians-abroad/2014/03/18/
432a1e60-ae99-11e3-a49e-76adc9210f19_story.html, last accessed
12 July 2022.

30. Qin Gang, "Remarks on the Current Situation in Ukraine," 2 Mar.
2014, available at https://www.fmprc.gov.cn/mfa_eng/

xwfw_665399/s2510_665401/2535_665405/201403/
t20140303_696318.html, last accessed 12 July 2022.

31. "Xi Jinping Holds Telephone Talks with Russian President Vladimir Putin," Embassy of the People's Republic of China in the Republic of Latvia, Press Release, 4 Mar. 2014.

32. Alexander Gabuev (2016) Crouching Bear, Hidden Dragon: "One Belt One Road" and Chinese-Russian Jostling for Power in Central Asia, Journal of Contemporary East Asia Studies, 5:2, 61–78.

33. "China's Xi Praises 'Best Friend' Putin during Russia Visit," BBC, 6 June 2019, https://www.bbc.com/news/world-europe-48537663, last accessed 12 July 2022.

34. Dmitri Trenin, Twitter Post, 4 Feb. 2022, 11:21 AM, https://twitter.com/dmitritrenin/status/1489544528088420352?lang=ar, last accessed 12 July 2022.

35. Bates Gill, "Endorsing "Self-Reliance", Beijing Raises the Geopolitical Stakes", March 9th, 2021, Asia Society, https://asiasociety.org/australia/endorsing-self-reliance-beijing-raises-geo-political-stakes, last accessed July 11, 2022.

36. Devlin Barrett, "FBI director suggests China bracing for sanctions if it invades Taiwan", *Washington Post*, July 6, 2022, https://www.washingtonpost.com/national-security/2022/07/06/china-taiwan-fbi-wray-sanctions/, last accessed July 11, 2022.

37. European Chamber Flash Survey "COVID-19 and the War in Ukraine: Impact on European Business in China", May 2022, https://www.europeanchamber.com.cn/en/publications-flash-survey-2022, last accessed July 11, 2022.

38. Mark Dittli, "China's Leadership Is Prisoner of Its Own Narrative", *The Market*, Interview With Jörg Wuttke, April 28th, 2022, https://themarket.ch/interview/chinas-leadership-is-prisoner-of-its-own-narrative-ld.6545, last accessed July 11, 2022.

39. Fourth Special Report of China Strategic Think Tank: "The Impact of the Russian-Ukrainian War on the World Landscape and China's Strategic Choices", March 2022, originally published as: "中国战略

思想库 2022 年第四期特别报告，
俄乌战争对世界格局的影响及中国的战略选择"

EPILOGUE

1. "Foreign Ministry Spokesperson Hua Chunying's Regular Press Conference on February 24, 2022," Ministry of Foreign Affairs of the People's Republic of China, Press Release, 24 Feb. 2022.
2. "China's Leaders Should Study James Bond Films," *The Economist*, 21 Mar. 2019, https://www.economist.com/china/ 2019/03/21/chinas-leaders-should-study-james-bond-films, last accessed 12 July 2022.

INDEX

INDEX

INDEX